T0208949

THINKING BACKWARDS

A ROSE IN FULL BLOOM

PATRICIA (MONROE) **HARBOUR**

BALBOA.PRESS
A DIVISION OF HAY HOUSE

Balboa Press books may be ordered through booksellers or by contacting:

Balboa Press
A Division of Hay House
1663 Liberty Drive
Bloomington, IN 47403
www.balboapress.com
1 (877) 407-4847

Because of the dynamic nature of the Internet, any web addresses or links contained in this book may have changed since publication and may no longer be valid. The views expressed in this work are solely those of the author and do not necessarily reflect the views of the publisher, and the publisher hereby disclaims any responsibility for them.

The author of this book does not dispense medical advice or prescribe the use of any technique as a form of treatment for physical, emotional, or medical problems without the advice of a physician, either directly or indirectly. The intent of the author is only to offer information of a general nature to help you in your quest for emotional and spiritual well-being. In the event you use any of the information in this book for yourself, which is your constitutional right, the author and the publisher assume no responsibility for your actions.

Print information available on the last page.

ISBN: 978-1-9822-3881-0 (sc)
ISBN: 978-1-9822-3883-4 (hc)
ISBN: 978-1-9822-3882-7 (e)

Library of Congress Control Number: 2019919334

Balboa Press rev. date: 12/16/2019

To my Mother and Dad
My children, Eric & Renee
and family and friends
who will read this book just because I wrote it

Introduction

The Sky is the Limit or is it Beyond? From the earliest moment we were BORN, we have been traveling 'Backwards' on a mysterious soul journey. No matter how many detours we have encountered, we have been 'planting seeds' to one place: The magnificent LOVE of the Heart. Love is the magnet which hold all life together and its attraction is so strong that nothing can resist it.

Upon entering, we have the astonishing revelation that the love we have has been in us all along with a gravitational pull that is not possible to release.

The tests and challenges we are meant to encounter on our life path are to drive us deeper into ourselves and to resolve issues and pass beyond the limits of thought in self-understanding and self-awareness. Through the scope of problems, I reached an opinion and learned to grasp the meaning to a clearer understanding that some things are way beyond the traditional view of reality.

Love is a big issue. I have come into the world to work through my emotions and love during this lifetime. It is starting to become clearer what I need and what is important to me. I feel I already know this but the enormous difference is I will be able to use it for a purpose. My growth path is through challenge and to appreciate the world as a connected path. I have been self-sufficient and overly self-reliant with the occasional blast of neediness, but as I start to become more comfortable with letting others help me I will feel happier lighter and more appreciated if I trust. It is a time to be brave and speak out my own truth with kindness and sincerity.

Without a past time would be standing still with an unspeakable dull childhood. I like using "analytical methods" to what happens within the mind of a person and I am very prone to exploring others from a psychological perspective. Some may think I might have a borderline personality disorder without having a mind of my own. But as it turns out, I absolutely do. I work so much through my own intellect that my 'Thinking Backwards' is repeated when I am making a point. I sometimes ramble on and on to cover all my bases. It may take a bit longer to get to the point but it is important to understand that a point is not a thing but a PLACE. Not everyone will agree but there is no use in arguing the point. I just try to ignore the {stressed-outedness}. The textbooks are not much help with the sounds of stressed and unstressed syllables, and it is just too stressful to even think about.

So, WELCOME to my persona of Déjà vu' in THINKING BACKWARDS at the center of the universe where everyone walks and talks with extra syllables. How else did we get foreign language? Have you ever thought of 'Childhood' being ahead of us instead of behind us?

After a trip through 'Thinking Backwards' in a deeper place of dreams' I found the magical garden of Wisdom' and I returned refreshed, wonderfully illuminated by the light of my newly awakened memory of a 'Past' before I was born and the place to go forward next in life. I began working on my 'soul's life plan' of experiences and the great challenges with illness, the death of a loved one, accidents and difficult relationships with 'Soul Mate Love' and finding 'The Inner Wisdom' with hidden purpose that was planned before I was born.

Aside from the pressure of THINKING BACKWARDS I began talking backward, and a new door opened to a sound of my own and I am waiting to go to the next level. It has been determined that I struggle with a 'Dutchly' speech impediment SAMENGESTELE WOORDEN that's 'Dutch' for the process of 'backward looking.' I find there is a lot to be said by doing things the hard way and living an extra- ordinary life. Due to our mother's people being the descendants of Holland during World War II with the invasion of Germany, I am wondering if my genetic engineering might have been altered during birth and brought into a culture without an identify. How else did I acquire such a unique way of talking with distinctive 'Old English,' akin to an 'Old High German 'lisp' used before the 12th century and wearing my hair pulled-up in a nutted-up top-knot?

I have heard the blurry explanation of how things were put together during the war and that science tends to provide the dullest possible answer. The greatest mystery of science continues as to how a man can father three kids and produce only one having stretched adenoids with a distinctive 'old English' & 'High German' lisp with a foreign accent. A bit of a lisp is used extensively for verbalizing espionage spying to obtain foreign government information for 'Artificial Intelligence' work and I know how to supply 'Dutch-German' into an English translation.

Labeled as "A Backward Kid" my family and friends try to correct my words saying "I speak gobbledygook." The truth is I try to make words sound more palatable from syllables left in my memory bank. Even though we are bordered close to a metropolitan area we live in a small backward central town of Indiana where everyone seems to be moving in an extra slow glide like 'country bumpkins' living in the backwoods of 'Timbuktu.' When people here me speak my words with extra added syllables it gives them something to think about and leaves timeless impressions in their bones for small town thinking.

I am worried however, that my parents will have a bad influence on the way I dress. I overheard them refer to the word HOODRAT in a sentence when talking. If it is any consolation, I have no idea what that means. I do not want to get too worked up about trying to understand as I always try to be understanding. After a painful search looking up the word HOODRAT for the meaning in a sentence "Does HOODRAT mean they will dress me in the most vulgar way they can?" It may just be a transcription error as I strongly suspect and 'backward' could be about "backwoods." Already I have been influenced to dress conservatively and I do not want to be attacked by their poor taste in dress.

When we go shopping for new clothes, I will make sure I get to pick out my own styles. No more high necks and ruffles with a lot of fuss. In my opinion HOODRAT could mean the exact opposite or have a lewd meaning. HOODRAT could mean a neighborhood is 'bending over' and is engaging in HOODRAT ACTIVITIES. (To make more sense, I would be interested in someone telling me which is correct.) I am worried that this will rub off on me.

HOODRAT could mean some kid from a rough neighborhood because It seems like some Writers desperately attempt to slang us, and it holds no place in writing personal without the experience and you first must have that skill with words.

Society shows us examples of exploring speech by contemporary thinking and falling into derogatory words of very informal slang never heard before at least not until I started school and watched ideological groups 'slanging one another.' At the end of the first school year I congratulated myself on successfully passing as 'normal.' Least I can continue talking my normal way at home where my lazy tongue can fall equally upon backward lazy ears.

Everyone has his or her own way of doing things especially when it comes to speaking. I stretch and pull my words like rubber bands to form a rhythmic quick step of syllables with an imperfect conjugation of nouns. I have a 'non-dis-functional' relationship with words that adapts me to speak with rhythm and I never miss a beat! Sometimes it is a battle of being understood and I always try my hardest to 'be understanding.' My goal is to work with my words until eventually they cannot say "It's a problem" or "It's being lazy." It knocks me out trying to fit in but words roll off my tongue and quickly betrays me. When I hear something, I feel it in my tongue, and it comes out backwards.

Inherent of learning, I wonder whose job it was in the first place to teach everyone to go forward without having a beginning place to look 'backwards.' Where did they do their thinking in a psychiatric ward? That could be at the heart of all my thinking and all that I do. I enjoy a joke and can tell one very well with my highly developed sense of humor and my tremendous quick wit. Neverless-ishly, I think that people who do not like animals, children, music or flowers, and have no sense of humor - are insane.

I like finding innovative ways of learning by adding extra syllables to nouns and verbs and giving words musical beats of rhythm with new goals to speak correctly with confidence and {op'tis'mi'ism} optimism. I am using my own words to change the course of life and I am standing up for what I believe in. It is a binding obligation to myself to make it my way and it is a test meant to drive kids deeper into their inner self, so they can learn 'awareness.' I am learning a clearer understanding of 'awareness' but some things are way beyond the traditional view of reality.

Childhood can set the stage for we came here to learn. Even in loving families a child can misinterpret loving behavior and form limiting fears and beliefs. If I did not receive enough attention and love and support in some ways as a child, then I believe of limitation can form in school, church, and in the interactions with siblings and playmates. It seems obvious how a family can highly contribute to a child's beliefs, with daily opportunities of believing their fears and limits and some more than others because of their challenging and troublesome childhood. Childhood is where we form our limited beliefs and fears and they are real as we all know. Fear can make us 'aware' of danger, so we act to 'Survive.' When someone is about to attack us most of the time we are not aware and being attacked is an 'Authentic Fear.'

A child being small and defenseless sees the world as a big place. Experiencing 'fear' becomes well ingrained in us as well as what we have been taught. I did not have the ability to solve big problems and my fears were recorded in my sub-conscious mind at a very early age. I have struggled with crashing feelings of inadequacy and my feelings of sadness have followed me. They sit deep in the nervous system and things keep happening to constantly remind me. I did not want to face real occurrences.

However, the times when I did feel the confidence and courage in wanting to face-up to a situation head-on "I was told that I would not be able to handle it that I was too emotional." Comments of excuses and 'Cheer Ups' did nothing to help and only made me feel silently inadequate and afraid. Despite the fear and terror and however long and hard the road might be it is a matter of {right behavior and unethical behavior} and a feeling of things out of sync.

The factual issues began, and others saw me as a challenge. Lies were always with a grain of truth and were enough for me to feel guilty and become inwardly resentful and more afraid. Emotionally, I withdrew more from the world with the fear of being hurt again and always feeling guilty. I focused too much on the external self and all these misunderstandings create barriers.

Growing up as the perfect doormat of give-and-take I gave they took. I just wanted to be accepted for me. I was always being compared with those of others often left with the responsibility and feeling like a third person manipulated and controlled like an object left for security in a borrowed pledge for someone else's 'self-esteem' or 'self-importance' or as a boost to someone else's ego.

My 'Awareness' was misled with serious conflicts and disappointments and my true emotions stayed hidden with a parent. I have 'a confidence and 'self-doubt' issue with criticism of myself and others. Influenced by my surroundings my conscious mind may not have recognized 'Truth' from 'Illusion' and the strength of my true self. The impact of my environment should not be underestimated. (I cannot reach my destiny if I am not aware of my true self and learn to have more control of it.

My career today is living, loving and being a little 'Pod' out of sync and I'm on the receiving end while waiting for my instruction today:

- "Eat Something" "Don't blow your nose on your napkin" or "Don't Lick your spoon upside down" "Don't twist your hair" or "sit with your legs crossed" "You could get Varicose Veins" - and "I need you to do (message) because you do it so well" (message) "And why didn't you stop your sister from" (message) "I'll teach you to do as I say when you come home late." One incident I had an accident on my bicycle and came home with my knee bleeding profusely and I kept it covered with my skirt so I would not receive added punishment for being hurt. I began growing into someone never able to meet the standards of the parent no matter how much I tried. I assumed everything for everyone else and everything that goes wrong must be my fault. Yet at the same time I knew I was needed and as a child I became the 'fixer of all things' and of people.

My "Manners and Etiquette" are very good but once they begin to control me they out-lived their usefulness. Have patience 'write poetry' I say and enjoy an occasional 'Twinkie'.

NATURE is my Consolation! My comfort is driven to abandon myself from everyday living. The place I feel most comfortable and safe is when I am gliding my feet effortlessly as I walk down our tree-lined street in a relaxed state of mind. I don't always reveal my 'consciousness' when I walk but psychologically I like existing only in the part of my mind that is almost {sub-conscious} but still familiar. It is the place where I am not thinking at all and things just seem to fall into place with good intensions. It is having {Sensory Perception} and short-term memory. It retains the impressions and all the facts and all the details in the mind after the original feelings and thoughts have ended.

The Golden Pond

In the early morning of exploring the mysteries of 'mystical truth' in my innocent childlike approach to the world I like taking a walk in a wanderous whimsical manner and abandon myself from everyday living just letting my sub-conscious mind whirl away to the next bit of creativity. That can be a phenomenal time of relaxation and 'healing' when devoting your pleasures to direct sunlight. Throwing back my head and breathing in the fresh air I let myself flow through the 'awareness' of the senses in the lilac blue of summer and follow silently through the generations of old oak trees lining the street sides. The essence of calming leaves rustling in the breeze were lightly touching and brushing together through the tall horizon of dense oaks and were flickering glimpses of splendor shining down from heavens blue and my consciousness raised-up from an emotional nature and into an illuminated awareness of 'Light' in my head and I became aware of my inner self like a romantic dreamer.

It is all about 'Love' and I could hear nature's music playing 'Maritimes' in a life of shadows that were echoing with deep lingering moods of what made me real and the memories were turned to 'truth' and the shadows were calling my name.

It was a lovely place to be when I found myself standing in front of a grand old 'weeping willow tree' bowing and expressing a strong likeness to the weeping willow tree just like the one in our backyard. I had never seen this tree before, but I felt safe and comfortable within a 'gut reaction.'

As a seeker with a powerful desire to know and learn I never forcibly end something when I feel it. Instead, I always go toward to what I don't understand. My feelings are deep in the nervous system and I feel compelled to put things right when I feel overwhelmed. I have an inner awareness and a feeling of discomfort when I'm called to the root of why

1

I'm here in the first place. It could be a SIGN of some sort giving me directions like a yard sign pointing to tell me which way to go when I am lost somewhere.

Summer songbirds were chirping and roosting high-up on a fresco lined roof of a two-story house wrapped with windows and covering all its bases and suddenly there was the beat of bird wings volleying from their roof line perches in downward flight and gliding into the unknown behind the willow tree. A branch bending inward led me into the blind narrow path through the thicket of willow and to the other side following my heart's desired to learn something new. I found myself exclusively in the backyard of a beautiful and magical 'Secret Garden.'

In the realm of giving presence is 'A Golden Pond' and a family of golden fish swimming and encircling the wide fresco ledge and extending an invitation for me to sit and listen to the babble of summer's sound and to taste the sweet air of nature's LOVE blooming in my heart with reassurance. I sat breathing in the scents of my childhood's budding lilacs giving immense pleasure for seeing, hearing and thinking about the delightful senses of mind and I began seeing the little maiden in me who likes to pluck flowers and radiate all of nature's love.

The Bible says, "For where your treasure is, there will your heart be also" (KJV) Book: Matthew Chapter: 6 Verse 21 KJV 1611

Oh, how true I thought, as I sat feeling the warmth of sun upon my face, I could feel the 'Love of Angels' through the spirit. Suddenly, the word 'REINCARNATED' channeled through into my heart and transmitted into my mind and suddenly found myself explaining "Why I have INCARNATED into this life!" I thought to myself "What does that mean?"

I did not know what "Incarnated" meant for me when I said it or how it happened. I only knew the word 'Incarnated' came from another place or dimension. After I heard what I said and looking up to the sky I wondered WHY I would say these words to God as I knew nothing of such things.

Looking into the face of the full sky through Heaven's eyes my heart filled with LOVE from the guidance of heaven's angels floating by in white pastel clouds of 'nature's poetry'. With the dependency of an innocent child I took several deep breaths with hope of inspiration 'Releasing' old feelings and difficulties awakening my insights and I could see clearly.

I did not know the word or a meaning for the 'metaphysical term' {Clair-cognizance} and having a 'Clear Vision' but I immediately knew that I was there to meet my 'Soul Love' so I began talking to 'God'.

- "Dear God I was 'Incarnated' here to keep an appointment and meet with my friend and 'Soul Love.' I'm merely five years old and don't know a lot yet about TIME. The thing is, I really don't know if this is the right time to meet my friend or if it's supposed to be at another time?" Through 'awareness' and anticipation I sat focused looking up to the sky with sighs listening for the hidden blessings in my 'sensitive nature.' Everything happens exactly as it is supposed to. Absorbed in nature I watched the clouds pass by and then I knew in the underlie of my senses that the meeting with my friend could only take place in the distant years of 'Tomorrow'…

God is the omniscient God knowing all and these impressions began transmitting through my {sub-conscious} mind and heart and I knew God thought {five years of age} was a bit too young to meet my friend at that time. Being the omniscient God' and knowing all I knew he would know the 'Right Time' for me to meet my 'Soul Love' and I left it in God's hands. My eyes still pictured on the clouds floating off I bid farewell and 'Thanked God' for listening to me. The birds were flying by and looking down from the sky waving, 'It's time to go' so I left for home feeling disappointed and closely resembling someone with 'a psychological dysfunction.'

The world is moving on and I began capitalizing on how the moons cycles can affect energy. In an afterthought, I wondered why God didn't capitalize on the moons cycles and instantly send down legions of angels in one thunderous gust and touch the hair on my head since God is a 'God of Love' with the quality of being 'divine' and letting every moment of every day be a 'mystical experience?'

I accept the idea that an omniscient God has cast me in his own image and that he watches over me and guides me from one place to the next and that my heart expands to encompass all the wonders and possibilities of the universe and that every soul has a 'divinely' guided mission and that 'I Am' being guided to the state of quality to enjoy the fruition of being 'Divine' BUT I wondered whose job it is to assign the 'spiritual needs?'

Every soul has a 'divinely' guided mission. Our mother was 'divinely' guiding my brother, sister and me to the side door steps of our paternal grandmother's church each Sunday while double parking in the middle of the street to quickly let us out of the car so we would not be late for Sunday school. Hidden in memory of that Sunday school class was the teaching and belief "that we are made in the image and likeness of God." Whenever I heard that statement, I would think "Well if 'I Am' made in the image and likeness of God then I must be God" because there is no difference between the person and the reflection. For me to make that kind of transition with my own reflection shocked me greatly and filled me with panic and fear. To my thinking, this could not be a God of love at any age. Treating someone or something as a god and putting them on a pedestal is the act of {hero-worshiping.} I did an advance search 'backwards' and I found that {hero-worshiping} is treating a mere mortal as someone godly and 'divine'. {It is the act of deifying and holding an immortal person sacred to the rank of a god}. I then learned that there are countless deifications including 'myth cults'

'religious formers' 'mystery rituals' and 'theologically inspired radicals' like in the first century and 'I'm none of those things'! I internally analyze the concept of attitude to something I believe in and I call for Inspiration with the quality that counts in 'Belief.'

I believe that God and Jesus were in a mingled error of 'Truth' in a continual religious conflict; and that ignorant men through centuries have tampered with the sacred writings that altered 'scriptural texts' and produced a set of beliefs intended by dark powers to divide us from God and Jesus with 'peace' in my heart. If the world was truly free then 'Why' was I not learning the TRUTH?' Mankind's energies have lopsided studies and religion and science had been taught with a selfish confusion with lies. Someone had done some tampering and my throat swelled up in protest!

I realized for me to think my own 'independent thoughts' I had to withdraw from this church as soon as I was old enough to do so, but in the meantime here we came repeatedly each Sunday morning and mother double-parking in the center of the street to 'Divinely guide our souls' quickly delivering us to the Sunday school door. I cried all the way up the church steps and looked for the miracles of God 'to save me.' This is where I began living a miracle as being more miraculous than ever imagined through the conscious mind. The conscious mind is remarkable but the {sub-conscious mind} is even more awe- inspiring! - I tried to think of something inspiring to say in a positive eager way to please and identify with my own feelings instead of seeking the approval of others.

I tend to daydream about the past and who I am as a small child or would be as a teen when life would seem more carefree and fuller of possibility. My nostalgia should not be to inform me of regret but to remind me what is important and what I value. I need to get in touch and connect to my sub-conscious thoughts about myself and what I need to embody more of to become the person I endeavor to be.

I need to own the decisions I have made that have led to who I am but there is also the reality to return NOW and just be me. I am finding that it could be dangerous to think nostalgically and have dreams about who I wish to be in the future. It is good to appreciate myself but I must not get distracted from knowing the reality of my personality at this moment so I can achieve my dreams.

I respect 'critical thinking' and it can empower me to make better decisions and cut through my memory bank of THINKING so I began following a new path in life to achieve my profoundest goals and desires with a crucial 'new inner-awareness' and through the spirit of 'Loving and Truth' I found the psychological process to think.

I started building a space for my greatest asset called INTUITION.

I have learned that INTUITION is "to see from the inside out." It is always more reliable than the 'thought-out' process of the brain and then everything you love you can understand. When you access the world from 'inside out' and not from 'the outside in,' it can give you a vision to knowing yourself.

INTUITION grows on the {right side of the brain} and it gives a deeper meaning of your purpose called {Recognition}. It is the ability to identify someone or something or a person from previous encounters with a previously experienced event. It is a 'declarative memory' with the ability to recognize previous encounters with people and events. It is the whole TRUTH and that is PURPOSE.

A single breath in 'meditation' may open the doors of 'Spiritual' perception so I let those juices flow and be creative bringing a banquet of 'miracles' from the 'subtle stuff' in my days. The secret is to learn to shift your focus from the world around you to the world 'within you' and have a more peaceful harmony between the brain and the heart. The heart has a similar 'Intuition' like the brain showing that it can independently learn. The heart can remember and feel and sense a link between the brain and the heart. It also helps with our 'Immunity' and 'Intuition' increasing our body chemistry and resilience. Science reveals that our hearts can access our intelligence of who we are so let those juices flow and let out the creative side and start dancing your dreams. "How do you do that?" The only way I know is to have a habit of practices that you practice every day. One of the things you can do are the MINDFUL practices of 'CARING' by putting yourself in other people's shoes and knowing what other people are feeling. When you do this, the little trivial things kind-of-wash-away and can give you so much more energy. It is a feeling of PEACE. I think there needs to be that SPACE in the school curriculum for students. It is essential! It teaches 'Good' from 'Bad' characters for a reason and it helps children to be 'Mindful' with the power of 'Awareness.'

– 'Saint Germain' in the eighteenth century learned how to use his powers of 'Sacred Alchemy' and poverty was dissipated with his 'Miracles' of base metals being transformed into Gold. The real purpose of 'Alchemy' is to 'change yourself' 'your nation' and 'your planet.' It is a 'Sacred Science' for transforming yourself.

This is a journey that all of us must take in 'awakening' from darkness to the self-conscious and to the key of 'Understanding.'

My brain is constantly evolving depending on how I feel, think, and what I experience.

I'm going to live by choice and not by chance
I'll make changes and not excuses
I choose to be motivated not manipulated
I'll have self-esteem and not self-pity
I'm choosing to see from the inside out
and not from the opinions of others
And I'm choosing to just be Me.

I will SPEAK the way I produce words with lots of extra syllables tripping off my tongue. It's a habit my tongue can't seem to break from the rhythm of my words. Sometimes I find myself in a raw space when people ask me if I'm punishing them for the way I produce my words? After a moment in awkward silence to meet my standard of manners and politeness I just answer back in 'a mantra' elevated in a utterance of sweetness and say, "Please Excuse Me" and then I dart off quickly with words not listed in the dictionary.

I am now making my talent more epic with achievements using a code of words when I speak

- but I have no idea what the words really mean so it is a perfect relationship.
- {Stra-trig -cally} {Stra'tragic'ally} Strategically, words were transmitting from 'Out of my Mind' and I began "Thinking Back-ward's" -
- {The voice will be translated backwards, and cannot be made intel'ligb'le by the voice lock control words The technical track of being translated Backwards leaps back and forth to extending to me I'm now turning into the frequency to CLARIFY the control} in 'Thinking Backwards' -
- finding a steady continuous flow and overlapping in 'creativity.' I felt 'bewitched' as an imaginative little girl. I sometimes need to go 'Out of My Mind' and bring in the delights of inspiration. I found that the answers to all decisions are 'within in my own 'Intuition.' I'm at the forefront of a human experience and began using this as a springboard to a more purposeful life. What comes next?
- "Knowledge comes, but 'Wisdom lingers" 'Alfred Lord Tennyson' a British poet.
- "Good judgment is the quality of being wise" Patricia Harbour American poet
- The 'Joy' in communication creates the values of trust I say, so I self-connect with trust and appreciate the 'little trivial things' that encourage me. Everyone thinks differently and I just happen to do a lot less than the average person and it reminds me that I'm in charge of my own thoughts and decisions.' Till now, I've made my contemporary life skipping along but now I find all decisions are truly intuitive and a sacred gift.

At eight years of age, I began having PRECOGNITIVE visions with a psychic ability and 'knowing' things before they happened.

Example: Relatives from California stopped at our home for a family visit on their way to New York and everyone sat joyfully in conversation. It was a cold December day and I sat next to my dad's chair on a warm floor register with heat pouring up from the coal furnace in the basement. I sat listened to conversations going back and forth from one person to the next as I began drifting into a subtle warmth from the floor register. Next, I found myself in KNOWING word for word what would be said next in conversation and with the exact words being said before they were spoken and to whom. Conversations continued from one person to the next back and forth for at least fifteen or twenty minutes with ten or more people in the room and then my senses came back into reality. Feeling strange, I don't know if I could explain what had just happened even if I understood it. It was like watching a movie scene as I sat in the audience as a bystander and knowing the whole scripted scene before it took place. It was like a movie rerun. I had never heard of anything like this before and I felt creepy and cray-cray.

Feeling I couldn't breathe I resigned myself to hoping that it would just all go away. I felt different and I didn't want to be different from other people. At times, there were things I knew by hearing, feeling, or seeing what my instincts and senses were telling me and 'aware' of the facts my intuition wanted me to know.

INTUITION is not some pink fluffy feeling It is the 'subtle stuff' that lots of times you don't really think about. It's the 'stuff' that I am aware of {unconsciously} every day. When I spend too much time having fun in my life and not paying attention to what I feel in my stomach and my 'gut feeling' I would miss a GOOD thing I could have done. Mostly what I do know comes from the 'gut feeling' and it's called Intuition. It takes a lot to know and to understand and if I am living in my head and not in my emotions how is it affecting my life?

I noticed that when I take a breath in and then another breath out I am learning to 'balance' myself like when I dance in my IMAGINATION or when I form words. When I see things from 'inside myself' it gives me a strong navigational compass to use and see which way I'm to go.

"Learn to abandon yourself in mindful awareness to inspire the Imagination to do something mentally creative" Patricia Harbour, Poet After being exposed to all this wisdom and knowledge at a higher level of "Who I Am" I found the missing link between my 'inner world' and the world around me and it's rooted in my own vision and imagination. Nature speaks with the Inner Eye and the Inner Ear through internal ways with knowledge and understanding of experiences in life, and through the senses of hearing, sight, taste and touch. They serve to keep the 'Sensitive Intuitive' alive to help provide a deeper meaning and recognition to PURPOSE.

When I experience answers deep inside telling me that I have PURPOSE and to move away from the distractions of this world, I then know that it's NOT somebody else telling me or a school telling me that I have PURPOSE but Instead, answers are whispered inside my ears and inside myself and for me to activate that PURPOSE. It's all spelled out for me here. The 'Spirit' is always guided by God and the 'Soul' is always guided by Spirit. However, the 'Soul' is always trying to discover the 'Personality' in my life's daily stuff so the personality can make the choice to 'consciously' or 'unconsciously' accept. The 'Soul' always seeks out the 'Personality' in the daily stuff of your life.

However, the Personality can choose 'consciously or unconsciously.' It's a CHOICE to accept or dismiss the inspiring feeling and guidance given to you by your 'Soul' your 'Spirit' and by 'God.'

- When my 'Personality' evolves with 'Awareness'

It must be shared openly with others and by doing so 'the 'Soul' evolves first and then afterwards the 'Personality' will evolve, and the 'Spirit' and 'Soul' will then shine a radiant future through the Personality. This is the GRAND JOURNEY through 'Spiritual Evolution' and it's guided by God's Holy Spirit.

NOTE: Childhood and Life Experiences are the tipping-point at which my minor changes became significant enough to cause a larger and more important change to where this book begins with everything I've experienced and 'True'. These are important lessons learned and to trust my 'inner self' and 'Intuition' my most important asset.

An Introduction:
- Mr. Willit's Garden
of Prized Tulips

When casting a glance back to my traditional self, it touches home base and I feel complete in my life. I am more convinced of the values of this practice. When somebody says to me, "Shhh, yeah, everything is just fine," I feel reinforced and it soothes the anxiety and puts me in a good mood. I like doing things on my own in my own way and to speak my own truth. This is what my whole mental process is like when I'm seeking new ways of doing things.

When I'm looking for fun, I never limit my natural abilities in competitive activities. I took swimming lessons and learned to swim distance without making multiple stops to rest and catch my breath. I just think 'backwards' to a solution and then would flip-over backwards to the backstroke like the teacher taught. In winter's dense snow and facing a problem of not knowing which way to go, I automatically 'think backwards' and track my footprints to where I started. I figured it's the right strategy in finding the right place to 'Go Forward' in all I do.

When I look 'backwards' for new stories or solutions to a problem, I take the back way the backstairs and backstreets and the back alleyways to the parks of nature and the 'Spirit' sores in my 'Critical Independent Thinking.' THINKING BACKWARDS is notable! It's the best way to go forward with 'Independent Learning.' Clear thoughts and order can move skills forward with becoming a confident learner without detecting any underlying sense of defeat; but sometimes, I do fall over backwards and drop under the force of gravity.

This morning, I realized I had never thought beyond this moment and I began THINKING BACKWARDS favorably and opening my memory up to the past times I was right and forgetting the rest. I do know the feelings of LOVE and the JOY of 'Words' are behind everything I do. Quick I thought, 'THINK! Wondering if I had disconnected some of my circuits because I've already lost a lot of time not knowing 'who I am' and 'what I think.' One thing I do want to say here if I spend a lot of time spying on my mind, then I could raise myself up to the occasion of 'learning' and have some powerful power surges. So, I'll be willing to make the sacrifice in the areas I have unconsciously lived in a low-voltage life.

I stood patiently THINKING BACKWARDS to the past and beyond in a moment of 'anticipation.' For instance if I had to stand in the same spot for the rest of my life it would be most boring. If you didn't have a past and know where to start your beginning, how in the heck would you ever know the experiences of your own childhood? It would be like having to share your bedroom with a younger sister and not have a private spot for serious thinking. That alone, can be REPITIOUS.

I have comfortable routines, but they're not mine. In my wistful thinking, I found the perfect opportunity for private consultation and sitting outside on the porch glider and talking things over with my stray dog. Her coat in tough short thick stubby white hair and her eyes speak volumes of having a painful journey of grief. I could see she had a very gentle and kind temperament so I named her 'LADY'. However, she wasn't a lady at all because I found out that LADY is really a HIM. OOPs! ... Oh well, Lady is my closet companion and friend.

As a child, the first act of will is to reach for the tenderness of mother for our comfort and nourishment. We grow-up reaching for our toys, treats, and for the things we love and want and reach for approval from parents and friendships to keep us company. We reach for the affection from lovers, and later for a partner with whom we hope to spend our life and have many beautiful experiences continue that love with children and grandchildren. However, we must redirect our search from reaching out to 'reaching within,' so we can retrieve the invaluable treasure that is waiting there for each one of us. Beginning here, is the story about that Journey to the heart and to learn how I found my way back to that innermost part of myself.

"MR. WILLIT'S GARDEN of PRIZED TULIPS

Our Neighbor's Garden became a distraction in my life this morning while I was on my way to my swimming lesson. Mother wants me to learn how to swim so 'I'LL BE PREPARED' so when we go to a lake for my dad to do his fishing and in case there is an incident and I get dropped into a lake someplace or fall out of a boat that springs a leak and will not float. I could become wet, 'wrinkled' and diluted' and I would not look the same.

Do you think I could DROWN? I would be nowhere to be found!

Mother says, I need to take responsibility and learn to take care of my body. I am being responsible. I am learning to swim, and I take-off my underwear before I put on my swimming suit, and I always bring my swimming towel with me for resting between my swimming floats. When I am doing my floating, I swallow too much water because my nose is floating too, and I start coughing and choking and spitting up.

Learning to swim is a tough thing.

I do not always know where I am going but I do know what I am supposed to do after I get there. Mother always says I am supposed to practice on my swimming float and learn to swim so I will always BE PREPARED. That is why I always say goodbye to my parents before I leave for my swimming lesson, it is the right thing to do, the thing I am supposed to do.

The Truth Is, I am feeling uncomfortable today and I do not like asking anyone for help. They might say 'No.' I feel like I am not accomplishing very much, and I feel like I have failed at what I am doing. I feel guilty going to swimming lessons for three summers now to receive a merit reward. The teachers are still sitting with me each lesson trickling little droplets of water down my nose so I will learn not to be afraid. When I get water in my nose it makes me cough and I start choking like when I eat 'Chop Stuey' and I don't always know what to do; and it's just like when I float and cannot breathe, and my nose starts to sneeze, and I cling to my knees as I start to SINK. And you know as well as me, when you cannot speak and breathe, and you sink and DROWN! And they do not believe me.

There are five of us in our family and sharing one bathroom can be some close sharing sometimes. My body is important to me. My actions are of a personal nature and I do not sit directly on a bathroom toilet without first lining the seat with tissue. I need to protect my body against whoever sat there before.

I looked up the word 'hinny' because that is what mother calls my bottom. The dictionary said the definition of a 'hinny' is {a hybrid that is the offspring of a horse and a donkey}. My eyebrows rose in thought like I was in a family's tragic comedy, just like Walt Disney's fictional character and the talking cricket chirping JIMINY CRICKET when things aren't right and I am rejecting what they wanted me to be! At least I am not one of them and living like a bunch of 'JACKASSES.' I have been raised to be very careful about catching someone else's germs and I take my body very seriously doing what I do. Mother says, "Sometimes you just don't question things and go on and when you ask too many questions, you're not being responsible." Then I wondered if I was being responsible without even knowing it: Because when I'm swimming in a public pool with everyone else, I don't ask questions to what kind of people they are, and I don't ask for their family history. I should not have to ask them question, but when I am leisurely floating, I don't want to be floating in a pool with a bunch of hybrid horses and donkeys and a spare angry JACKASS here or there. I am trying to learn more about what to do and what not to do to protect myself and my health. I could just evolve on into a part of me I do not understand, or I could make a run for it and go somewhere else. Regardless, I am like a bad doctor and don't have any 'Patients!' Still, I need information for the medical terms of infectious diseases including:

{White Spot Syndrome, Ebola, Yellow Fever, Plague, Influenza, Diphtheria, Whooping Cough, Scarlet Fever, Tuberculosis, Mosquito-borne bug bites, Impetigo, Strep Throat, Streptococcus, Mad Cow Disease, Bird Fever, Hybrid JACKASS diseases … and of course 'Diarrhea,' did I leave anything out?}

Early this morning mother was reading a book of QUOTES: A quote is when old people say things but cannot remember what they said, so others write down their words for them. When old people stop talking completely and still have a few more words yet to say, they have 'Ghost Writers' write their words down for them to complete their memoirs.

This made an impression on my mind. I am not old yet, and when I want to say something I just speak up and say whatever is on my mind.

I like to talk, and I have plenty of words to say. If I cannot find the right word, I just make up one for the occasion. The imagination always shows me the way to absorb positive knowledge. I already know how to be 'faithful and tell the truth and judge fairly.' I like to share new thoughts when I am THINKING BACKWARDS and set a good example. That is cool but I do not do difficult.

I have been waiting for boring to pass, so I can have FREE WILL to think and do real stuff with my own imagination. When fantasies hit me in the gut, my brain opens with excitement and inspiration and my INSIGHT helps me to feel within. It is called EMPATHY with the experience of understanding another person's condition. I like checking things out for myself and I looked up the word EMPATHY; that is how I know I have it! The hidden INTUITION of magic inside began to unlock the doors I have not been through before and my fascination became super adventurous with my own clever ideas. When I go out into the neighborhood I like to see where I am going with my really clear eyes. You just do not know what an impact eyes can make when they are detecting light. Mother has a high second sight too, and we both can see through the 'Biggest Boon' of INTELLIGENCE! Of all the good qualities to consider in another person, intelligence is at the top of the list. It is the most stable quality over time. Intelligence can either be 'controlled' or 'spontaneous.' 'Controlled Intelligence' is deliberate with abstract thinking and 'Spontaneous Intelligence' provides the ability of information automatically with a sudden creativity just like me. It's like when I control flowers to grow and create seeds to automatically grow and bloom

Standing here in front of Ole' Mr. Willit's garden of prized tulips, I became distracted by the divine infinite colors of something immeasurably great. My clear unobstructed vision could see the unlimited brilliance of colors not invented yet. Ole' Mr. Willit, is noted for his 'First-Place' grand price winnings' with the distinction for his divine 'Prized Tulips.' I know I am supposed to be on my way to swimming lessons this morning, and I know they are expecting me, but I got sidetracked and I will not be arriving today. You can call it an unconscious connection with the ability to be open to other possibilities that may not be obvious, like having a sudden creative insight without deliberately working on a problem. It is important sometimes to be defocused,' and allow for on-the-spot problem-solving. The brains flexibility knows when to completely 'deactivate' and remove the CONTROLLED learning and to switch through other unplanned strategies and ways of action.

My actions are so intensely sensitive with peeking into Ole' Mr. Willit's private garden, it would never occur to me that anyone would be watching. Clutching my fingers through the chain-linked fence for a closer look at the 'prized tulips,' I felt like a peeping 'Tom' but my name is not Tom, it's Patty Ann. I tried not to think about the 'prized tulips' but I couldn't help it, and I hated my brain and mind for thinking about it.

The fact of matter is, TRUTH revealed my inner self. I have no boundaries just like the Universe has no fences, and my inner self cannot be fenced in or out. I found myself FLOATING in a fantasy of big bold Reds and Sun Swept Oranges, Apple-Blossom Pinks and Buttercup Yellows, like when I'm floating in the colors of my DREAMS at night. and {All the rest are the colors of what I am inside that have not been invented yet.}

- My Imagination opened to a new inspiration of colors, appearing in dazzling and vibrant colors unimaginable to the mind, like the iridescence of the magnificent Northern Lights. The overlapping waves of warm and soothing sensations danced with beautiful melodies of color in new experiences, profoundly connected with the infinite imagination. I was drawn into a multitude of waves with flowers touching each other through the light breeze of indescribable bliss. The award-winning silken petals of the bright REDS, WHITES, PINKS, YELLOWS and ORANGES of shimmering tulips were dancing in featuring watercolor shades for welcoming the joys of spring and summer. The mind has such a wide range that I can carry on without giving notice to what I'm saying or doing and leaving my mind FREE for the important matters and finding my creative goals. It's like taking a walk in the park and someone suddenly waves a magic wand to resolve a CONFLICT seen through the vision of 'extraordinary eyes.' Some people call it 'daydreaming.' However, the problem in Mr. Willit's garden was very apparent. The 'prized tulips' were standing in a 'hot bed' and would fold like an accordion when their TIME is up. In other words, they need to move on.

"Old Time is still a-flying; and this same flower that smiles today Tomorrow will be dying"

Quote: by Robert Herrick (To the Virgins, to make much of time)

(Poets.org/poems/ virgins-make-much-time)

The day the tulip bulbs were planted in the ground, step-by-step they started growing old with nowhere to hide from the light. Already, they are in the SPOTLIGHT and will not be here for long before their out of time! When they reach their final destination, 'they'll die' and 'they're' done! It is like a 'timed test:' when a bell rings, it is saying to you, "YOU'RE DONE!" and it is time to hand in your answers. It is like when you are standing under the starlight and watching 'a dying star' disappear POOF! Its TIME is up, and it's done! It is gone, like coming to the end of a life.

- I like to pass on useful information before it is done and GONE! It is usually the only thing I have to do with it, because it is never any use to me. However, for your information only,

- {There are seven STARS in the sky that reflect WISDOM and KNOWLEDGE.}

- Mother once said, I was born under "A LUCKY STAR" and when I asked which Star -

- Am I? She replied, "There are lots of other stars too and I forget which one you are."}

That explained to me that I know there are things I cannot do, like remembering the things I can do! So this morning, I'm giving myself A FREE PASS beyond anywhere I've ever been before and I began breathing with a sigh of relief with the things I can see in my 'mind's eye' and I turned full attention to focusing on saving Mr. Willit's 'tulips' with LOVE. 'Love Drives You Mad'

QUOTE: Love drives you mad

from revelation to revelation
through ordeal after ordeal
until humble and broken
you are carried tenderly
into the heart of the rose.

Poet: -Jalal-ud-Din Rumi

I didn't expect it, but I knew I would have a long busy day. The 'prized tulips' would always be on my mind. I tried not to think about it, but then I would think it, and I knew I would never forget the tulips in Mr. Willit's garden. They would always be there in my mind for me to do the right thing. When I think I'm Right, then I must be Right.

I looked for a way to STOP TIME from coming around and knocking down the tulips. No one is perfect, and ideas are scary and messy sometimes, but I'm 'the best' when something isn't right! The clock is still ticking and the 'prized tulips' are still growing and ageing, while waiting for the end of their blooming life.

TIME changes lots of things, and I dislike 'time schedules' and I don't have patience!" All the years of being a kid I have had to watch the clock and be on someone else's time which is different from mine. The clock hands are always going to the RIGHT and that is the way I was taught when I started to walk. But now, I am going to lead first with my LEFT foot as I Am 'Left-handed.' Whenever I THINK BACKWARDS about going forward, solutions start popping into the 'right side of my brain' with clever ideas and the WISDOM in how to stop TIME. I believe if the clock hands are set to go backward to the LEFT, then the clock will run down! "Wouldn't it!" I always like to 'Validate myself even when I already know that I have the right answer. 'ALL IDEAS' deserve an extra clever start! Watch when I plug the clock's cord into the Sun Whoops! The cord was a bit too short and wouldn't reach and the clock ran down. WOW!! TIME STOPPED!

It's off the clock! This just goes to show you never know if a clever idea is a good one or a bad one until you try it and I am a firm {believer} in "EQUAL OPPORTUNITY."

That is why I am writing this down. Everyone has their own EXITS with specific RULES to follow. When it is a flower's turn of being in the SPOTLIGHT, it's a moment to remember living in joy and harmony and must MOVE ON. Everyone goes through some SHOCK and HORROR sometimes, so get ready to take a deep breath and have your MIND BLOWN. Now follow me and don't breathe till I tell you again. I am CLIMBING over Mr. Willit's chain-link fence to make room for a radical CHANGE with a new kind of technology. The only concern I have, is for the tulips to stand tall in the morning light, so they can gaze and blaze in the Sun with allowing themselves to MOVE ON with guidance and reverence and showing honor with deep respect for the dead. I will guide them to a new view and to a new beginning. Now, I am getting somewhere and you and I can breathe again.

(If any prying eyes are watching with yakking blabbing tongues flapping their loose lips and spreading gossip throughout the neighborhood, then I don't care what they think!}I'm not afraid to grab an opportunity in a CALM and Peaceful way. My mom teaches me to be strong and brave and like an old man once said, Quote: "One-part brave three parts fool" Attributed to Christopher Paoline (Quote about Brave)

I say, one-Part does not cry and three parts does not laugh so I only fight the fight I can WIN and do both or there could be a very loud THUMP when I hit the ground.

Finally, here I am. Standing in Mr. Willit's tulip garden. When I don't know the Right way to start, I always start with my LEFT foot. The tulips are standing and blowing their magic in the warm air begging to be SAVED. It is the responsible thing to do and save these incredibly 'Divine Prized Tulips' with dignity and self-respect of their own. My heart filled with LOVE bringing a smile and a tear to my eye as I felt impassioned with feelings of 'Empathy' and in sharing these feelings of LOVE with another.

Without any further hesitation I then did the responsible thing and WACKED-OFF the bloomin' flower heads from Mr. Willit's prized tulips. No longer will they be under the control and power of another. They have 'Free Will' now with the 'Freedom from Thinking."

The naked tulip stems are now standing straight in their tall BARE BONES with a new- found pattern fashioned with jig-sawed jagged edges and reaching high to the sky and pointing their dreams of happiness to a new well-planned future.

In sheer and positive determination, I SWOOPED-up the whacked-off tulip blooms and piled them into a bundle in my swimming towel and made ready for our journey. We are on our way to their new HOME out of the sun, over the fence, and out into the blue, and never returning to this world they knew, and NOBODY will ever know what happened to Mr. Willit's tulips but me and you!

Lying on my bed still wearing my 'lucky tennis shoes' It was time for a TIME-OUT, and I thought about a QUOTE mother once read:

-"Progress is not an accident, but a necessity. It's part of Nature" - Attributing Poet (Robert Browning)

I thought about my world being the TRUE world and all the MAGIC I've had in my life I've made myself. Today's MAGIC was made right around the corner in Mr. Willit's garden and it's the place where my dreams were born and began to grow.

The 'tulip blooms' were floating FREE and calmly in mother's new 'Jewel Tea Bowl' in a lovely sea of cool water sitting deeply under my bed.

Then, this afternoon we received a knock at our door. Voices were echoing up the stairway to my bedroom and I recognized the voice of Mr. Willit. He must have come to pay his respects for my helping hand in his garden today, and saving his tulips from DISASTER.

I heard mother's footsteps coming up the stairway and wondered if this is one of those trick situations when you need to talk to someone or just be left alone. I'm here, and I don't remember WHY? It will come to me, but I'm having no response. It reminds me of when I use to sleepwalk at night with my 'eyes wide open,' carrying my pillow over my shoulder and making my entrance to the downstairs living area journeying in and out between mother's card tables with people sitting at mother's Bridge Card Party. I must have been travelling in one of my hypersensitive ambivalent auras' through a 'Time Warp' of 'some mixed feelings' while astral surfing at a higher level than my personal aura. I'm waiting to be perceived as the 'uninvited guest' and recognized but I must have been judged for a lack of information in my life and psychologically evaluated! Bored out of my mind my trip ended quietly, and I found my way back upstairs carrying my pillow over my shoulder and putting myself back to bed. My only Explanation: (I must have been in a time lapse of an 'epic dream' while passing through a 'vortex' of whirling energy while looking for an 'Escape Hatch!') -

I felt a big knot form in the pit of my stomach. What to do beside hold my breath and I've already done that before. I know how it feels to go without Oxygen. You grow dizzy and limp and then faint and fall on the ground. If someone isn't there to catch you before you hit the floor, you could land on your head and it could come loose and 'roll-off' somewhere and disappear. Nobody would ever see you again and losing a head would be a 'DISGRACE!'

Mother's High Command was advancing up the stairsteps. I thought she might have a purpose for coming and I remained very quiet while I looked for 'a safe house,' but then I remembered we didn't have one. The clock began ticking 'BACKWARDS' and the plot thickened. "Is this the beginning of an end or an end to a beginning?" I don't have a clue if I'll ever cross this threshold again, and I don't always think before I speak. That would take all the fun out of it for me. I do think there could be a problem and the worst possible thing that could happen, HAPPENED!

At this awkward moment, I felt surrounded in a hostile territory of unfriendly people with a black cloud hanging over my head. Am I under some sort of suspicion? I think I must have made a terrible mistake somewhere and I am feeling panicky. I have a pounding that is spreading from the heart to my gut and I think I have a temperature. I am running hot and cold and it is spreading quickly through my body to my brain. I feel stressed and nutted-up, like I am going a little crazy. Now I'm feeling cold, stiff and numb and I can't move my fingers. I am sitting on the edge of everything that matters to me and I am hyper-ventilating from the silence. What to do? I haven't even begun to cover all my basis and I don't have a {Do Not Disturb} sign for my bedroom door.

It is now PREDICTRABLE! Mother is HERE and she is standing in front of me! How do I deal with this situation? I looked at her 'neck' to see if the veins were sticking out. Then I looked at mother timidly for her support! At first, I thought I would pretend to be deaf or that I couldn't speak English. I am a faithful TRUTH teller and I lose trust and respect in someone if they lie and try to pull a fast one on me. My inner world then opened inside, and I found a deep truth to myself! WHY? I know too much!

Here comes the QUESTION!

Mother asked, "Did you pick Mr. Willit's prized tulips today?" "Yes, I did," I replied. "Where are the flowers now?" She asked. I'm thinking that while I am on a dedicated path to my connecting with strong relationships and that my relationship with mother is very strong, I'll do the right thing to make everyone 'happy' and including myself through my activity of LOVE. Reaching under my bed, I pulled out my mother's large 'Jewel Tea' bowl with the swimming tulip blooms I gave them for their new home.

I knew Mother had purchased the bowl from a 'Jewel Tea' salesman who comes to our front door from time to time and sells his array of 'Jewel

Tea' dishes. Mother likes to buy dishes at the front door and to pursue her ambition for shopping. The latest of her shopping expeditions is this new 'Jewel Tea' bowl and being the right size for scooting under my bed. "The tulip blooms are homeless hybrids, and they love the 'Jewel Tea' bowl with its tulip flower design painted across the sides" and it's the spitting image of them calling this their new HOME."

"SEE!" "The tulip blooms are in love with their new life and are bobbing happily as they float in the 'Jewel Tea' bowl." "They're not wet, withered and diluted or chocked-up while they swim and they are not drowning with their WHACKED-OFF HEADS still attached. They LOVE being FREE THINKERS and they don't have to bloom at someone else's command when they're told to do something. And, I have taken on another new responsibility today also I have learned to perform the Heimlich Maneuver." Mother smiled with a twinkle in her eye as she often does and asked: - "Can you tell me why you picked Mr. Willit's prized tulips?" "And why have you put the tulip blooms under your bed?"

With the slightest amount of preparation, I was prepared to do what is necessary to come forward, and I chose to come forward with my courage and honesty and have a clear conscience and tell the TRUTH. I do what I do for showing Respect and some things you just don't question! It's important to answer as best I can of what happened to me today.

"The TRUTH is, I was having a perfectly nice day as I was hurrying along on my way to my morning swimming lesson. But then I got side-tracked and I didn't get to my swimming lesson. Instead, I peered into Mr. Willit's garden of 'Prized Tulips' and I got lost in a mind-boggling fantasy of colors as I was travelling by and squinting closely into Mr. Willit's garden with a very clear observation' and I suddenly felt the empathy and the concerned feeling for the tulips standing there desperately struggling in the heat and begging to be SAVED. I UNDERSTOOD what it means to take RESPONSIBILITY and of putting myself in someone else's place, and I could suddenly understand and share the feelings for something other than for myself. I care deeply about what would happen to the tulips, "I LOVE THEM" My emotions rose-up in me with personal identity of another. I knew the tulips wanted to feel LOVE and be loved." "The answers of 'FREE WILL' popped-inside of me with a simple TRUTH and I was challenged by 'Right and Wrong.' I understand the values of beauty in 'remembrance' and sweet-scents fading in moments that can live again and I can see the beauty in what one has with a 'Moral Lesson.' "Mother, a 'moral lesson you once told me was that the biggest challenge in understanding a situation is the ability to THINK deeply and take Responsibility." So, I went deeply into my head and began searching for answers. The fact is: A sudden lesson of something rare and different happened to me with an insight of 'Right and Wrong'

"And I saw heaven opened and behold a white horse. And he that sat upon him was called 'Faithful and True,' and in righteousness he doth judge and made war."
The Holy Bible: King James Version (KJV) The Holy Bible, Revelation (Chapter 19) (Verse 11)

Then {THREE WISE MEN came with something for everyone and to celebrate the manifestation of a 'divine' NATURE with planning a 'Celebration' for new life to grow in Mr. Willit's garden.} I learned the core VALUES for taking care of something or someone else with LOVE and with it being the essential key to happiness inside ourselves. {Through the unfading sweet-scents with our moments of REMEMBRANCE their TRUTH will live again with LOVE in our life.

The tulip stems are rooted with a good start for new blooms and they will re-grow in a remarkable eye-catching graphic design of jig-sawed edges that complements the bare- bone naked stems pointing to the sky and for catching their own true DREAMS of JOY.

The 'tulip blooms' under my bed speak for itself:

"Loveliest of lovely things are they," "On earth that soonest pass away" "The tulips that live its little hour" "Is prized beyond the sculpted flower"
William Cullen Bryant, an American romantic poet -
"Look deeply in sleeps gentle sleep

> Sweet tulips grow in gardens deep
> Unfading sweet-scents blooms to be
> With 'Love and Joy' to greater dreams"

Patricia Monroe Harbour Poet

The reassurance of what is most important was seen in mother's face and heard in her voice and I could feel her unconditional LOVE resonating her smile without limitation

"The next time you pick flowers try leaving the STEMS on them."

"And why not set the dish of flowers on the table so others may enjoy them also."

Through mother's 'Wisdom and Knowledge,' the most important lesson to be learned was in her message of knowing: Mother understood that kids need to be educated, but she also realized that learning can be found through individual experiences. Mother gave us 'Trust, Belief and Values' with a profound sense of 'Courage' that is not found but learned through experience and understanding.

The picking of a few flowers was not for what I wanted but for what I needed:

Understanding and knowing 'Where I am going' 'What I am doing' 'Who I Love' 'Who loves me' and 'Who I have helped.'

When you 'UNDERSTAND' what you have learned, that is all that really matters. Our deep family love for Mother shines brighter than the brightest spark of any star in the Universe and her 'Love' lights the way for all.

CONCLUSION: "There is no happiness without challenge and feeling the LOVE through the highest standards of ethics and values. Explore the creative imagination through problem solving and you will find the solution to ideas through the SENSES of the heart and mind.

> Quote: "A creative skill is worth growing and developing and becomes mature upon Understanding." Patricia Harbour

Introduction to "A NOSE is A ROSE"

"Last night's north winds howled through the night leaving carved traces as it rushed by Patterns of breaking ice cling tight with breathtaking snowflakes frozen in flight. Chips of ice were plucked from chimney's smoke while the sun's breaking smile blinks and winks over blankets of white celebrating all moments of life.

It all began with my brother and me wearing twenty pounds more clothes. The longer we stood there the shorter we grew hoping a revolution doesn't start during our lifetime or we would have to be physically removed. Comfort has its place but dressed as we are with beads of sweat above the lip seemed rude and even in confined spaces on a cool day.

THE NOSE is A ROSE

The early morning encircles two freckled faces wrapped in scarves hats tight on heads mittens pinned and dangling from coats so they would not be lost and boots tied with shoelace so they would not fall off. Being unqualified as we are and just a step above a toddler, my brother, Johnny and I had no other option but to stand like a 'tree' and be decorated like a 'Christmas Fruit Cake.'

The weather outside from last night's snowstorm looked like a complete whiteout of zero visibility leaving behind high drifts of snowy powder-puff mountains." Mother began peering out of our little sashed kitchen window with concerns for the weather but after seeing the sun pop-out shining brightly she felt easier for our winter's outside adventure of "tracking" down through the snow in the backyard giving her last few warning orders

24

in her parent's voice to motivate our minds with SAFETY! 'Safety First' to mother meant "To be 'Free' from hurt and injury!"

"I cannot stress enough the Must-Nots the don'ts" "The Should-Nots and the won't" mother said wearily ending with saying "It is chilly outside when it is cold, and the streets are long and deserted in snow and anything can happen when you are feeling cold wet and damp." Her voice reflected with fear and doubt as she continued saying "Listen to what I am telling you and you will not get 'bit by frostbite." "Are you both listening to me?" We nodded and said nothing. "May I please have an actual answer?" "Un-huh," we replied. "Un-huh is not a word," she said. "Okay?" Mother barked with frustration, asking "What is okay?" "What can you hear, the difference in my words?" We said, "Yell, that!" Due to our mother's maniacal unlimited discipline her last few orders of parenting wisdom left us clearly unqualified without an option by the time you read this.

Dressed and looking like of a couple of 'fruit cakes' tied-up with extra adornment hanging around our necks like a couple of 'Christmas' turkey birds, we started 'yawning' and stretching our eardrums to cool the brain and to help stay silent and not be noticed. It is like when we are eating and keeping our mouths shut so we don't make noise. Personally, I always hate it when forced to express my verbal skills on the spot when I am not ready.

The miracles of snow falling outside last night filled our dreams of mind-bending adventure consisting of an unfamiliar word in most people's weather glossaries called "Graupel." "Graupel" is the frozen participation of a water granules or snow pellets also called soft hail. - Graupel Definition by Merriam-Webster/ dictionary Definition of "Graupel" sounds more like a German dish of food rather than a weather event.

Mother took her post beside the back door giving one last tug to our scarves before saying "You are now ready to go!" My brother and I respectfully paid our courtesy to mother with saying our "good-byes," like we always do, giggling, hopping and skipping out the backdoor to embrace life freely with a renewed sense of liberty. FREE to hurry along lost in a fantasy IGNORING we fettered the air with laughter in the great white swell of an Indiana snow tracking our footprints down the backyard to the alleyway. With the instincts of the pioneer spirit leading the way with our remarkable ability to walk and to run we began setting new goals 'in a gallery of memories' to open our minds and thoughts never explored before.

- "If you come to a fork in the road, take it"

Attributed to 'YUOGI BERRA' Quotes USA Today. Com/2019/03 The 50 Greatest Quotes

- "I Learn by going where I have to go" Attributed to THEODORE ROETHKE - (Selections) 'The Waking' by Theodore Roethke

And without hesitation, we moved on down the alleyway to feel the pleasures of DREAMING BIG … and discovering new horizons with the opportunity of discovering skills of throwing snowballs and learning to make perfect 'snow angels' representing our very own human form with wings and a long robe to show the 'spiritual' side of us. It is essential to your well-being that everyone has access with a pathway to personal safety like disease prevention nutrition health and welfare maintenance with the protection of First Aid giving assistance with a quick insight of concern with suffering a sudden illness or injury.

What I find appealing in life is the inevitable sense of helplessness and escaping in a wonderous climate with five basic survival skills to know: 'Fire' 'Shelter' 'Signaling' 'Food/Water' and 'First Aid.' Last night's winter storm 'Signaled' my brother Johnny and me to get up early besides, everyone knows only 'worms' sleep late' and you cannot be a sleepy head if you want to enjoy the new fallen snow in the real-time of 'Tracking' and breaking through the new drifts of snow soaring high overhead and with staying on top of all your 'Critical' tracking accomplishments of pride. This is called the FREE action of 'Experiential Learning' and it is learned through the reflection of DOING!'

Johnny, my wondrous wise brother is an unbiased expert and an alleged genius in Mathematics and began informally saying

"An ellipse is an oval or a 'squished' circle." In primitive geometrical terms, an ellipse is a figure you can draw in the snow, and calculate the circumference of the circle giving the unlimited capacity of "An Icicle's Alternate Life and Demise. Icicles hang in a row upside down by their roots and are made of a fusion of Ice holding a lot of heavy water without a long shelf life. Icicles are made to live in winter's cold so when it is warm, icicles must die and let the years go by and you have to move on!"

Continuing down the alleyway and tracking through the large drifts of snow thinking about the unlimited capacity of "An Icicle's Alternate Life and Demise" our heads were titled high to the sky with eyes squinting from the sun and turning all at once to look at the most 'Magnificent Icicle' ever made visible to us. We stood together directly under the longest three-foot icicle ever seen searching to get a closer look OOPS! With 'A Shout' 'A Crash' & 'A Fall' my brother got 'WACKED & SHALLACED!' I am afraid he got a little too close and a piece of 'Icicle Sky' broke off spinning out of control and attacked his NOSE and Down he fell collapsed and sprawled on the ground like a corpse with his arms arranged in an 'eternal embrace' and ready for an 'Eulogy.' My brother's nose looked like "A Bloody Red Rose" SLAMMED & LOPSIDED and had developed a breathing malfunction. Looking like CRAP and completely out of character for the Christmas holidays, who would have known a tragedy of this nature would occur?

Revaluating the situation by using mother's way of 'healing powers' I knew that without having a cup of hot soup or tea and a hot water bottle and 'mineral oil' to soften the stool, I would need to improvise using her remedies. I started taking my brother's vital signs and taking his pulse feeling his head to see if he was still alive and "yes" he was still alive!

His blood is definitely 'Red' and it is coming from his Nose.' He thinks he might overflow and drown. I find it is more advisable to take a step backward to 'Think' - when confronted with a difficult problem and a sign of Danger.

THINKING BACKWARDS can bring triumph in finding bits of information in mother's healing powers and the wisdom stored in the brain. Gazing across the blanketed winter's snow and letting the mind go blank, I held focus from the 'inside' of the mind's eye and the solution appeared through my thoughts. I began removing the mittens pinned inside my coat and pack them full of snow to make a cold icepack for my brother's hurt nose.

With a storytelling mindset - I tried sounding businesslike and world weary offering love and hope to my brother, rather than practice my irregular verbs, syllables and assorted nouns or try to make sense of the day so I passed time updating the day's minor details while my brother was healing his sore nose. Oh, what a day!

My brother now wants to run away saying!

- "I think I could turn and live with animals. They do not sweat and whine about their condition. Not one is dissatisfied" Attributed Poet: WALT WHITMAN

He said he would find a place to hide and he almost cried. He is afraid and dreads going home. His nose is hurt, and Mother will be upset. She exhibits the wrong reactions when we are physically hurt. He cannot hide his blackened bruises with swollen lips and a bloody nose and they are enough to stop Mother's heartbeat.

The love I have for my brother and the pain of parting would take some swift action to persuade him to come home with me. I predicted an image of UTOPIA

Highly desirable for my brother to come home with me. I promised to guard and protect him from getting a spanking and that I would make mother understand. While at loss to explain some things, I take boundless joy in explaining others. If you are going to make a statement try to sound intelligent. Through my bravery and solid determination I added one final thought:

"Good things will be heading your way." Mother cannot claim she warned us of an icicle attacking your nose!" My brother agreed with saying, "That's good judgement to follow." "You cannot deny the evidence of science and reason in the future" he said.

I have stronger memories of the past than normal and it will start to become clearer what I need to do to fulfill this task. It is time to be brave and speak out my own truth with kindness and sincerity.

The sun popped out in full strength and the drippings from the thinning icicles melting on the gables and eaves became more clearly seen. It was as plain as day there was no way around it.

> "We have to flee! We must leave!
> I held my brother close Down the alley we goes
> Wearing our bloody clothes Blazing tracks through this poem
> Chasing our footsteps HOME." Patricia Harbour, Poet

Arriving back home we found mother standing at the back-kitchen door watching for our 'SAFE' return. Her eyes grew wide carrying a distinct hint of judgement with a frown of disapproval.

According to the facts, my brother was wearing blacken bruises, swollen lips with a bloody nose still qualified as an announcement of being HURT. Mother's temperament is not based upon good and bad days, but only when her children are hurt regardless of how it happens. Mother's bullish appearance started laying the ground way for a 'spanking.' I like having goals and I was determined to create some sort of 'identity' for taking the responsibility for the wrongs between "Blame and Empathy." (The ability to understand and share the feelings of another.)

The storybook quality of telling a story is to arrange the order of events, movements and things that follow each other. - I began telling the facts and speaking out my own truth of how my brother was hurt. Mother was obsessed with the fact that harm had come to one of her children that she was not listening to what I was saying. I began shouting in a higher pitched voice to be heard like one does when getting upset… and I began crying and filling the air in a resounding echo to the point of hysteria and screaming

"Johnny was afraid to come home and be spanked. He was going to run away but I promised to protect him and make you understand. I stood in front of my brother as to guard him. "It is not his fault he is hurt, and it was not a crime. It was an accident." "I Promised Him" "I Promised he would not be spanked if he came home with me" - and my voice descended into a low whimpering whisper of broken sound.

I trust that if I had been more imaginative or intelligent with a deeper connection to my thoughts in telling the story I would have been clearer and fresher as the sky.

I took on the responsibility bringing Mother's love back to a clearer understanding in the family and I felt responsible for failing in my determination. Mother has a tendency of being too strict and then favors one attitude over another. It is like understanding a good thing from a sad thing and being 'Mindful of others and their feelings.' My personal support and passions are always with what is call the 'underdog' with needing love and kindness based on the understanding and the feelings of another. I believe when you are influenced by such a powerful and strong emotion as a mother's LOVE it can become a feeling hard to express between a COOL and LOVING emotion.

The fact remains - A straight forward icicle hanging by the wall fell and hit my brother's nose looking 'red and raw' freaking him out and the birds sit brooding in the snow" to-wit! -

(Bird Forum) In the snow ("Tu-whit, Tu-who")

'Shakespeare was right'

Mother was shaken taking a short step backward with a tear appearing in her eye silently reaching out as she began listening to 'the truth.' Silence is a wonderful substitute for brains when you run out of words to say and silence is great because it prepares you for a deeper connection. When you listen you can learn how another person feels and learn the wisdom of sympathetic love and the trusting of another.

Mother's smile returned to her face with a loving and sympathetic kindness of sincerity -understanding the valuable virtues, that we learned at her knee. This day I learned the self-appreciation of mother's dearness with giving everything its value and keeping our family tradition great. In my mind it keeps 'time and nature alive.'

My brother Johnny and I shares the same nose. It's a refined and highly cultured nose and it goes back to our birthright showing our good education with taste and manners. In this nature, I am attributing to my brother Johnny, this dedication for what he knows by all modern standards and methods, very few men can do the painful and necessary work of a nose-cracking. 'The Nose is the Rose' of the cultured world.

- "To arrive at understanding from being one's true self is called Nature.
- To arrive at being one's true self from understanding is called Culture." - Attributed to (CONFUCIUS) A Chinese philosopher

Introduction 'Family' & The Great Depression'

A time when many poor families were forced off their land losing their homes and unable to feed their families. Many people set out on foot looking for ways of survival and hopping trains to look for labor or the hand-out of a meal. The American classic written by John Steinbeck's "The Grapes of Wrath" published in (1939) as a realist novel of the times gave some of the happenings during the depression. It was an incredible time to be living and I began having my first conscious thoughts. I knew that when I prayed, I would pray for the folks that are alive not knowing which way to turn.

Raised in a fairy tale life of belief like my books and fantasies, my thoughts were in beautiful poetic language, but I did not understand what I was experiencing about living. I desperately wanted someone to help me discover the truth about myself. In my own mind, I knew I was very loving as I searched for thoughts and ideas that made sense to me. But I felt unlike anyone I knew or seemed to think like me and I didn't know how to articulate such thoughts and questions. With no personal growth and self-help except for my manners, I felt only awareness about things I could see feeling depressed in the need for deep soul-searching.

In an unpretentious family environment this was the time when fathers went to work all day and when mothers wore aproned dresses and cooked dinner wearing spiked-high heel shoes and could still have dinner on the table at a specific time. We always sat down together for a beautiful meal prepare by mother for our breakfast, dinner and evening supper meal. These were also the days of having a clean house which suggested that we were important besides being clean and going to the movies seemed to suddenly qualify as an intellectual accomplishment on par with devoting time to serious thought. My thoughts were always serious to me and in the form of questions coming from a deeper place inside of me. After listening to an afternoon lifetime radio drama that mothers liked listening too I knew these programs were made for a large audience of bored children with catchy tunes and jingles playing with words to ring in the ears of children and to nag their parents into buying the products the jingles were advertising when they would go to the store with their Mother.

I remembered, Mother listened to one radio drama called "Stella Dallas." When the dialogue would hesitate and drag on is when I learned that it was simply easier to reply with a question. Like in the radio drama of Stella Dallas, they would ask, "I know what Stella means to me, but what do you think of her?" While waiting for the answer a commercial break would drop-off to advertise their products and leave everyone hanging in midair until the next day's drama and still waiting for the answer. This is how I learned about the products that large people like to eat. Others were products of deodorizing soaps designed for those who needed to take a bath.

Remembering in 1939, there was a new product advertised called "Tangerine." It was the first real lipstick on the market for women. I was a child of 'Three' in a time even everyone was talking about the oncoming of WWII and doing their part in the War. The conversations sounding dysfunctional to me. I watched the mechanics of women's red lips stretching in movement when they talked and all were wearing that same red lipstick advertised on the radio called "Tangerine." This was so important and the song writers made a song called "Tangerine" and I wanted to know more.

One Saturday afternoon trip downtown with mother to the 'Woolworth five-and dime store we stopped at the candy counter which held large glass canisters with assortments of chocolate candy. Mother often brought home little bags of chocolate candies for us as treats. While standing at the candy counter my eyes strayed off to the cosmetic counter I call {cosa'med'ics} in my limited way of vocabulary pronunciation and I suddenly saw the new raving "TANGERINE" lipstick that everyone was wearing and talking about. I wondered off to that counter and lifted a tube of "TANGERINE" lipstick holding it tightly in my closed-up hand. As we left the dime store

32

and reached the sidewalk outside I found myself being marched right back inside with my personal apology for the crime I had just committed. I stood watching my hand open up and giving back the lipstick as it was required by law. - The only silver-lining I could see through this 'Epic' at the age of being three years old, is that I was 'being saved' and NOT taken away by the police and put in a chain-gang to build roads on top of a mountain. Who knows what type of people I would then be associating?

I began directing my goals more gracefully and called for a truce with my mind before it was wiped clean and was cleared away in a non-thinking existence. I am still a kid, and I have more things I need to learn and do. My thinking grew wistful with adventure and learning to do my best no matter how tedious and repetitious it is for me to understand. I always try to be understanding, kind and sincere and mindful in a place where I can continue to be me and learn to understand the joys for happiness inside me.

My Dad's Theme

Struck by the sort of man my father is and under the right circumstances he might have invented the transistor radio so he could listen to every broadcasted ball game at once. Taken to the Cincinnati Red's Baseball Game with daddy and his friends, I was able to see what it was all about while watching a sport that did not grind on the nerves with everyone screaming at once. So young and not knowing the game, I was quite content sitting with people and enjoying a more civilized sport. I gained great enjoyment in the beautiful evening sitting outside in a quiet stadium and thoroughly enjoying myself as I watched interesting people eating hotdogs and drinking Cocoa-Cola.

You certainly couldn't accuse daddy of being unsupportive with remembering one day while conducting my confidential business in the privacy of our one bathroom, I accidently locked myself inside and couldn't get the door unlocked. I panic when someone knocked on the door. However, my doubts and fears began to dissolve when I suddenly saw daddy climbing to my rescue through a small bathroom window and it was a real problem when he fell into the bathtub. He also fell flat when it came to charge my 'Imagination' in teaching me how to unlock the bathroom door by picking-the-lock. It was a beginning course in how to plunge headfirst into an active life of crime again. The only reward would be the sense of a social life on the other side of something and the practice of picking locks could only embrace life with a renewed sensed of liberty. Childhood is unspeakably dull and if I was charged and convicted at the age of three I was willing to make the sacrifice to improve my vocabulary. I 'think backwards' when I speak and I could do it with a flowing rhythm of unfamiliar words to impress my parole officer

Another Story about my Father

In 'Thinking Backwards' there was another bathroom incident but this time it involved my dad. He was unapologetically blunt and pounding from inside the bathroom and screaming in a very loud manner. The door was locked inside, and mother and I couldn't get in to help him. "Holy Might!" daddy yelled. He must be having a hard time, I thought. Then a roaring thunderous banging was heard from the other side of the door with an intense sound of stomping and pounding. Thunderbolt screams followed with some newly chosen words I had never heard before. As it turned out daddy had been sitting with his trouser pants dropped to the floor and a little bald- headed gray mouse which was living in our house had climbed into daddy's pant legs lying on floor. When daddy stood-up pulling up his trousers the gray mouse must have been scared out of its wits feeling trapped and squealing vigorously running up and down daddy's legs while looking for an 'Exit.' Later mother and I learned daddy felt so obliging and obligated he accommodated the mouse and helped him to find his way out with an Exit.

In finalization when daddy opened the bathroom door and reaching into his pocket, I perked-up thinking it was the little mouse but instead his hand returned bearing nothing be a 'Cigarette.' I watched and admired the way he could smoke an entire cigarette and blow smoke rings at the same time without ever taking the cigarette from his mouth. It was a skill he had mastered and one that continues to elude in the physics of motion, involving and interdependent and symbolic relationship with the wind. It could have been a lesson from 'Jerome Kern's 1930's 'Movie' I once saw with the movie presenting a new song entitled "Smoke Gets in Your Eyes." Daddy must have learned then exactly when to turn his head in order to keep the smoke out of his eyes.

My Mother's Theme

Thereon I began expressing my enthusiasm for my mother's hobbies but with one notable difference my playroom was suddenly being re-evaluated and converted into mother's new business "A Home Beauty Parlor!" Mother said, "She didn't know what to do with my hair as it was straighter than a stick and stood up on end. "Magically, the beauty parlor hair dryers arrived and were installed along with the new hair sink and tables. Then came a free-standing permanent wave machine and looked like a 'coat tree' and surrounded with a round top dome encircled with mysteries hanging tentacles in mid-air holding metal clamps attached to the ends of the wires. The machine had a distinctive look of something to be used for an 'Electrocution' and ready for action. Suddenly clamps were applied to my head and the switch was thrown. Out came the electricity in the tranquility of my own home and with mother's assistance. I sat gasping for breath 'feverishly' until the electricity was released from my head. This is when I began leaving my own signature mark on the world. A had mirror automatically appeared in front of my face for a sufficient view of myself and "I had been FRIED!" Looking deceitful my hair was now standing 'at attention' from end-to-end with combustion of little piglet ringlet curls and swirls. Mother said, "Now you are wearing a brand-new finished product of beauty and tested by a real machine!" "All I needed now is a hair bow" she said. It was my cue to act I a way of being grateful and impressed and with only having my offer of kisses. It the truth be known I thought 'I was in a real 'Transition' of needing emotional support. I felt my hair had been caught in a shock of a gravitational ORBIT and should be listed as a subject for 'Investigation.'

The Guest

Uncle Harley, half-brother to our Paternal Grandfather Monroe, had been living an eventful life in Paris, France studying European History and hanging out with other poets such as 'Ernest Hemmingway' and 'T.S. Elliott' writing poetry in the Paris Cafes. Due to the talk of the coming war and with the unsettling events beginning to take place in Europe in 1939 Uncle Harley wrote the family of his coming home for a visit. It was then debated by the family as to who would take in Uncle Harley? Words upon words and non-actions were conveyed in the fact that 'no one' wanted our dear Uncle Harley. The talk was, "He might be Gay!" You would think that in a democratic country there would be room for a well deserving 'family guest' as Uncle Harley.

> "And the second is like unto it" "Thou shall Love thy neighbor as thyself"
>
> King James Bible Version (KJV) Mathew Chapter 22 Verse 39

Uncle Harley a very refined gentleman with ultra-intelligence and compassion for a high capacity to comprehend 'words' is magically on his way from Europe to become 'Our House Guest!' Without hesitation mother popped-up with quickly saying "We would be honored to have Uncle Harley stay with us and that ended the discussion!

Upon Uncle Harley's arrival from Europe, mother quickly pulled-out an 8 x 10" photograph of Uncle Harley seen as a fastidious dresser favoring a high winged color, tie and vested suit, and was seen sitting perched high-up in a tree. His deep brown eyes and clean-shaven face and big smile were shining tentatively without effort as if time were to be spent slowly with just family.

After Uncle Harley's arrived the early bright morning brought him towering expectantly in the traditional sense in suit and tie and took his place at the head of our detailed 'Dutch' painted kitchen table where our father would be sitting if he were home from work today. My brother John Frederick and little sister, Frances Sue and I were already sitting in our designated places at the breakfast table and happily awaiting our first moment's experience with Uncle Harley. "Life is a reality to be experienced" I thought, as our kitchen was like a sun-filled garden of life and where mother would often throw open the little sashed kitchen window and sing out "It Might As Well Be Spring" with an onsite of nature's first pure green growth pushing-up through the winter's snow. Those moments are honored in my memory just as Uncle Harley is today.

Mother began serving nicely poached eggs sitting in little demitasse cups. The white linen napkins were placed properly with needful silverware. This is one of our mother's 'fortress' of defining "Fine Dining" and "Good manners." We sat quietly and mannerly taking our cultural 'que' from Uncle Harley and to improve our kid's humanly good health and the ways of the world. Picking up his table knife Uncle Harley softly began cracking it against the shell of the poached egg, until the shell broke open and fell like 'Humpty Dumpty' (in our eyes like in the storybooks) but the egg was still sitting in one piece. Without having instructions as how to open an egg sitting on its end in a demitasse-cup we wondered if we would discover a distinct new species while eating but it was the perfect egg without getting it all over our face.

After we finished breakfast, Uncle Harley gently folded his linen napkin laying it to the side of his plate and we followed accordingly. Politely, Uncle Harley said "Now children we can excuse ourselves from the breakfast table and go directly to the library cabinet to find a book and I will read to you." Quickly following behind Uncle Harley to our little library cabinet and watched as he pull a book of 'English Classics' from the shelf and saying "Now follow me children the weather is nice outside and we can sit in the morning sunlight on the front porch steps and I shall read to you "Shakespeare's Sonnet," -"Shall I Compare Thee to A Summer's Day?"

- My little sister, Frances Sue was sitting on the porch steps starring up at the sky in some distant faraway place, and without the benefit of 'sunglasses'. My brother Johnny was pretending to be assigned to an 'ant colony' transporting crumbs and estimating how many trips it would take to carry a crumb between one slab of cement to another. If an 'ant' came back with an empty load and not carrying a helping crumb - SLAP - it was gone and stuck to the end of a rock. 'It seemed unrealistic to live your life as an 'ant' I thought, and within such strict parameters.' That sort of thinking only wears me out in advance and I just try to ignore the 'stressed outed-ness. tie and vested suit, and was seen sitting perched high-up in a tree. His deep brown eyes and clean-shaven face and big smile were shining tentatively without effort as if time were to be spent slowly with just family.

After Uncle Harley's arrived the early bright morning brought him towering expectantly in the traditional sense in suit and tie and took his place at the head of our detailed 'Dutch' painted kitchen table where our father would be sitting if he were home from work today. My brother John Frederick and little sister, Frances Sue and I were already sitting in our designated places at the breakfast table and happily awaiting our first moment's experience with Uncle Harley. "Life is a reality to be experienced" I thought, as our kitchen was like a sun-filled garden of life and where mother would often throw open the little sashed kitchen window and sing out "It Might As Well Be Spring" with an onsite of nature's first pure green growth pushing-up through the winter's snow. Those moments are honored in my memory just as Uncle Harley is today.

Mother began serving nicely poached eggs sitting in little demitasse cups. The white linen napkins were placed properly with needful silverware. This is one of our mother's 'fortress' of defining "Fine Dining" and "Good manners." We sat quietly and mannerly taking our cultural 'que' from Uncle Harley and to improve our kid's humanly good health and the ways of the world. Picking up his table knife Uncle Harley softly began cracking it against the shell of the poached egg, until the shell broke open and fell like 'Humpty Dumpty' (in our eyes like in the storybooks) but the egg was still sitting in one piece. Without having instructions as how to open an egg sitting on its end in a demitasse-cup we wondered if we would discover a distinct new species while eating but it was the perfect egg without getting it all over our face.

After we finished breakfast, Uncle Harley gently folded his linen napkin laying it to the side of his plate and we followed accordingly. Politely, Uncle Harley said "Now children we can excuse ourselves from the breakfast table and go directly to the library cabinet to find a book and I will read to you." Quickly following behind Uncle Harley to our little library cabinet and watched as he pull a book of 'English Classics' from the shelf and saying "Now follow me children the weather is nice outside and we can sit in the morning sunlight on the front porch steps and I shall read to you "Shakespeare's Sonnet," -"Shall I Compare Thee to A Summer's Day?"

- My little sister, Frances Sue was sitting on the porch steps starring up at the sky in some distant faraway place, and without the benefit of 'sunglasses'. My brother Johnny was pretending to be assigned to an 'ant colony' transporting crumbs and estimating how many trips it would take to carry a crumb between one slab of cement to another. If an 'ant' came back with an empty load and not carrying a helping crumb SLAP - it was gone and stuck to the end of a rock. 'It seemed unrealistic to live your life as an 'ant' I thought, and within such strict parameters.' That sort of thinking only wears me out in advance and I just try to ignore the 'stressed outed-ness' tie and vested suit, and was seen sitting perched high-up in a tree. His deep brown eyes and clean-shaven face and big smile were shining tentatively without effort as if time were to be spent slowly with just family.

After Uncle Harley's arrived the early bright morning brought him towering expectantly in the traditional sense in suit and tie and took his place at the head of our detailed 'Dutch' painted kitchen table where our father would be sitting if he were home from work today. My brother John Frederick and little sister, Frances Sue and I were already sitting in our designated places at the breakfast table and happily awaiting our first moment's experience with Uncle Harley. "Life is a reality to be experienced" I thought, as our kitchen was like a sun-filled garden of life and where mother would often throw open the little sashed kitchen window and sing out "It Might As Well Be Spring" with an onsite of nature's first pure green growth pushing-up through the winter's snow. Those moments are honored in my memory just as Uncle Harley is today.

Mother began serving nicely poached eggs sitting in little demitasse cups. The white linen napkins were placed properly with needful silverware.

This is one of our mother's 'fortress' of defining "Fine Dining" and "Good manners." We sat quietly and mannerly taking our cultural 'que' from Uncle Harley and to improve our kid's humanly good health and the ways of the world. Picking up his table knife Uncle Harley softly began cracking it against the shell of the poached egg, until the shell broke open and fell like 'Humpty Dumpty' (in our eyes like in the storybooks) but the egg was still sitting in one piece. Without having instructions as how to open an egg sitting on its end in a demitasse-cup we wondered if we would discover a distinct new species while eating but it was the perfect egg without getting it all over our face.

After we finished breakfast, Uncle Harley gently folded his linen napkin laying it to the side of his plate and we followed accordingly. Politely, Uncle Harley said "Now children we can excuse ourselves from the breakfast table and go directly to the library cabinet to find a book and I will read to you." Quickly following behind Uncle Harley to our little library cabinet and watched as he pull a book of 'English Classics' from the shelf and saying "Now follow me children the weather is nice outside and we can sit in the morning sunlight on the front porch steps and I shall read to you

"Shakespeare's Sonnet," -"Shall I Compare Thee to A Summer's Day?"

- My little sister, Frances Sue was sitting on the porch steps starring up at the sky in some distant faraway place, and without the benefit of 'sunglasses'. My brother Johnny was pretending to be assigned to an 'ant colony' transporting crumbs and estimating how many trips it would take to carry a crumb between one slab of cement to another. If an 'ant' came back with an empty load and not carrying a helping crumb - SLAP - it was gone and stuck to the end of a rock. 'It seemed unrealistic to live your life as an 'ant' I thought, and within such strict parameters.' That sort of thinking only wears me out in advance and I just try to ignore the 'stressed outed-ness.' I found my place sitting next to Uncle Harley looking up to his very dignified 'Shakespearean face.' His mouth began to move as his eyes widened in drama with each stimulating indescribable word 'Changing Everything' for me with provoking wonderment.

A door opened to a sound of my own and to something familiar that I can hold onto in a new and brighter world. In my adventures of 'Thinking Backwards' I summoned-up the remembrance of things past whispered with reflections in ways of my own spiritual seeking through life guiding me to speak from the 'Heart' and to be heard. Memories of Uncle Harley's spiritual power moves through my life and has supported me with his advanced knowledge and guidance with this dedication and 'Poem' speaking my Truth.

"Uncle Harley"

"Shall I compare thee to a summer's day?

- "Full many a glorious morning have I seen"
- Above the street where birds sing on every tree
- His voice raises, words pour out left and right into quietness!
- From the steps boundless flows to the sky breathing there
- The essence of past days and where they start
- Foundations and roots, the very heart
- Uncle Harley in vested suit, short hair and tie
  Reads 'Shakespeare in the morning breeze

Sonnets plunge and roar

- The strum of throated cords
- Falls slightly past syllable
  Slides into a minor key and penetrates the Soul

More real now than the trees

- Love awakes Beauty
- Where shadows only be
- Souring, Surrendering to the Spirit"

- Patricia A Monroe Harbour - Poet

Free and un-encumbered, I need to travel in 'Light' along my way not having any burden or impediment and only identify myself as an 'Optimist.' I'm a walking talking 'Brushfire' in 'Beat Poetry' and there is no shutting me up! My brother Johnny remarked "He knew there was something special about me as I ran through the house screaming "I Know Shakespeare." I flirted with the idea that I might be a philosophical genius or a Clairvoyant and can {See Clearly} and only communicate with the dead.

Dad said, "That's the way it goes and then you know you have peace of mind." At the time I thought a good affirmation would be

- "Health is not always defined by a test result" -

However I was surprised by the JOY our parents took in saving a few dollars and I finally had a new role to play. Applying HOT hand held rags to STEAMING OFF wallpaper before the walls could be re-plastered. In my thinking this procedure is not because our family has settled on being cheap because that does not make us any more valuable than the next guy… it is only because we are "SCOTTISH Irish".

My Brother the Taxidermist

Decided to change his goals, and through his scientific curiosity blossoming he took up being a 'Taxidermist.' He was more willing to take the risk than admit defeat and knew enough to keep his experiments to himself.

There were ample bottles of beer sitting on the shelves in our icebox all belonging to our beer enthusiast father. I could never find the milk! It was always hiding behind a carton of glass beer bottles! When my brother had an experiment fail, he would put it in the icebox with the bird's beak filled with BEER and packed in ice. The icebox was a good place to store my brother's failed experiments because every time the icebox door opened the ice would grow larger on his failed experiments. Later he unpacked the ice from the experiments thawed-out and the bird -was 'REVIVED' remembering nothing of its previous life as 'An Alcoholic.' Then our father discovered a colony of stuffed animals suspended in animation in the basement, but Johnny chose not to explain his complex theories that failed in 'Taxidermy' and it is a point I cannot really argue!

My Sister Frances Sue

At an early age exhibited a remarkable talent for drawing. She was born with what our parents define with having an 'artistic temperament' as she would stare dreamily up at the sky as often, she noted, "The sky is blue." While walking she also could trip over stones twisting her ankles with falling off curbs. My daily instructions: "Hold onto your sister so she does not fall down."

When winter snows arrived she could not walk without holding onto my arm. The fact being she was so tiny and light that I could pick-up her feet hydroplaning in a blissful haze from a ditch of snow. I always wondered why she could not walk, talk and think backwards like I do without consistently falling down? I told myself that my interest was being compassionate and that my presence to hold her upright amounted to a demonstration of support.

Mentally, nothing bothered her. You could tell sister Frances something in the strictest confidence and within five minutes she had blabbed it to our parents or anyone who would listen. She followed her own rules and customs in some faraway foreign exotic nation as a double-agent informant living in our house and being my roommate! There were times she would sit straight-up in bed with eyes wide open and carry on a complete conversation in a foreign language. How in the heck would I know what she was talking about? In my 'Backward Thinking' I have not even mastered English yet.

Sister Frances and I do share a bedroom together with twin beds and we even had our tonsils removed on the same day together at our local hospital and with a private nurse who would stay in our hospital room with us for those three days and nights we were in the hospital. Mother would then come early in the morning and again in the evening to check on us. When released from the hospital and returning home we opened our bedroom door to a Fairly Tale and the delightful 'Gift' of mother's Love. Our bedroom had been transformed into a child's beautiful dream and completely re-decorated from top to bottom. The walls and ceiling were newly wallpapered in a delightful pale pastel of yellow sunlight and blossom-to-blossom flowers floating in a peaceful bliss of dreams.

Daddy's glass perfume bottles made with his love from the molds he had designed sat on our long double dresser reflecting light from the dresser mirror. Our windows were sashed with the same print and colors of the wallpaper and with matching ruffled drapes. The dressing table skirted to the floor with a gathered ruffle of matching color and design. A white iron mirror sat on the ruffled dressing table in the front window reflecting all our heavenly dreams to come true.

We were like two little girls in the room with a view at the top of our kingdom waiting for our white knight to come with a cup of tea. Mother gave us a 'bell' to ring when we needed something during our recovery from the tonsillectomy. My sister was sick and throwing-up. I didn't get sick, but I didn't talk for ten days either. We sat writing notes and ringing the 'bell' when we wanted something. Our Mother was having a lovely time running up and down those stairs to see about us and bringing our meals on a tray. But then the final straw was broken when mother finally picked up the telephone and called Dr. Painter to tell him of our bell ringing and her running up and down the stairs - Dr. Painter said, "Then take the damn bell always from them," and she did! - I do believe we were bored.

Winter's Wonderly Grandmother

T he best of times were the snappy winter days when Christmas is not Christmas without the 'shopping crowds.' People were so quick to apologize when stepping on your foot. If you get pushed, sat on or knocked down I never even complained.

It is a time of year the vast stretches of snow covered the sidewalks on 'Main Street' glistening with starry moonlit and packed full of memories with a 'Christmas' Card Spirit with Mother and me sharing together the heaven sent moments of Joy as we waddled quietly down the street under heavenly starry skies and our boots crunching the snow 'In a Memory' I can hold onto forever.

GRANDMOTHER in her 'Model T Ford'

{Act 1}

A week before Christmas Grandmother was making one of her famous December visits to our house. Long after her arrival I could still here her old model T Ford chug-a- lugging in forward jerks and stopping with a hiss and then dying right there on the spot in our driveway.

Grandmother smiled with a glint in her eye saying "Oh, it isn't dead not dead it is just resting." Equally distressing in the great scheme of things is the fact that I had been the one 'chosen' to ride back home with grandmother to keep her company.

"ALREADY!" shouting out from her Model T Ford "I only have

'breaking' in the rear wheels and if I need to make a quick stop I want to have plenty of time." Getting into the car was equally confusing. The side doors opened backwards and towards my body just ready to throw me straight out on my head in a quick stop. {Now, I can understand the crusade for 'Universal Health Care.'}

Grandmother squinted a smile with a twinkle in her eye as if she knew something I didn't know. Regardless of her never coming right out and asking I always had the distinct feeling that she had no idea who I was and that fact coupled with not ever remembering her calling me by my name.

Grandmother Cora, my dad's mother is a very tall religious woman and always manages to get 'scripture' into the conversation. You have to wonder where you had gone wrong with earning such a distinguished invitation to travel through the center of town in her provincial 'Model T Ford and at the same time be transformed into a citizen of the world with 'Bible Scripture.'

{Act 2}

"A Model T Ford is easy and fun to drive" grandmother spouted in a continuous rant and said, "It is built to go on forever." "All you have to do is follow 'The Instruction Booklet' and gain an understanding of what to do when you drive. "This is the car that got the world moving" she said, but nothing could be further from the truth and the car suddenly died! We were NOT moving anywhere...

Sitting dead in the center of town at a 'green light' in an old Model T Ford was all I could take. I tried to express my displeasure and think of a new word with Double -Bubble Activity but all I could think of was an old 1940's song that said, {"I'm Laughing on the Outside and Crying on the Inside"} twisting my face into unpleasant contortions to express my pain and disapproval - along with remembering some words to another song in the way this situation and I looked to everyone in the world with drawing attention to myself and "The Crowd Sees Me Out Dancing Carefree"

{Act 3}

Grandmother had caused us to be in a line of 'BOTTLENECKING' and with weird people hanging out of their car windows to look and wave as they are slowing moved around us from behind and in just the moment grandmother decided to hop out of that old Model T Ford with her 'daddy long-legs' and with the usual look of her dress hiked- up in the back and her slip hanging out below the hemline.

Bending and stooping over grandmother started hand-cranking the engine of that old Model T Ford while praying silently to get it started again. I knew she was praying because I could see her lips moving with that same flash of light reflecting out in her eye. Suddenly with a sputter and a chug-o-lug hissing sound of a sucking noise so loud you would have to shout to hear yourself. The engine finally turned-over and started while grandmother remained there with her lips moving quickly in self-empowerment. Jumping back inside the car and shutting the door with this statement:

"HEALING starts by clearing your mind of doubt and knowing you can do it."

{Act 4}

At this point the stop light turned to 'RED' and just at the moment grandmother elected to drive out in front of all the incoming traffic while nodding her head freely and waving her hand with grace and gratitude and showing that same little remote sparkle of light in her eye. A big smile appeared on her face as she looked at me in surprise as I was picking myself up from the car floorboard after this eventual cessation of all my vital body functions. Grandmother then returned to her exhortation and the ones based on a 'text of Scripture' saying

"The snow is a pure white symbol of loyal love and kindness." "It is God's narrow way to the world's wide highway."

This was grandmother's equivalent term to "Freeway Motorway" and her way of knowing that if you 'think you can do it then it must be right, and you will do it.'

THIS FINALE of a childhood episode is one of my personal highlights when I am 'Thinking Backwards.' It also leaves me with the memory of sitting in grandmother's dining room at her very large dining table and eating homemade sugar cookies from the large cookie jar. I prefer however to concentrate on the single caged asthmatic yellow canary sitting perched all day in her dining room and singing 'JOY to the WORLD' in a 'high-pitched' tweedy-bird delightful chanting and with a pleasant song like the calm bubbling sound of moving water 'gurgling.' Grandmother said the canary always catches a cold at Christmas time but with a bird-breathing humidifier 'Tweedy-bird' will be ready for singing the Christmas Holidays.

The Railroad Tracks

Days flew by with the birds and now I am wondering what my first day at Kindergarten will be as I hung onto daddy's every word while we walked together down our 'Main Street' sidewalk. When I perform thankless tasks I like walking fast and I don't mess around. Daddy didn't mess around either as we took long strides together and with only a general comment now. Daddy then said, "I was walking his legs off of him." By the time we reached the gates of the town's railroad crossing daddy suddenly stopped saying, "this is my corner where I will leave you now to go on by yourself" and cross- over to the adjacent street to where I go to work. "WHAT?" I asked. "You're not going to walk me across the railroad tracks until I reach safety on the other side?" "No" he gently remarked, "I will stand on the corner and watch you cross by yourself until you reach the sidewalk to the other side of the tracks" and all will be well" with his trying to re-assure me.

Left standing there alone with a shell-shocked expression I turned and looked back at the train rails CRISSCROSSING back and forth and compounding more fear and terror in my imagination. The picture in my mind was clearly taking shape and like in a dream. - {I began imagining my foot caught between the rails as I twisted and tried to pry my foot loose, but to no avail I was TRAPPED! The train was rapidly barreling down the train tracks and coming quickly towards me spitting and hissing hot steam from under the heavy steel wheels and with plumbs of smoke pouring out from the engine's stack and into a whirl of casting unwanted images ... Frozen in place and unable emotion, I couldn't move and knew that I would soon be gone. The loud train whistle blew with a blasting and deafening last moments warning and signaling an alert warning of danger. I stood completely breathless in motionless unable to move or scream. I was finding myself in a fussy mist of another time land in a frightening drama I could not stop. The train suddenly overpowered me with its big steel wheels sweeping and wept me under. I had heard before a train's hard hit can rip the clothes right off your body and drag you for a block or more along with the process of being scalded and MASH'D. No one would ever find me again if they chose to submit a claim for my injury. - SO PLEASE let it be known "I am wearing my best clothes for my first day at Kindergarten".} And that is all I have to say at this point of non-existence.

I said 'Good-bye' to everyone in my remaining thoughts. However, I am still standing here on the corner in front of the train tracks and faced with making a tough call. I thought for a second that 'this is my duty everyone does it' and I kept my true emotions and conflicts hidden inside myself behind closed doors of self-doubt so no one could see while I took a BIG deep breath and I "CHANCED IT." I began crossing the train tracks all by myself and being one of the most frightening experiences I had ever encountered along with the 'FEAR' of drowning. In my senses I knew the criss- crossing of train tracks would be like walking on an imaginary tightrope, but if I could conquer my fears, I would do it! and I did it! Then quickly, I turned around to see if daddy was still standing there watching me from the other side. I needed to feel the pride and be recognized for doing a good job with such a big 'fear.' I was almost afraid to look around and for the 'fear' that daddy may have abandoned me and not be there altogether but "Yes" there he was still standing and with his hand extended high in a big wave to me. I could also see the brightest beam of light I had ever seen coming from daddy's face and I instantly knew that "I was Loved." That day, daddy taught me to cast out all my fears and to TRUST MYSELF.

The Beginning of School

In the first days of school I could clearly see that having 'Virtues and Values' were not something to be ignored but I also found out that it was not cool to not know what you are talking about. On my first day I was asked to define what my father does for his living? All I knew was that he did something with 'Moles' and I proudly said, "My father is a "Mole Maker!" Soon afterwards, mother received a note from the teacher and I watched mother scream relentlessly of embarrassment and said quickly, "Your father is a MOLD MAKER" and began spelling it out for me. - "He has nothing to do with moles!" "Moles live in tunnels under the ground!" "Your father does not live underground!" "He lives above ground with us!" "Moles are mammals with a cylindrical body, and they live in a whole different lifestyle." "Don't you see your father come home each day to live with us?" "You father works hard, and he contributes a very important part for the war and the good of the country!" I then began to wonder if I had backward lazy EARS also and could not hear properly?

Lunch for Daddy

Mother packed a small lunch for daddy and had put it into a paper bag saying, "Come on Patty, let's go!" We drove to daddy's workplace and of which I had never seen before from the backside of the building. Driving up to the StreetSide curb, Mother stopped the car and said, "Patty take this brown bag inside and give it to your daddy for his lunch."

I looked out of the car window and up a hill with seeing nothing but a widespread rust of utter devastation. Mother then said "Now go on Patty he will be waiting for you." The thought of having to travel through the smell of hot rusty gloom was overwhelming and not knowing where to go was terrifying and I might get lost and not be able to find my way out. As I looked again to the banks of rust Mother then said once again "Just keep walking until you can see a large open garage door and to walk inside and there, I would see daddy.

As I picked-up the little bag of food stepping out of the car, I felt I was walking in a nightmare. I began walking up the hill and continued walking through the center of red-rusty iron and steel and until I could see a large garage doorway. As I approached and looking upward to the top of the surrounding walls I could only see one small window located high-up towards the ceiling. I couldn't imagine WHY the one small window was closed for there wasn't air-conditioning in those days and it was a very hot scorching day of July. The humidity in the Midwest is smoldering HOT that time of year.

As I entered the large open garage doors I found myself standing in a dim mist of light smelling like steel floating through the air. The noise was so loud and ear-piercing into a deafening crescendo. I stood there with total inability to move like 'a frightened child' - and suddenly I could see a shadow coming towards me and as the shadow came closer I could see it was daddy with the biggest smile lighting his face. I was so happy to see it was him but I was struck with shock and honor and seeing poor daddy in the misery of what he had to go through each day at work without ever a word of complaint. Yet here he came with the proudest smile on his face with pure delight to see me. Covered in black grim and suit partials of steel sweat was dripping and running down his face with flies swarming eating his eyes as I extended my arm out and holding the little brown bag of food clutched tightly in my hand. Daddy reach to me so graciously and still holding such a large smile on his face and saying 'Thank You' and still standing there smiling to me as I turned to walk back through the hot grim of rust and back to the car where mother was waiting.

Immediately, I told mother of seeing only one little window where daddy worked but it was shut and I was still wondering WHY on such a hot humid day when he needed air to breath. Mother replied by saying, "There are those who wanted the window closed for this or that reason and it had come down to threat to anyone who objection.

My feelings rose-up in tears in such love and compassion for daddy and experiencing what daddy must go through each day. I learned to understand the awareness and 'Compassion' with the ability to understand the feeling of 'Empathy' and the sensitivity I felt for daddy. He chose to go to that place of work each day and in those kind of conditions for a wage of survival not just for himself but for his family. This is when I began learning what many of us go through together. The 'Sweat Shops' of Endurance I call them as it was a classic time of neglects for many during times of the Depression Era. I later learned when my grandfather, Monroe had a heart attack my father was in his eleventh year of school and had to quit school to help support the family of which there were four others. One left to make his own way My dad went to work to support his mother and three younger sisters and did so with grace.

With warmth and affection giving a heartful of love for daddy and for his unconditional love of guidance and support - I write the following words expressing 'My Tender Love' for Daddy and the 'Remarkable Power' - 'In His Silence' -

THE MOLD MAKER

O' Black Raven! burning still

- Out of perilous pits of HELL,
- What drill shriek'd? what grind shrill
- Could burnish thy molds of steel?

In what grey and grimy heat

- Burnt a lash dead on the cheek?
- On what lathe dare hot sparks fly?
- What dare blind the mocking eye?

And what cloud belched pollut'd spews,

- Could dare its noxious carbon fumes?
- And when thy throat began to choke,
- What rust corrode? And what dread smoke?

What racks the joints? what fires the veins?

- In what sweatshop was thy brain?
- What dread heat? what burning eyes?
- Dare deadly sweat on hungry flies?

When he cast their desperate death?

- Did he breathe their dying breath?
- When molds were cast, did he know it?
- Did he mold an ever poet?

-Patricia A Monroe Harbour Poet

Beginning School & Bullied

The pressures from 'Bulling' are big problems. It can make a kid feel hurt, scared, sick, lonely, embarrassed and sad. 'The Bully' hits, kicks and pushes to hurt people using ugly words of name calling while threatening, teasing, scaring and terrorizing, and it became a continued problem affecting me.

The stress of dealing with bullies made me feel sick and I no longer felt safe in school. It became a place of fear and violence for me and I never wanted to go outside for school recess or when leaving the school building at the end of the day. As a little blonde girl with big blue eyes and wearing a little 'red coat' resembling "Little Red Riding Hood" I was the constant appetizer for big bullies and in FEAR of being attacked. Through this I learned that 'Bullies' love having brute power and superiority over someone smaller than they are. And when bullies speak, the 'Verbs' seem to all be the same and would NEVER win a prize when it came to the NOUNS and objects. I found that the 'Bullies are the 'lowlife' of low moral character and they are clueless and dumb learners not wanting to help themselves or learn. Through school, they afre held back academically and usually never promoted, but only when it is necessary, and they are too big to fit in their seat. Along with this, I also learned the aggressive pressure of worry or the intimidation of being persistently harassed in hostile situations and bullies at the 'end of a knife of their wanting physical contact. This is how I learned to become a very fast runner without any strings attached. In school, I withdrew inside myself scared out of my wits most of the time and couldn't concentrate. My 'Running Away' was not in keeping with my character, but it became a matter of survival. In school, I gave names to all big letters and number and called them hateful words.

Bullies use strength or power to harm or intimidate those who are weaker or smaller and force others to do what they want. A big part of my beginning years in school was in an environment of learning FEAR and I learned to DISTRUST.- My personality, nature, temperament and psychological psyche constitutes the opposite and often in school I looked for someone bigger and stronger or an upperclassman to walk with me from school for protection. Most of the time I was alone in getting home but I did learn to become a champion runner through my survival. I attended this same school until my fifth grade year and mother asked for my permission to attend a different school. Upon acceptance I was then thrown quickly into summer reading lessons and searching deeply into 'PHONICS' for developing my ability to hear words distinctively and correctly to develop my speaking ability. But even then, I still identified with the rhythm and beat within me and manipulated the 'linguistics' of my own phenomena speaking dialect.

After beginning the new school that fall there was a powerful turn of events starting within me and I was off on a serious path of growth that was being set in an inevitable motion. I immediately became a team player in attitude loving my teachers and every new classmate. Freedom had brought a whole new change in limiting the FEARS I had previously lived through and survived. In a new appreciation nothing else mattered. I immediately began with 'commitments to myself' with a new change of goals and circumstances of achieving. I suddenly had new skills in responsibility and with new beginnings. I found for the first time free from emotional chaos. New doors began to open my own independence and freedom and new people came into my life bringing the joy and feelings of motivation and happiness.

The Growing-up Years

The next few years I felt very driven and flew with new feelings, hanging-out with positive people and experiencing new and unusual ideas. I began feeling like a person of the 'Avant-garde' and especially in the arts and the 'works of artists in visual, literary, and the musical arts and classics, including poetry.

Transportation became a crucial factor in my life with depending upon myself to travel to and from the new school as well as traveling on to another school for band lessons. My dad could see the importance of learning to help myself and took me to a premier Schwinn bicycling shop to buy a girl 26" bike with brakes so I wouldn't fall over when I needed stop like I always had to when riding my brother's bike. I have always put a lot of thought into something when choosing a color and I figured it must be some sort of decorator's bent. I chose 'Blue' for the color of the new bicycle as I had been riding a 'Red' bicycle belonging to my brother and without breaks I learned to stop by falling over sideways always causing cuts and skinned up bruised knees.

After shopping for the new bicycle and back at home, I was suddenly in the spotlight on the front sidewalk with a new Schwinn bicycle to call my very own and I was ready to perform once again. I felt so proud with daddy saying, "Now let me see you ride that bike!" Pushing my limit of achievement, I shoved-off down the sidewalk but soon became 'aware' that I was quickly approaching a curb-crossing at the end of the sidewalk leading into another street. I screamed back to daddy asking "How do I stop this bike?" "Where are the brakes?" Then I heard Daddy "You'll figure them!" Daddy's way of teaching was by self-experience and to my amazement, I did just that and peddled 'backwards' like I do in all my 'backward thinking.' After I stopped the bike short on a dime I thought

WOW! Daddy's inspiring way taught me to think for myself. I began experiencing a new kind of 'self-awareness' with new lessons learned in the freedom from self-doubt as I began cycling from one school to another across town and with a new-found confidence in myself. Daddy gave me the 'Belief' in myself in new ways of learning.

I began piano lessons at an early age and continued for thirteen years. In between time, my parents decided I needed to also play a horn. One day a 'Trombone' showed-up. "Here is the horn you always wanted to play!" I never wanted to play a 'Trombone' and was sure that they had me mixed-up with some other kid. However, I did end up playing the Trombone and taking lessons from the high school band director. I suddenly had the new inspiration of riding my bicycle twice a week across town from one school to another with eventually ending -up and playing in the high school band as an eighth grader. I felt comfortable sitting in the placement of third chair Trombonist and after two seniors but in first and second chair being good on the Trombone. I did like doing this for a while, but I never expected it to be my heart's desire. Sitting directly across from the trumpet section in band where the trumpets sat next to the clarinets, I - noticed one Trumpet player named 'JIM' who was also an expert on - the Cornet and played 'Trumpeter's Holiday' and won first in state competition. WOW I thought! That would be great to make music like that! I didn't know him but later I learned he lived around the corner from me in my neighborhood. However, I don't believe he ever recognized me living in that same neighborhood.

Becoming A Job's Daughter

My father being a 'Mason' and consistent in a fraternal organization tracing its origin back to the fraternities of stonemasons of the fourteenth century daddy was always studying rituals as a Mason and attended the Mason lodge as a member. I remember once, asking daddy to tell me about what he was studying. He said it was a ritual of secrets. I said, I am very good at keeping secrets and remember begged him to tell me. His eyes lit-up with a spark looking back at me with one of his big smiles and saying, the rituals were only for other Masons to hear.

Mother became a member of the 'Eastern Star.' The 'Eastern Star' is an order of the Masonic and is also a Masonic appendant body open to men and women with chartered chapters throughout the States. The 'Eastern Star' was established in 1850 by a lawyer and educator noted as a "Freemason" and with chapters based on teachings from the bible and open to all religions.

Though the order of the 'Masons' and 'Eastern Star' I became a member of 'Job's Daughters.' 'Job's Daughters' is an order for the daughters of the 'Masons.' As a daughter of the 'Book of Job' we delivered the messages telling the story of the book of "Job" and of his misfortunes. In a ritual epilogue of prose narrated in a dialogue of monologues consistent with statements from sages and wise men offering their judgements and wisdom we learned the benefits of 'Divinity' and 'Virtue.'

{Given the honor of helping to choose mother's silvery gown of sparling stars} My most cherished and fondest memory in Job's Daughters is remembering mother as choir director, singing 'Franz Schubert's 1825' "Ave Marie" I still see mother standing in that beautiful gown of silver sparkling stars singing from the deepest depth of her heart and soul with her beautiful classical soprano voice ranging from middle C to high A and with the voice of an angel sent from heaven in continuous breathtaking dreams streaming of love's miracles for all the ladies to hear bringing the tears of a thousand years in 'Loving Joy' - and the giving of mother's love with moments to remember in time and through all the darkest moments of my life. The fun part of Job's Daughter was inviting a first date to my first 'Job Daughter's Party! A close school friend of my brother's played the clarinet and looked just like the movie star 'Roy Rogers' 'one of the good guys' in the movies and always riding a horse. He would come often to our home as he and my brother worked on their studies together. So, I had the opportunity of inviting my brother's friend to my first Job's Daughter's Dance and with my brother, Johnny accompanying a Job's Daughter friend of mine and we all sat together comfortably drinking Coca-Cola and giggling. I wore my first formal of yellow looking as if I was taking a walk through an old fashion garden and with my date bringing beautiful 'yellow Daffodils' for my very first corsage are often toted as the beacon of spring.

Brownie Girl Scout Hospital Volunteer 4-H Art & Music Dance

Piano 3- Mile Club and Life Saving Swimming.

After beginning as a 'Brownie' and then as a 'Girl Scout' through my high school years I carried a food tray into a little sweet looking man and looking to me with the most loving eyes. After I sat the tray down in front of him I began spoon feeding him as his birdlike mouth opened automatically for each little bite. I sweetly talked to him as if I already knew him without his ever saying a word as he looked adoringly at me. When I came from him room, a nurse grabbed my arm and asked in a sharp voice "what were you doing in there?" In a calming state I said, "He has been fed and I spoon fed this sweet little man." The nurse then screamed out saying "No one not anyone has ever been able to get close to that man as he only screams at all of us and throws trays at us from across the room. 'Well, that gave me food for thought!'

I remember being told to not ever go into any room with a closed door. However, on another occasion I walked into a room where the door was not closed and was slightly ajar. I entered carrying a food tray and found a sweet little looking lady wearing a pretty bed jacket with the sincerest sweet smile on her face as I approached with the food tray I kindly pulled out the floor table and sat down the tray placing it before her. I smiled again with saying "Please Enjoy" and then I left. As I came out the door another nurse grabbed my arm asking "What was I doing in there and then asking if I had touched her or anything belonging to her?" I said "NO, I have not" and I further explained that the door was ajar. The nurse remarked "That woman is in ISOLATION and she has "LEPROCY." I suddenly remembered reading in my history books about the 'Leper Colonies' and known as 'Hansen's disease' with the inability of feeling pain as they deteriorate into death. It is a long-term infection and everyone is at RISK who comes in close contact of a LEPER. Immediately, in my course of action I left the hospital in 'Fear' and quickly took off running until I reached home drawing a bath of the hottest bath water I could stand and quickly climbed in. I sat soaking for at least an hour or two. All I knew then through my reasoning I WAS NOT CUT OUT TO BE A NURSE.

A Turning of Events

I have been sleeping on the edge of the world and the next few years
through school

I began finding 'New Way of Thinking' and feeling very driven with
new feelings and 'Intensions.' I hung-out with positive people hoping to
experience new and unusual ideas. I began feeling like a person of the
'Avant-garde' in the 'works of Art' with a very visual, literary and musical
regard to 'dance' and the 'musical classics' and writing poetry in my quiet
moments.

A powerful turn of events started within me on a serious path of
growth that was being set in an inevitable motion. I became a team
player in school with a new attitude and loving all my teachers and every
classmate. Freedom had brought a whole new perspective of change in
my direction with helping to eliminate the FEARS I had previously lived
through and survived. I had a whole new appreciation for life and nothing
else seemed to matter. Beginning with new commitments to myself with
intensions and new goals circumstances of achieving began to change
through achievements with giving new encouragement and hope through
responsibility. For the first time in my life I felt free of emotional chaos
and new people came into my life.

– New doors were opening-up with independence and I felt free with
happiness and motivation.

Teachers found my talent in 'Art' and making posters for the walls
for school exhibits and extraordinary events. I began participating in
competition with running the 100-yard dash and relay events against other
schools. From experience, I have much experience with 'Running' for my
life so now I can give something back for the good of becoming a 'Runner.'

Also found were my talents in a 'Geography' class and learning the calls of different birds. By giving a required weekly book report of 'Bird Calls' I became proficient and historical with 'talking to birds' by picking up the echoes of birds and communicating with them daily and become a nature lover also talking to the 'trees.

My parents decided I needed to play a horn besides taking piano and dancing lessons. One day, a 'Trombone' showed-up. "Here is the horn you always wanted to play!" But I never wanted to play a 'Trombone' and I was sure that they had me mixed-up with some other kid. However, I did end up playing the Trombone and taking lessons from the high school band director. I suddenly had new inspirations as I rode my bicycle twice a week across town from one school to another and eventually ended up playing in the high school band as an eighth grader. I felt comfortable as I sat in the third chair placement with two Trombonists [both seniors] mostly playing their musical vibrations in a fashion of a 'jazz trombonist' and so fun for me! I did love sitting in third chair until it was time for the two seniors to graduate from school and left me to play first chair. Well, I had second thoughts about that as my heart was NEVER into playing the Trombone and I would be the first to admit that! I began wondering what it would be like to play the clarinet or a trumpet as I looked across the band section.

One Trumpet and Cornet player was an expert on both horns. He wasn't in any of my eighth-grade classes, so I didn't know anything about him but he played the 'Cornet' like a dream and I was drawn into a 'Magnetism' when he played 'Trumpeter's Holiday.' It was announced in band that he went on to State Completion and Won first place. I thought WOW! It would be great to make music like that with your own sound. I didn't know him but later learned that he lived close by and around the corner in my neighborhood.

Music Swimming 4-H Baking & Sewing Art School Events

DANCE

LIFE was an 'UNCHAINED MELODY'

Taking 'piano' lessons close to thirteen years I thoroughly enjoyed the classical music -and the thirty's and forties with 'David Rose' playing soft instrumental romantic songs and 'Glenn Miller' playing the lead in all the 'Big Band' music. Now however, we were going into a new horizon of music of several generations all rolled-up together in one which all lead to ONE BIG GLORIOUS TIME in the 1950's. The music of 'Rock & Roll' and the 'Jitterbug' were in the height of splendor with glorious times of fun and romance in THE NEW and dancing to it all!

Some things began coming to an 'END' and I quit being a Trombone player in band and chose to be where I wanted to be and that was in 'Cheering Block' with all my classmates and friends. Now in our 'Freshman' year of high school and feeling revitalized, young and optimistic in myself I felt an effort and a new faith as a class team member with others. Our class did everything together. Yearly, we wrote and memorized giving 'Orations' to our school class members or in a convocation. Regarding our school classes they consisted of either 'Science & Math' or 'Business' and 'History' or a combination with 'Home Economics.'

I worked on the school newspaper in business class and participated in competition running 100-yard dashes and relays against other schools

Teachers found my talent in art making posters for special school events. I also became proficient and historical with the echoes of bird calling and still communicate talking with birds today as a nature lover and as well as having an interest in all humanity and the preservation of it.

Having had years of swimming lessons to help get over my 'fear' of drowning I found myself becoming a summer swimming instructor of children from ages three to adulthood and sixty-five or beyond with learning to have self-confidence in myself and helping others. One of my childhood visions was to swim and perform like "Esther Williams" in summer 'water ballets.' All the swimming teachers swam together each summer for the public in beautiful Water Ballets' and 'Dolphins in Sea Life' and accompanied with musical scores as the background of our rhythm and strokes. During these summers, I took courses of 'Junior' and 'Senior Life Saving' and finalized my summer senior year of teaching with swimming 'three miles' and becoming a member of the 'Three Miler's Club.' It was a personal 'healing' for my 'fear' of water and drowning.

Baking and sewing also became a big part of high school summers through '4-H' judged with winning ribbons each year in the community and going on to State Fair competition in Indianapolis, IN for Judging and received a ribbon. One year in '4-H' Baking I baked 'Chocolate Chip Cookies' {with mother's help} for competition I remember so well that morning with mother lighting the pilot light with a match in hopes to get the oven started. It took a little courage and if the pilot light didn't light the first or second time around, the gas would become overwhelming. Mother was also good at helping me pull out the many trays of cookies from the hot oven and in hopes of finding the right looking cookies for presentation. Mother was also very good with 'presentation.' She placed a beautiful 'doily' {a small ornamental mat made of paper lace with a lace pattern} on the plate under the three chocolate chip cookies. I could not have done this without mother's help and instruction. Mother drove quickly to meet the truck at the school building and the cookies were the last entry placed onto the truck just before leaving for the Indianapolis State Fair. Surprisingly we received a phone call from school stating that the 'Chocolate Chip Cookies' mother had helped me bake for competition WON SECOND PLACEMENT at state.

My family and I climbed into the car and drove to the Indianapolis

State Fair to see the presentation of cookies for which I was being awarded and seeing all the other entries of competition in judging. Awarded a state check of 'One Dollar' I still have the check as it became a wonderful keepsake of 'Good Luck' and represented a wonderful 'Omen' like finding a 'Four Leaf Clover' and regarding it as a 'Miracle.'

My brother, Johnny and I were dance partners in early life as we took 'jitterbug' classes together and found the expression of dance within my own powerful vibrations of rhythm falling in love with all forms of 'dancing.' I began dancing for business and social groups in the community later dancing and performing before school audiences for entertainment. I preformed 'Tap Dancing' and 'Interpretative' and I found myself in my 'Soul' even when I was never awake. Performing arts are a form in which artists use their voices or bodies to convey a conscious artistic expression. It is a way of making known one's thoughts or feelings and voicing a declaration of words in a rare delicacy of romantic expression. My body dances through a secure foundation of trust and truth and here I found LOVE within myself of the highest 'Reverence' of respect. It is a PROCESS of vibration and HEALING and 'a gift of healing' for me when I feel unbalanced.

DANCE is a powerful form of prayer. DANCE is an Art a discipline, a meditation. DANCE is a vehicle for personal expression and storytelling. This is what we need in this world.

- "Whoever knoweth the power of the dance, dwelleth in God"
- Jalal-ud-Din Rumi "Dancer and Poet"

Don't forget to walk in the rain

- "Every raindrop has its own melody when it falls on the earth
- And if you listen closely you can hear the unspoken messages of the heart
- And the dance of the Soul"
- Patricia Monroe Harbour "Soul Dancer"

Introduction Life's Coming Attractions

'The Halloween Party'

The 1950's opened the door for NOISE! It was at a time of loud car mufflers, and drive-in waitress's on roller skates delivering a quick food order on a tray that would attach to your car window. The 1950's also opened the door for delivering new sounds of nerve-shattering' 'Be-Bop!' The fun part was that we all danced the 'Jitterbug' and that was essential for the 50's. TV was then introduced to our lives and it became a system designed to eliminate pleasure but except for comedy and one called "All in the Family." 'Laurence Welk' came to be known with his elevator music for parents and older people. We were just coming out from the '1940's era with the 'Big Bands' we danced to it all!

Our high school class was known as a very ongoing party class and we all stuck together in our friendships as classmates. We loved talking about our next party coming up and at who's house it would be held and knowing the next party would be held on October 31, 1951 the night and preview of 'Halloween's coming attraction.

"The Halloween Party" A Beginning A Soul Mate Showing-Up

I n Life's Coming Attraction and Journey and "I found God to be the 'Holy God of Wonders" beginning with the celebration of "All Hallows Eve" {An ancient Celtic Scottish Holiday} and to honor a holy evening of 'All Saints' and souls with a sacred purpose. Today, it is called "Hallowe'en." It is also called 'All Hallows Eve' being the 'All-Hallows' or 'All Saints' Day and the last day of the Celtic calendar. It was originally a pagan holiday created by Christians to convert pagans and was celebrated on November 1st and a time for honoring saints on this designated day.

The Halloween culture signifies 'summers end' and a harvest festival with huge sacred bonfires -marking the end of the Celtic year and the beginning of a new one. Gifts and treats were left out to pacify the evil and ensure next year's crops would be plentiful. This custom evolved into 'Trick-or Treating' including spooks, ghosts and walking skeletons that represent the contact between the spiritual and physical world and between the living and the dead. Figures of witches and wizards were all seen to have the power to contact the spirit world. Bats, blacked cats, and spiders were often connected with the Halloween night with the darkness of witches and wizards. -

In the moon glow of October 31, 1951 and a freshman in high school I attended the 'Halloween party of a classmate - and led to a basement adorned with many bales of hay carved pumpkins and trails of long hanging tussles of yellow corn enhancing the appearance of the holiday where an abundance of small sandwiches was served with 'Coke-a-Cola' and the traditional 'Apple Cedar' for October's Hallows Eve' drink. and is how this 'Halloween Party' began.

The 'Halloween Party' began with finding myself crouched on my knees and allowing my face to plunge down into a tub of water sitting on the floor, and bobbing, dunking and biting into the water to retrieve a floating apple in the mouth, it was a game all the girls and I liked playing on a traditional Hallowe'en. The object was to be the first person to retrieve an apple in the mouth and the winner would be the next person to marry. After several dunking's and plunging my face into the water barrel I found myself thoroughly wet, from being submerged like an aquatic plant reaching above the surface of the water. Drenched and soaked gasping for breath steeping to extract the apple flavors from my mouth Standing up and brushing at a mop of wet hair I heard laughter from across the room and began observing a crowd of boys.

Classmates were all standing in a huddle laughing as they tossed their heads in festive cheer. I stood casting a wondering look and falling into a vacant mood I gaz'd and gaz'd looking wherever the eyes wondered. Suddenly a pastel reflection loomed into view like the unveiling appearance of a 'spirit' being propelled from behind or from beyond and something was moving into a forward direction.

At that very moment Information dramatically began unraveling from 'beyond' and into pieces of a dramatic past and future. I began experiencing messages instantaneously in the mind's eye with a sense of stunning facts and bring my heart to the attention of the past with a direction to an immediate reality. "Cognitively Thinking"

– I could see pictures with messages appearing and projected vocally with knowing stunning facts and knowledge.

I could barely breathe. Silently, a mere shadow of a profile appeared as if a mortal was slowly being refined from behind a strange transparent veil like a 'spirit' in celestial glow coming to celebrate 'Holy Saints and Souls' for the "Hallow-Eve" celebration. A 'Precognition' of knowing a future not yet experienced came to me with a 'clear sight' of 'Clairvoyance' and I could 'hear' the 'psychic' information through an inner hearing of 'Clairaudience' A flash of messages from 'Source' and 'spirit world came with this future message: "This is the meeting for which you were incarnated to meet on this sacred 'Hallow-Eve" After sensing this stunning fact in questionable disbelief my attention was directed to an immediate reality standing across the room in the crowd of boys and in a powerful and instantaneous deep gaze of electrifying vibrations the most amazing 'Liquid Brown Eyes' turned quickly gently meeting mine with 'Love.' Sparks transcended between the two of us without a word in the same purposeful moment and I began receiving God-like flashes in the heart and from 'somewhere within' a sea of silence of 'New Life'

- "This is the man you will marry in this lifetime

The 'Friend and Soul Love' you have been waiting for since childhood.

There may be some problems with an air of melancholy - You are strong and have the strength and ability to handle it." -

I stood in 'Silent Joy' remembering other people saying that his name is "Jim." I also knew this good friend and I had come here from another past life and now we are on 'God's Time' and I'm meeting the ultimate connection to my heart.

Mystified and overwhelmed I fell into a connection of mental bliss and not sure of what just happened. Everything was happening so swiftly I stood motionless dazzled in flashes of 'messages' of what was happening on a sub-conscious but higher level. In all due respect to the 'Divine Spiritual Source' and the messages sent I was propelled to see the truth of life and with my eyes still fixed upon the profile of this boy named 'Jim' across the room I could hear the direct communication of CLARITY coming again 'Affirming'

"Jim is the love for which you have been waiting"

I knew that 'True Love' can be drawn only from 'God's heart' with the mighty flame of Love but was I being 'Divinely' guided from being a 'seeker' to a 'seer?'

Still feeling dumbfounded I began feeling the inspiration of the Universe as a 'Psychic Medium.'

"The best and most beautiful things in the world cannot be seen

- or even touched; they must be felt with the heart"
- Attributed to Helen Keller

"The eyes are the windows to the soul" and with a quick turn Jim's eyes met mine in a direct eye contact with a mutual depth of love ever present in my soul and like we had known one another for a long time. In deep eye-contact we had an 'Instant Rapport of Connection' and it was immediate! The deep intense connection of love's rapture was as if time had not been lost since we were last together Time and Space had no meaning.

Instantaneous charges were electrifying and powerful that words could not be described. It was like making 'love again' the first time we met. It was like your partner's eyes drew you in looking right through you with an immediate 'recognition on a Soul Level.' I seemed to know that it was truly 'my Jim' and the one I had been waiting for but didn't know who he was or what he looked like. I felt like a 'Bride!' In silence my mind was saying {"You, many years late. How happy I am to see you." "The air of this October night found you and replaced my heart with your name Jim" I felt a deep sense of sacredness of learning the 'oneness of God' as though I had never lived before.

Jim and I were attracted to one another like magnets followed by an intense attraction and full of uncontrollable passion. Intuitively, I felt connected by 'attraction' as we could feel what the other was feeling or thinking before words were ever spoken. We both felt overcome by a pleasant buss-like sensation throughout the body and into the limbs and extremities. The sensation was physical and pulse-like almost like an electricity coursing through our system. 'Soul Love' knows no physical boundaries and is always followed with dreams.

There are no barriers between the two of us. Our relationship became totally an open one. Our conversations seemed to go on and on forever and we have a special sacredness transcending beyond anything I have ever experienced. A strong spiritual sense of unlimited eternity gave feeling without a doubt and that we were brought together for a reason inspires our sameness. I could see us as 'God Mates' with purpose and meaning through our living in harmony of whispering winds and our hearts as well as our brains were acting in the same wave-length destined to enter our lives to bring about 'Change.'

When two lovers connect on a spiritual level the 'soul' sex is amazing transcending all physical parameters. Only passions great passions can elevate the soul to the 'Next Level.' Spiritual supports are very much at play and more so than any physical ones.

"I am in you and you in me, mutual in divine love"

Poet: - William Blake -

"Open the memory and embrace the Love and who we are." Poet: Patricia Monroe

"My own thoughts propelled longing for more understanding, more learning, and deeper spiritual experiences of searching seeking self-help and seeking the truth of life. As I peered within 'Thinking Backwards' to life in this incarnation I could see clearly that there are no accidents in this universe. "Truth" applies right from the moment of our creation in an infinite universe going on forever.

There is truly NO ending but the beginning of a new beginning."

-Patricia Monroe Harbour

The world's greatest mystic poet has the electric eloquence of innermost Truth. A visionary's incredible life work "Poems" and a spiritual genius at the highest level.

-Attributed to Poet RUMI

I felt rapture and wonder in awakening to 'Divine Love' like to a Wild Rose of fearless courage awakening the senses with such humility and clarity

Love at its peak is euphoric. From the beginning of when Jim and I first held hands magnetic bolts of electric shock were triggered flowing through our blood together. Emotionally obsessed with each other, we put each other's love letters under our pillow at night when going to sleep longing to be together. We could embrace and kiss forever if we did not have to go to school. Just looking into one's eyes sparked dreams as 'one' in marriage and ecstasy. We had the illusion of a marital bliss to make each other supremely happy and it was nothing but perfect. Of Couse, we are not totally naïve and knew intellectually that we will eventually have some differences but we would discuss openly any problem and would always be willing to make concessions and reach agreements. Caught-up in the beauty and the charm of one another's personality we have the real thing, and nothing could ever come between us and 'Our Perfect Love.' 'Our Love' will always be through Eternity.'

Through research I found the "Coulomb's Law" which means "Electrostatic Forces" and those forces are very important. The magnitude of force of an electric charge bears a strong attractive force and it is the same forcer as opposites repel and attract using a little reasoning. They are some of the most important things on the Universe because they keep us together.

When a 'Soul Mate' is supposed to appear they will come into our life and very often when you least expect it. Realizing at this point I didn't know Jim, nor had we ever met or spoken with him in this life before. We were in the same grade in school but not in any of the same classes. I only knew through others of his name to be 'Jim.' However, by "Coincidence" which has an apparent connection, I knew he lived around the corner in the neighborhood I lived in.

I began 'Thinking Backwards' to the time I fell into a spiritual connection in a conversation with 'God' with prayers as I bask in the sunshine of a summer backyard garden sitting next to a 'Golden Pond' of golden fish and remembering I had asked God for help to find my friend and the soul love I had incarnated to Earth and to be with. It was a 'planned meeting' by Source long before we were incarnated here to Earth. 'Prayer Changes Everything' and everything I had asked and wished for in prayer is now being granted and honored.

- When a true friendship catches fire it turns to deep love Who doesn't desire such a foundation through special Love and Hope and bond dreams to BLOOM? Through mystic sweet inspiration of 'soul love' images of romance and romantic candlelit evenings with passionate embraces while looking at the moon is perceived as somehow being superior to what others settle for. The ultimate connection with one another is portrayed by peers as being 'SOUL MATES.' Struggling with the concept and pondering the idea of 'soulmates' leaves much conjecture and misunderstanding concerning the subject. A relationship with a 'Soulmate' is likely to be CHALLENGING testing one's abilities and demanding.

- "The whole point of a 'soulmate' turning up in your life is to show you 'YOURSELF' that is the person drawn into your life is there through vibration and nothing else. They are present because your vibration and their vibration are matched the same way."

Mention the word 'soulmate' to a group of people and you are bound to get a few eye rolls. The idea that there is one magical person for you who you will fall in love with instantly and never disagree with is just not realistic.

What does exist at least for many people, is a person who you know instinctively who you connect with on the deepest level and who allows you to grow as a person within the relationship. When that person is a romantic partner you have come across something "Truly Special."

How do you know when you have found 'The One?'

Some telling signs are when you're not capable of being separated. 'Soul Mate' love is so strong and pure that even death cannot quench the feelings or tearing them apart. They will reunite here on earth through love, relationship and marriage as 'SOUL MATES' and is linked to the concept of 'Reincarnation.'

What causes individuals to be drawn toward one another?

The answer can be both by accident and a destined meeting between two people. It can be purposeful and both random and existential as well as being something emotional or intellectual. More than that 'Fate' plays a role in our lives.'

SURPRISE is an element Jim and I have set off on and a course not accounted for. Jim had a sharp awakening to the 'nature of his social values and style' while I was being made to see the reality of my own unconscious desire for change. We were always having unusual effects upon others and one we had not been using too or had not reckoned with. I knew our relationship was only as stable as our 'awareness' of what it was about and where we would be going. It was dependent upon our having longer-more lasting and stable interactions or we could be picking ourselves up and WOW!

What Happens Next?

Jim and I have 'efficient teamwork' which is what I find unique about him and makes him constructively aware of how he should or could fit better into the the status quo. Jim shows me new ways of looking at life to clarify difficult issues. Impartially, he points out where I am my own worst enemy. We do have a mutual problem-solving element which is useful to one degree or another with working on some specific project together.

If our relationship was sound and sincere we could have drawn upon our friendship in an "Unconditional Comradeship' and take it still further as a pair or part of a team. It would be instrumental in helping others in a way through difficulties.

If Jim and I could have stabilized our fears and secured a solidity and steadiness and owned-up to the projection of putting everything onto each other instead of the {'Realist' versus the Dreamer'} and having "self-honesty" it would have been the best exercise to do because in time and as it stands now the "muddy pool' will turn into a swamp."

This is a call of the NEW

And it is a generational interaction for us as individuals. This interaction is saying that such qualities are central to our being together. We were both born and grew up in a time that we saw the same technological advances and changes in social and political values. Wek are the same age and therefore we are subject to similar cultural, spiritual and musical influences in our lives and they are the general underlay of compatibility and are thrashed out through sexual forms that make up our relationship. This interaction makes it clear that giving into our passions leads to some kind of reckoning and sooner or later ethical standards would have to prove themselves to be more than just opinions.

Having the intensity of a 'Close' generational contact we have similar psychological, political and global changes in our lives, and a number of passionate, obsessive contacts between the two of us and this makes it all the more so because our social environment would encourage the same.

As perceived we could have a business-like arrangement which is an extremely down-to-earth interaction. It would allow Jim to help me to find my place in the world and give stability to my insights or feeling of loneliness. My part of the 'deal' would be to allow our relationship to conform and intensify Jim's sense of authority at a DEEP LEVEL.

Friends and associates have always noticed our harmonious vibrations and liked to be around us seeking our help and sympathy in times of trouble. However, much we make of this or don't is still the question.

Ideally if we both evolved of 'Spiritually' then we could use the 'Spiritual' energy- to achieve greater good. Compassion and good-will are the basic ingredients of this basic compatibility.

The possibility of blame and recrimination is strong in my emotional urges or convictions and it clashes with Jim's beliefs but the contrast between could serve to make us both more aware of where we stand with respect to these issues.

Jim and I are both after some form of philosophy that goes deep enough to enable us both to understand what it is about human nature that can draw up downward and inwards despite our best intentions or sense of {what is right and what is wrong}.

Jim and I are interested and involved with metaphysical subjects, and the frontiers of science and 'Understanding' the human nature through the HEAD. HEART and 'HARMONY.' This interaction could greatly contribute to our progress of individually or together. Jim offers 'Scientific' explanations and formulas to my 'psychic impressions' while I introduce a vision or myth to inspire Jim's models or theories. With our other creative interactions between the two of us together we could make a very original and innovative duo.

"Faith is a passionate Intuition"

- Attributed to Poet: William Wordsworth

The ability to understand something immediately, and without the need for conscious reasoning is to allow the 'Intuition' of the 'Sixth Sense' of Clairvoyance to guide us. It is the ability to acquire knowledge without proof, evidence, or conscious reasoning and it is being unconscious in patterned-recognition such as {Instinct, Truth, and Belief} and meaning in the realms of greater knowledge: Whereas, others contend that the word

'Intuition' is often misunderstood and that it means instinct, true belief's and greater realms are the inherent mental and physical powers of instinct, beliefs and intuition and they are all factually related.

On the face of all this the subconscious describes something that is just below the 'awareness.' In time, Jim's and my 'awareness' will surface and maybe we can get to the root of why we get so nervous in the first place. "The subconscious" is also a dark place and fits beautifully with what the 'Dark Mojo' is trying to explore.

In Accordance:

- 'When we remain 'unconscious' the 'ego' only sees what it can see immediately ahead Ego is identified as the "I" and is blind and protects the space we know. 'Ego wants to be in control with having power and attention and always wants more. I was engrossed in the top of my mind with other things to the extent of exclusion of others and their thoughts including my marriage and portrayed an image of what my 'ego' was all about as I understood it to be as my reality.

– 'Unconsciously, 'the ego was busy telling me that I am not that bad and I was in 'a place of limbo.' Confusion is good if you have lived many years in confusion as I have wanting to know 'who I was' and 'what I was meant to be' and 'what I was supposed to do in my life.' -

Jim and I were not willing to reach agreements or make confessions and we failed to reckon with the reality of human nature. You might say that we were both egocentric and our world revolved around ourselves.

Jim became increasingly distant around me and our hearts went on into sweet escape. Jim walked away completely ignoring me. I couldn't figure out what I had done wrong or what he was thinking. - Then out of the dark of day he approached me there on the spot and announced that he thought we should 'Separate' not get a divorce but just 'Separate.' Blown-away and I asked for a reason and if he had someone else? After several seconds he answered "NO" but continuing to say we should separate!

A THOUSAND KNIVES CUT THROUGH MY HEART. The living breath was knocked out of me and I couldn't breathe. Feeling lightheaded and like I was going to faint I managed to swallow taking a deep breath and said "Well, you know what you can do about it." He answered: "I can't because you are here."

Those were his last words to me with no explanation. My breath fell with the deep plunge shattering my heart into small pieces that lead further into a cruel non-existence of communication. Had I been living and loving this man in a marriage for thirty-five years without a reverence for honor or without deep respect regarding mortal values?

In this an 'Unchained Melody.' I felt undervalued as a person in every way without respect and personal quality or ability. "The mind is for seeing" and "the heart is for hearing." Had I been living and loving within an illusion all these years? I have always been a romantic girl; and now there was a break of 'balance' or contrast between us.

From the dark side of time Jim came down with "Leukemia"

"Where is the Mind?" Was it the 'Last Lullaby' saying 'good-bye to old times' and the best to you too? We both had failed to reckon in the reality of human nature of the highs and lows in life. The "RAIN' began falling in life within the heart of one another.

Jim was checked by health doctors regularly but only after getting him to 'MD Anderson' in Houston it was found that he had "Acute Leukemia" causing cancer of the blood cells of the bone marrow with a limited time to live 'two to six months' and with constant weekly blood-transfusions. Of course, it was Jim's decision whether to stay in Houston at MD Anderson where he would have the finest of doctors to make him more comfortable but Jim CHOSE to come home for the remainder of his time. He composed and record music pouring out from within. His feelings were so telling through his music. I could feel Jim deeply through his music and I knew exactly what he was saying but of course in a psychic way.

I don't know how I found the strength but saw to it that our transportation was made via a bus or others donating their time for our transportation from Rockport to Corpus Christi for his cancer treatments weekly and increasing to three times a week.

That last day at home before Jim decided he was ready to go to the hospital I tried to resign myself to the fact that Jim would not be coming back home again. Before calling the ambulance to take him to the hospital I asked if he would like for me to fix him something to eat? "Yes Please" he said, and asking for a fried egg sandwich with all the trimmings. I remember him looking up at me as I sat the plate down before him with the sandwich and saying, "Jim you can have anything you want" and he gave back a sweet smile. After being admitted to the hospital in Corpus Christi Daughter, Renee came to relieve me after four days and nights at the hospital sleeping in Jim's hospital room. I could go home for one night and shower and get a good night's sleep. That same day was our wedding anniversary July 29, 2007.

That next morning July 30th one day after our thirty-fifth wedding anniversary Renee called saying to hurry back to the hospital; Jim's Leukemia was ending. Having to depend on someone else to get me back quickly to the hospital felt like a very slow and painful operation and I was at my wits-end that I would not make it back in time to be with Jim.

Upon my arrival at the hospital a few close family members were ushering in and out of Jim's hospital room and I waited till all others had paid their last respects before I entered his room and stopping at the end of Jim's hospital bed. As he looked at me, I finally got up the nerve to say -

"Jim, I know you can't talk to me right now but I here you I know that you love me and I love you"

Walking closer to the side of Jim's hospital bed I picked-up his hand and held it locked tightly within mine speaking volumes to him without a word in a deep inseparable kind of love that is carried through many lifetimes. In the same breath there was a look and feeling which only the two of us would know with a likeness of the deepest kind and I felt I had known Jim for a 1,000 lifetimes through intimate experiences and knowledge.

Our gazes were matched whispered in the same breath of life and Jim rose up in bed towards me touching my heart. His glance suddenly turned looking beyond me to his loving angels at the end of his bed and where spirits of loved ones were looming and waiting by the ivy gate. With one large last breath, I smiled to Jim embracing his face with love the deepest kind in a sacred moment and his soul was elevated to a higher level with his last breath.

"I began walking through the 'dark night of my soul' without moon glow looking backwards."-

Patricia Harbour - Lost and Hurt, I looked 'backwards' to 'Ancestral

Legacy' and looking within to find my authentic self to re-learn how to be myself as I looked to the Angels of Hope. -

I knew in my heart that I had no qualifications, definitions or descriptions blazing in a reflection of life and that the man to whom I have been married existed no longer as I watched the brilliance of our life together disappear into a new light of death and a 'Sacred' moment.

Let's not talk about the 'Embarrassment' and the discomfort I have experienced with my loved one and the unacceptable emotions of non-communication and pure silence at the end of our marriage. I was left with the feeling that I had been eliminated for greener pastures.

I began taking smaller steps and with each step I looked deeper and deeper within myself. Why was I being treated in such a way? Was I climbing a mountain of 'betrayal?'

I do have a pure 'Imagination' and I questioned myself in my own responsibility of life and I knew I needed to learn new things to a level of consciousness. I had to expand to a higher level of experiencing and then eventually, I would be led to 'Who I Am' and Why I was let go.

I had diminished 'trusting' and I began feeling how NATURE is close to me. I do have difficulty receiving offers of gifts and I don't know how to look at my relationships. HERE is where I began looking backwards at myself. Feeling unworthy I seemed that I didn't know how to receive the LOVE I so desperately wanted and needed.

I tried this and that anywhere from becoming a 'Docent' as a guide for giving tours through an old historic mansion and bringing about others to the ways and times of family living and thinking. I then joined a class group of 'Online Dancing' learning to consolidate my personal thoughts into something I could 'Believed and could Change.' I began searching to find my 'authentic self'within me.

"I 'Awaken' in a sea of silence as I forged deep within the DARKEST corners of myself "THINKING BACKWARDS." Patricia Harbour, Poet

Floating through the meadows of my life as a child I wanted to understand WHY I felt not loved or not as good as a sibling and the many times of closing myself off 'without an ability to receive'. I would always give to others and Not to myself. Learning how to receive must start when you are small and I was overwhelmed at what I found out by looking at life as a child.

I needed to learn how to Give to Myself First in a completely new shift of 'Awareness' and bringing in the new ways with a new beginning. LETTING GO of the old ways and the things that are no longer of any help or good for me with endings beginnings and transformation. I started seeing the wisdom stuck in the dark knight of the soul's sexual energy and emotions that must be extracted. I am a wounded healer with a beginning in a brand-new Life and new Beginning. In 'A beam of Candlelight' I learned BLISS and the bliss of love. It's (Giving and Receiving with a higher level of 'Understanding) and which is coming into NEW TECHNOLOGICAL ABILITIES. There's the quick pace of technological change and it's scientifically applied. This is a framework to 'analyze the general environment relating to industry' which has impacted the politics of technological change and new factors in human resource.

There is a NEW and NATURAL step occurring with an 'Eternal Wave' and I am allowing myself to say how I really feel trying to get over the painful experience and heart break. I've tended to stuff it down and push it away pretending it doesn't exist. I didn't even realize it was still hurting me because it has hurt me for so long and I refused to face it head on. Now I am choosing to face it with saying:

"I felt rejected with pain and I felt numb but I'm telling myself that I'm okay and that I am going to be okay. I've felt like I was nothing and all those things have made me feel this way. In this acknowledgement I'm honoring it even if it does evoke bitterness again. These are natural emotions and I am choosing to face them head on."

"I am always about feeling 'Positive' and I am not naive in facing and showing experience or wisdom and judgment. We must face what hurts us and I am facing what has hurt me and what has damaged me. It's not fun but it is so worth it. Day by day I'll slowly get over you as it is a different energy Jim that you are in. I'm finding what has damaged and caused me mental turmoil and I'm going through all the emotions that have accompanied it and I will HEAL. Today it is not so deep and it's a good day to "Apologize."

"I sit now in prayer and Meditate to the Universe and cry myself out to the Universe. I am saying this HURTS and I wish it wasn't but it is and so I want to FREE MYSELF and the other person involved. I want us both to HEAL and I want us both to move on and I want the best outcome for everybody that is involved. I am coming from a place of hurt and I want to prevail so I'm staying in this good source of energy and stepping out of it with saying "NO." I am not coming from a place of hurt emotions and I'm keeping myself perpetuated. I don't want any kind of cord connecting us because I'm NOT forgiving what you did to me and I am FREEING myself. I do want the best outcome for everybody that is involved so I'm stepping out of it. I want you to be fine and I want you to heal. I want us both to heal and move on. I want to be free and in saying that, I give you and I to the Universe and I want us both to HEAL. Whatever happens I took the Universe's Way in all this and the pain was not for nothing as I'm learning the 'Experiences and Lessons' in the Healing process.

My consciousness has expanded and I'm realizing that all I've been through is not for nothing and that it is TRUE HEALING 'TRUE FORGIVENESS and an EXPANSION of FORGIVING and I'm letting the Soul guide me."

"I am forgiving myself and you, my husband and soul mate and YOU HAVE HELPED ME TO EXPAND IN WAYS THAT I NEVER COULD HAVE SEEN. When someone has screwed you over and betrayed you it's not for nothing and once I had moved through this - I started seeing the WISDOM and the STRENGTH within me and I' m letting this be my lesson for today."

TODAY "I say to the Universe I am crying and I AM asking for your help to guide me:"

"I AM ALLOWING my feelings to heal and I'm facing it head on. I have felt rejected

– Belittled and put down and I am honoring it. It's been hurting and I'm all about what has hurt and damaged me. I'm looking for balance and I'm facing it. I am rejecting myself and I'm asking to heal and for my friend, husband, and soul mate to heal also. As I hone into the hurt, I will find BALANCE and I'm facing it."

"I am putting in details of the past and the things I didn't wish to remember and I now am beginning to see facts and I ask to reclaim the parts of myself I felt impacted over in myself and with others."

I am "remembering evil acts of cutting-off others in traffic while driving and many sometimes without knowing I was doing so. It was brought to my attention that I had even cut-off my daughter Renee in traffic and I didn't realize it. There were times I wanted to cut-off my sister from the love she was given in childhood out of some satisfaction and to feel that love I knew she had. I wanted to feel that personal value of the TRUTH and the truth of love. One day, I even went to the extent of pouring a glass of water over my sister's face as she could sleep and not help clean the room, we both shared. I believed the responsibility in our space should be shared by both of us as a duty and not left only for one to do all the cleaning all the time. These facts left me feeling not worthy and Jealous. These actions also poured-over into my marriage and I treaded on my Soulmates personal space. This action resulted in a violent reaction from him that was UNFORGIVING. At the time, I didn't realize the hurt and distrust that I had caused. Through an astonishing DISAGREEMENT with a case of good Judgement I'm showing a lack of refinement and perception to judge well in these activities and I've learned WHY knowledge is important. THE LACK OF PERCEPTION 'TO JUDGE' leads into hurt feelings and mistrust and suspicion and deep doubts set in.

Through the feelings of being hurt more, I tried to make jokes about the lack I felt with making things sound to be the fault of the another and the one closest to me, and the one I have loved and cherished. This has led to other situations known as A DIVISION IN 'BALANCE OF POWERS' which has led to a situation of risk. There were no treaty terms to follow or were discussed let along the ones I had NEVER LEARNED. DISTRUST -simply divides the responsibility to Checks and Balances. The phrase TRUST AND VERIFY " refers specifically to Distrust! I was no longer Trusted to Remix or Transform or Be Respected Enough to build upon a marriage for any purpose with my 'Soul Mate' and he turned away from me.

"AFTER A PARTNERS DEATH YOU NEED TO ASK YOURSELF IF YOU TRUST THOSE WHOM YOU'VE BEEN IN PARTNERSHIP WITH. - IT IS ONE OF THE MOST CRUCIAL ASPECTS YOU NEED TO HAVE IN ORDER FOR THOSE CONNECTIONS TO BENEFIT YOU. Make sure you give enough of your time, energy and resources to your investments The more you put into them the more they will give you back. "WHEN YOU HAVE TRUST WITH THOSE WHOM YOU LOVE AND WORK WITH YOU ARE MUCH MORE LIKELY TO BENEFIT FROM YOUR PARTNERSHIP WITH THEM

INCLUDING THE FINANCIAL ONES INSTEAD OF BEING LEFT IN THE DARK."

"Today I am filled with a creative fire that burns bright and true. It is an opportunity that's not to be missed! I am letting this energy boost and carry me forward in a creative endeavor expressing myself boldly and truly By tapping into my own life force and giving it shape and form. This can inspire others to do the same."

"It is easy to come to terms with the darker, less pretty and polished parts of my being. I'M LEARNING HOW TO BE IN TOUCH WITH MY SHADOWS and reflect on all the deeper questions. WE ARE SO CONDITIONED TO REJECT CERTAIN PARTS OF OUR PSYCHE, AND THE ONES THAT WE'VE BEEN TOLD ARE "UNACCEPTABLE" "INAPPROPRIATE" "IMPOLITE" YOU NAME IT.

What ends up happening is that we put those parts of ourselves away, the parts which are just as valid and valuable beyond all human ones as another one. This causes those rejected parts to lurk in the darkness where they've started to wreak havoc upon our lives without us even being aware of it and because they're invisible to us. It's time to reclaim all those parts of myself that I have put away and recognize that there is nothing "bad" or "evil" about them. On the contrary I'll bring them into the light of consciousness and relinquish their negative control and the impact over myself and others."

"I've asked if these are reflective of personal values or not? If they are not, then seek out the ones that are personal that I do reflect upon because at the end it is so worth it. Surround yourself with people that bring you closer to who you want to be."

"A 'Soul Mate' SECRET Never Admitted: But WHO'S Secret is it? Is it Pure Love {Unfinished Business} (A connection that was Not Grounded) and NOT BALANCED?"

"We both were lacking patience and felt insecure and no longer TRUSTED or believed the other. After my 'Soul Mate' had passed on behind the veil to the other side with distance and time between us I'm here on earth in body, mind and spirit. With a bit of a distance between us now twelve years later and I have never given-up on the strong intimate bond between my 'soul love' and myself.

With much meditation and wanting to reconnect with my 'soul mate' 'Source' 'God' and the 'Universe' could see my desperate attempt and sorrow of longlines and an emotional response to isolation, including anxious feelings about a lack of connection or communication with my 'soul mate' after so much 'unfinished business.' I gradually began receiving information coming to me from many various places and ways. It was not just in meditation but through the Internet and many different people writing to tell me the most shocking news about my affairs. This has been happening for several months and I've really been feeling confused and SHOOK with knowing what to believe any longer. I began to lose a lot of my Positive Feelings and I dug deeper into the reality of myself with more research of learning and with more knowledge through research. I've learned the facts that Source, God, and the Universe all the Archangels friends family and loved ones on the other side were all rooting and standing in my corner as well as my Spirit Guides and Angels. Suddenly, I'm feeling the Divine Universal knowledge of being completely loved and helped and guided towards the 'Change' and a Transformation into an 'Alchemy' of divine energy of 'Oneness' for helping all others in need. I began meditating on this each day with my 'Intensions' and establishing oneness with my Christ Self and freeing myself from self-limiting concepts and bondage to others. Through the VIOLET FLAME.

I Begin with the protected connection of my 'Higher Self' to stay centered and at peace

The VIOLET FLAME BOOKLET By: Elizabeth Clare Prophet and the book of "Saint Germain on ALCHEMY" and his Formulas for Self- transformation - Attributed to "Mark L. Prophet * Elizabeth Clare Prophet".

Saint Germain tells you how to do it. He reveals secrets he has used for centuries along with Techniques you can use today to duplicate his achievements. St. Germain illumines and inspires and gives you the keys to SELF-TRANSFORMATION

- Saint Germain's is the ALCHEMIST -"Voltaire" (Francois-Marie Arouet) French and known as 'nom de plume Voltaire' and a French Enlightenment writer, historian called SAINT GERMAIN "The man who never dies and knows everything." And that is an understatement. The Count Saint Germain turned base metals into gold, removed the flaws from diamonds and discovered the magical portion of youth granted to induce and he is the confident of kings and a friend to the poor he used his alchemical powers to dissipate the poverty so prevalent in the eighteenth century. But his well-documented "miracles" were really the natural outgrowth of his practice of alchemy. The real purpose of Alchemy is to change yourself. Your nation. Your planet.

Through deed and thought:

> "We can bring about a heartfelt connection of service and bring on a light never done or known before."

> - 'Patricia Harbour' -

(FLEXIBILITY)

Flexibility is one of my best characteristics but also one that sometimes complicates my life. I am most comfortable when I'm not restricted by a plan. Today I'm wonderfully OPEN to any twist or turn life presents. It's also hard to focus on the path Well, I'm forgetting it! I'm going with the flow as it takes me to some wonderful places. I don't feel urged to "do anything" but to just rest in the emptiness and be. It is a crucial aspect of 'self-love' just allowing yourself quality alone time to refill your energy reserves and rejuvenate.

Today I deserve to allow myself to come first and prioritize my needs to feel safe and confident in being. The common belief that putting our self-first makes us "selfish" or "narcissistic" but that isn't true. The only way we can show up for the rest of the world is by showing up for ourselves first. By constantly giving others and neglecting yourself our reserves will empty and how will we keep on going? To be of service to the world, we need to replenish our energy by doing the things that nourish and support us then allows us to offer the same to others. Before pouring out to others, we need to make sure that our cup is full.

Our current energy will be open to discovery and strokes of insight and learn to live with your eyes and ears open and make sense of it all later. I look forward to having a common project that I can work towards with a romantic partner and create a much healthier and successful relationship dynamic. I'm setting my intentions of practicing more of that. So many relationships don't succeed because the people involved don't feel like they can relate to their partner on a bigger level, and one that extends outside of the personal relationship and doesn't neglect other aspects of your life. We owe it to ourselves and the world to share whatever gift we have to offer. Also, at the same time, we need to learn how to find 'balance' between those two parts of our life and find the fulfillment of a meaningful life.

As two independent and fulfilled beings of our own allows us to be much less likely to fall into patterns of codependency. When we are full of love towards ourselves, we can share it with others without feeling resentful or desperately wanting anything in return.

I am getting more in touch with my Confidence and Ability to take initiative to make what I want to happen. It is important the way we hold and present ourselves creating an image as someone who can take the lead and has self-motivation. Others look for someone who embodies these qualities.

I set my INTENSIONS for meditations each day with an invitation of prayer:

I have complete Optimism and Faith in myself for whatever I can dream up, and I have complete utter faith in myself to carry it out and I'm planting the seeds of some new beginnings on the social scene feeling uplifted and secure in the process. I am entering a period of reflection and releasing some secrets of self-finding my best work happens alone. Alone time will help me to attract some lucrative opportunities, both in love and money over these next several weeks. I am willing to bring myself as fully as I can in a relationship to one another and be present in the true sense of the world. If there is something lacking in the partnership, then I need to get curious about how that can be shifted? - Make sure that my partner is seeking the same things that I am and is willing to show-up fully in a relationship with me, and vice versa. Having a healthy strong element of TRUST. Mutuality doesn't mean expecting something in return! It's the sharing of a feeling, action, or a relationship between two people with RESPECT for each other's "Expertise." When we expand our mind and wrap it around new unfamiliar concepts we can be wide open to anyone who wants to take advantage of this fact and can be easily taken in. -

- A smidge of skepticism is a health thing. -
- I could not forge TRUSTFUL relations with my soul without acknowledging my errors and with sincerity, and I emerged from the materialist age as it has nothing but 'EGO' and the 'ego' only sees what is immediately ahead. I wanted to be in CONTROL with power and attention and was blind to opening myself to all possibilities and I settled into the same space of comfort I knew. -

(INTUITION)

After being exposed to all the wisdom and knowledge at the highest level of who 'I Am'

I found the missing link between 'my inner world' and the world around me rooted in the word INTUITION a world of vision, feeling and imagination.

Today I sat quietly after my morning meditation in my little garden of nature and just 'letting go' as I allowed myself to peacefully rest my eyes, my heart, and thoughts as I look deeply into the little tree I had planted just two years ago. The morning of the season was changing from summer to the fall of autumn with an overcast and the slightest of a raindrop allowing myself to drift into a feeling of peace. Words from 'within' the heart and mind' began speaking with an {inner eye and ear} as I began repeating each word coming through from internal ways and my 'third eye' opened wider and suddenly, there was strong sunlight shinning directly into my eyes turning everything into a guiding 'White Light' with others and as I am sharing this experience with you now.

In doing so, the 'Soul' evolves and afterwards so does the 'Personality.' The 'Spirit' and Soul' are to shine radiantly through the 'Personality.' This process is guided and inspired by God and 'God's Holy Spirit.' This is the GRAND JOURNEY through 'Spiritual Evolution.'

NATURE speaks with the {inner eye} and the {inner ear} through internal ways. The knowledge and understanding of my experience came through the senses, of hearing, sight, taste and touch. They serve to keep the 'Sensitive Intuitive' alive and helps to provide a deeper meaning and recognition to 'PURPOSE.' When we experience an answer deep inside our bones, telling us we have purpose and to move away from the distractions of this world, then we know that it is not somebody else telling us or a school telling us that we have PURPOSE. Instead, we will have several answers whispered in the ears 'inside ourselves' to activate that PURPOSE and it is all spelled out for us.

God always guides our 'Spirit' and our 'Spirit' always guides our 'Soul.' Our 'Soul' always seeks out the 'Personality' in our daily affairs of life. However, our personality' can choose {consciously or unconsciously} whether to accept or not accept the guidance given to us by our Soul our Spirit and by God. It is really a matter of CHOICE.

I am choosing the GRAND JOURNEY through 'Spiritual Evolution.' I think our world has a long way to go to be able to really embrace this growing movement of 'Intuition' and to recognize it is not soft but hard stuff and it is just as hard as math and science and economics. When you learn to breathe from the 'Inside out' your world 'sees from the inside out' and not from the 'outside in' and you will know yourself in the form of our inner worlds.

-Wangari Maathai the Kenyan visionary and internationally renowned Kenyan environmental political activist received the Nobel Peace Prize for the simple act of {planting trees} with strong roots creating social and political changes in her country. Her greatest legacy is to teach us all, that by attending to our own roots that go deep into the unknown of our own Energy Chakras and into each of our own souls, we can enable All Living Things and individuals to thrive through time spent in NATURE and in MEDITATION giving a sense of belonging and happiness and a sense of the past world around us.

IT TAKES MORAL COURAGE to change and {We Must Let Our Heart Break}

to find what we can do for the rest of our life and redistribute what we have learned and understand. When our sense of ego and personality are set aside and we keep our mental energy intact, we can become conscious of the non-physical our 'inner self and the subconscious through different practices to activate the 'light in the head.'

(GRIEF) And the Grieving Reactions:

Crying is a normal and natural part of grieving. Cry and talking about the loss is not the only healthy response. If it is forced or excessive, it can be harmful. Lack of crying is also a natural, healthy reaction, potentially protective of the individual, and may also be a sign of resilience. Science has found that some healthy people who are grieving do not spontaneously talk about the loss. Pressing people to cry or retell the experience of a loss can be harmful. Genuine laughter is healthy.

There are five identities of grievers:

1. NOMADS: Nomads have not yet resolved their grief and do not seem to understand the loss - that has affected their lives.
2. MEMORIALISTS: This identity is committed to preserving the memory of the loved one that - they have lost.
3. NORMALIZERS: This identity is committed to re-creating a sense of family and community.
4. ACTIVISTS: This identify focuses on helping other people who are dealing with the same disease or with the same issues that caused their loved one's death.
5. SEEKERS: This identify will adopt religious, philosophical, or spiritual beliefs to create meaning in their lives.

In the case of death, not providing adequate or appropriate adjustment to the environment or situation A maladaptation trait such as increasing consumption of alcohol, excessive daydreaming associated with excessive fantasy is a complicated grief and can be defined as a more persistent form of intense grief in which thoughts and dysfunctional behaviors emerge along with continued yearning and sadness or preoccupation with thoughts of the person who died.

(RISKS)

Complicated grief is characterized by an extended grieving period. An important part of understanding complicated grief is understanding how the symptoms differ from normal grief. When the reaction turns into complicated grief, the feelings of loss become incapacitating and continue even though time passes. The signs and symptoms characteristic of complicated grief are "extreme focus on the loss and reminder of the loved one, intense longing or pining for the deceased, problems accepting the death, numbness or detachment ... bitterness about your loss, inability to enjoy life, depression or deep sadness, trouble carrying out normal routines, withdrawing from social activities, feeling that life holds no meaning or purpose, irritability or agitation, lack of trust in others. The symptoms seen in complicated grief are specific because the symptoms seem to be a combination of symptoms found in separation as well as traumatic distress. They are also considered to be complicated because, unlike normal grief, these symptoms will continue regardless of the amount of time that has passed and despite treatment given.

Many of the "Bereavement and Late-Life Depression: Grief and its Complication in the Elderly" were symptoms correlated with cancer, hypertension, anxiety, depression, suicidal ideas, increased smoking, and sleep impairments at around six months after spousal death.

(DEATH of A SPOUSE)

The death of a spouse is usually a particularly a powerful loss. A spouse often becomes part of the other in a unique way. Many widows and widowers describe losing 'half' of themselves. The days, months and years after the loss of a spouse will never be the same and learning to live without them may be harder than one would expect. The grief experience is unique to each person. Sharing and building a life with another human being, then learning to live singularly, can be an adjustment that is more complex than a person could ever expect.

After a long marriage, at older ages, the elderly may find it a very difficult understanding to begin anew; but at younger ages as well, a marriage relationship was often a profound and an emotional intense one for the survivor.

The factor is the way the spouse died. The survivor of a spouse who died of an illness has a distinct experience of such loss than a survivor of a spouse who died by an act of violence. The grief, in all events, however, can always be of the most profound sort to the widow and the widower. Emotional unsteadiness, bouts of crying, helplessness and hopelessness are just a small sample of what a widow or widower can expect to face.

Depression and loneliness are very common. Feeling bitter and resentful are normal feelings for the spouse who is "left behind".

When an adult child loses a parent in later adulthood, it is "timely" and to be a normative life course event. This allows the adult children to feel a permitted level of grief. However, research shows that the death of a parent in an adult's midlife is not a normative event by any measure, but is a MAJOR life transition causing an evaluation of one's own life or mortality. Others may shut out friends and family in processing the loss of someone with whom they have had the longest relationship.

An adult may be expected to cope with the death of a parent in a less emotion way; however, the loss can still invoke extremely powerful emotions. This is especially true when the death occurs at an important or difficult period of life, such as when becoming a parent, at graduation, or at other times of emotional stress. It is important to recognize the effects that the loss of a parent can cause. For an adult, the willingness to be open to grief is often diminished. A failure to accept and deal with loss will only result in further pain and suffering. "Morning is the open expression of your thoughts and feelings about the death. It is an essential part of healing."

Severe reactions: Occur in people with depression present before the loss event. Severe grief reactions may carry over in family relations.

(IN ANIMALS)

Grief was thought to be only a human emotion, but studies have shown that other animals have shown grief during the death of another animal. This can occur between bonded animals which are animals that attempt to survive together.

"The soul comes from without into the human body as into a temporary abode, and it goes out of it anew and it passes into other habitations, for the soul is immortal" Dedicated to Ralph Waldo Emerson Philosopher and Poet -

Issues with family can be difficult. -"I feel unconditional love for my family" Family karma often carries on from one generation to the next reminding us to pay attention to the habits and ways we have inherited and to keep a careful watch with awareness. By healing our relationships with our parents and even if they have passed on, and with our siblings and our children we can heal our personal and family members karmic patterns. This can be the bonus of our 'awareness' in life. Beyond our family blood exists our tribal family and our families of choice. Letting go of judgments and any sense of separation can help us in feeling connected with the whole human family.

"Open the Eyes of My Heart

- I am the light of the heart and see that light in others
- I intend to dissolve a sense of separation in all relationships
- and trust that everything works out for the best"
- Patricia Harbour Poet

(NATURE & EARTH)

I have always had a strong connection to NATURE and EARTH ever since being a small child and in doing so for me, it was good to be outside with nature as much allowed.

– I never missed a meditation day but only except for circumstances. Meditations can be done whenever it it appropriate for you. I have tried both early in the morning and at night. At night, I would feel too tired from the day that I would fall asleep.

Morning is the best time to meditate. A lot of times we are meditating even when we don't realize it and when we feel something loving in our hearts.

I began feeling and seeing the positive changes happening to me in my live through prayer and "From the Light, Love, Power and Heart of the Universe that I AM" I 've learned that God works in a myriad of ways to bless me. If we open our mind to receive our good there is nothing too good to be true. Nothing is too wonderful to have happen With the Universe as my Source, nothing amazes me.

No longer am I burdened by thoughts of past or future. One is gone. The other is yet to come. By the power of belief and coupled with your purposeful fearless actions and deep rapport with the Universe, your future will be created, and an abundance made manifest. When you ask and accept you will be lifted in this and every moment into Higher Truth. Keep your mind quiet. Don't forget to give freely and fearlessly into life and Life will give back to you with magnificent increase. Blessings will come in expected and unexpected ways The Universe provides in wondrous ways. Be indeed Grateful and let it be so. -

Things to Remember:

DON'T let anyone make you feel inferior and DO believe in your own skills and show others. Don't be resentful and too sarcastic even it the other side deserves it. Be the bigger person and just withdraw from a debate if you sense it starts to deteriorate to a quarrel. Don't allow your inner fears and insecurities to be visible for everyone. Do try to look invincible from the outside.

"True happiness lies within yourself." Patricia Harbour, Poet

The Secret Challenge: Take out the photos of moments in your life you perceive as perfect and ideal. Try to really remember everything from back there, to the smallest detail.

Was everything really that perfect or did your memory mislead you to imagine it perfect? Take an imaginary 'photo' of your current situation. How does it look like now?

Be careful and think twice before deeming any undertaking void of potential, because chances are, you're too impatient or too tired to wait for the results to come. Don't launch anything significant if you're not prepared to work hard and for an extended period before you can finally see the fruits of your labor. You'll be very motivated, but also very impatient to see results right away, so projects, which require your full attention for a prolonged period without imminent gratification are not a great idea now.

DO'S and DON'Ts:

DON'T be quick to give up undertakings for the lack of imminent results. DO be patient enough - to bring them to full fruition.

DON'T launch anything significant if you're looking for instant outcome. DO invest your time in shorter and less important projects.

DON'T exaggerate past failures and DO stay open to new ways in which to enjoy old skills.

> "Everything that I've done, I've learned is a steppingstone towards my future success."

Patricia Harbour, Poet

Secret Challenge: Make a list of all the things you've learned from your first job; think about the skills which a hobby of yours has taught you.

HELLO FROM HEAVEN:

SIGNS from the AFTERLIFE (Rainbows Feathers Butterflies)

I remained living in Rockport, TX after Jim's passing and began searching for answers which never stopped with me always searching for signs from the afterlife. I made several different calls to psychic mediums for connecting with the spirit world on the 'the other side' and talking with Jim on specific dates; one time I remember being on the exact day of Hallowe'en October 31st the day we first met at a Halloween party. Other times were on July 29th of each year being our Wedding Anniversary. I wrote bits of poetry specifically for him with readings through mediums. I never wanted to lose touch with Jim and the angels were more than enthusiastic to provide extra signs I was experiencing.

I would watch rainbows while driving along with others in a car. Rainbows became such a significant sign for me, I began seeing rainbows in my bedroom as a sign and to what they wanted me to learn and be aware of when they came knocking. I mean that literary. One night I awoke at 3:00 AM hearing a knocking at my door. Stunned I couldn't imagine who would be there at 3:00 AM in the morning and fearful as I was living alone with my little dog, Shariz, at that time I needed extra assurance and confidence as I carried little Shariz to the door with me but no one was there. After going back to bed a few minutes later I would heard the doorbell and this time I checked the back door. Again, no one was where.

Then my phone would ring and again no one was there. This went on for some time. I was flabbergasted! At first, I thought someone was playing a joke.

Then one night I was sitting up in bed listening to music and writing and the light was clearly on. Suddenly I saw a string of small white 'Orbs' as if they were tied together one after the other and attached to one large 'Blue Orb' leading the other smaller orbs around the top of my bedroom walls next to the ceiling. Suddenly, a larger 'golden-white light' attached itself to the large teak Armoire bookcase sitting adjacent to the side of my bed where I could see this light so very close. What a heartwarming way for the angels to reassure me, I thought. I couldn't have been happier It was a miracle of how God and the angels were wanting to communicate their love to me showing me that I was not alone and I am loved.

I had been feeling very alone since Jim's passing and not understanding WHY he pulled away from me towards the last of our marriage. Rainbows began appearing here and there and without any rain and were very vivid when I saw them in my mind.

My mind began remembering our beautiful Black Labrador Retriever named "Max" which Jim and I both loved so very much and adored. Max came down with cancer at thirteen years of age and daughter, Renee being a Technician and Manager of a veterinary clinic at that time, came to the house with the doctor to Euthanasia the ending of Max's life for relieving his pain and suffering. Max served to bless Jim and my life with so much love. Our beloved "Max" died in my arms as I kissed him and taking in his last breath. Jim and I both were very heartbroken to lose Max as he was a beloved member of our household.

I talked to Max in heaven through Mediums and "Max" asked me to please not forget him. How could I he was a champion of beauty and the delightful joy of love from God and his angels.

The next thing I knew, Renee was calling to say that it was time for us to have another dog and companion suggesting a newborn from a rescue dog having a litter of nine pups. All the pups had been asked for but one and this last one was needing a home. Jim was in the last of life with Leukemia and was venomously spiteful and objected to my having another dog.

After the third phone call from daughter Renee saying it was her last call about the pup needing a home and without a decision from us, she would find someone else who wanted a dog. I immediately reached a decision despite the fact. I grabbed the car keys saying I will give a home to this little newborn pup as I walked out the door to the car. Jim came quickly behind and got into the car with me as I was starting the motor. After seeing the sweet little powder-puff pup which Renee presented and having the largest innocent loving eyes I had ever seen and immediately said, she now has a home and I'm naming her 'Shariz.' She didn't look like a 'Shariz' as you might imagine but she was so beautiful with a gorgeous blond-platinum coat and such trusting eyes.

After bringing her home - Jim wanted nothing to do with her and I managed to keep her away from him. Then one day soon after I found Shariz sitting in Jim's lap as he sat in his wheelchair in his bedroom and petting her. I yelled "Shariz" come out of there you don't need to be in there." Jim said, "No let her stay here with me we are bonding." I thought how wonderful! That was such a beautiful time I will never forget. Shariz's Love was something in which Jim was really needing help with through his last days. Soon after is when he passed in the hospital. I somehow knew this was meant to be with Shariz and Jim finally bonding. "Shariz" found him and gave such love to Jim. It's like she knew how ill he really was.

Later, after Jim's final wishes were upheld with his cremation and our jointly agreeing for the cremation of our dear "Max" as well their ashes were presented in a beautiful cemetery in our hometown cemetery where I had previously purchased plots for us. I had the head of a dog's silhouette with a likeness to "Max" engraved on the stone making three places for "Jim, myself, and a third place for Max and Shariz together with the stone engraved "Beloved Friend Max & Shariz." This is 'Our Home away from Home' as I like to refer to it as they are 'angelic angels'.

I Wrote the Life Celebration Ceremony for JIM and I tried to keep it light with an 'Upbeat' of happiness' for the Celebration of Jim & Max. I had asked the Archangels and all the angels for their presence during the ceremony. I remember Archangel Uriel 'bringing baskets of flowers' to help keep everyone happy and 'Archangel Gabriel making his presence to keep

'Harmony and Balance through any Conflict.' They weren't the traditional things people say in a formal setting but I kept things more in the relaxed environment of 'spirit' with a little humor and loving fun. I was so grateful to the Archangels and their attendance as well as 'Saint Germain' and all of God's heaven and friends for being with us on that blessed day. How comforting it is when your heart is saddened and heavy with grief, and everyone conveys their eternal love.

Continuing on my Journey of 'Thinking Backwards' I remember later having a phone conversation with a 'Psychic Medium' and a conversation with 'Jim' about my words I had written and presented for his life celebration and burial. Hoping my thoughts and words would be accepted by him in a positive and just way, I hoped he would be proud and feel a deep sense of pleasure and satisfaction from the result as an appreciative and proud husband.' Quite the contrary I received the opposite from him and perversely disagreed and annoyed by thinking I was NOT 'dutiful' or 'RELIGIOUS' enough in the sense of not being ordained enough with the words of a clergy and I was left with feeling of being 'not enough' 'not good enough' and 'too common or insufficient' for the purpose to give or satisfy. I felt I couldn't meet the demands or what was expected of me even from the dead.

Continuing my life with 'Shariz' helped me to become stronger and she supported me with courage. The two of us together have faced storms with lightning bolts entering the fireplace chimney and doing surmountable damage. We still managed to come through it together leaning on one another and learning to resolve the hassles of daily life.

The soul is destined to experience everything life has to offer in ways that may not be immediate but we are led and directed through hints, messages and SIGN of warnings. The amazing life transformations occur when we learn to see the messages angels give us in life throughout each day and some are so big in the subtleness of unapparent awareness. We all need to learn to see the messages that angels give us each day even in the SMALL situations and they are our life transformations.

Some signs are so monumental and can help us find our life purpose with guiding our decisions that support our path and goals. Listen to the new realms that open-up for you and be receptive. Our job is not to search but to notice the signs given us. Usually they are very subtle and if you try to seek them out like most things it will only cause setbacks and tension and will not go forward.

Heaven delivers messages in all different ways Some are with clouds coins, feathers, rainbows, while others can be through meaningful songs and which only you would recognize what it means to you and this happens in many ways.

EXAMPLE: A time out for dinner with a very good friend in Houston, Tx still sitting in a restaurant after having dinner and getting ready to leave and the piano player suddenly began playing "Misty" a song which I knew immediately. It was meant for me. My friend looked at me and we both sat back down to listen through to the end of the song. After a few seconds we stood up again to leave our table and the piano player looked to me across the way and suddenly began again playing "Misty" but this second time around he sang all the meaningful words of "Misty" and which many people would not know for this is a much older song. Sitting back down again I began crying blissful tears of joy for I knew it was truly a 'Sign' and 'Message' from my beloved "Jim." It was a song in which Jim would lead with from his heart when he played the piano before playing his own musical compositions he had composed. It was such a personal moment from my 'Soul Mate' bringing me an abundance of love from Heaven. I knew then that people on Earth can be guided, protected, and healed with 'Angel Signs' from heaven.

"We are what we think, having become what we thought." said India's Poet and Writer Gautama Buddha,

The mind can be the conduit for the consciousness of our Higher Self or for the pride of the Ego. In either case, our thoughts are a power force.

In my senses I began allowing myself to bust through obstacles that were a problem in the past and the things that use to stop me from being creative and expressing myself. I am setting boundaries for it's all about acknowledging your power and claiming ownership of it. I'm moving ahead on my path for it's time to recognize everything wondrous and miraculous that I've noticed outside of myself, that exists inside of me and that I am unique. I will do things the way that I do them and if I am comparing myself to other people, it's time to recognize the beauty that's inside me and how I can uniquely express the qualities of the Divine in the world. It's time to acknowledge myself and appreciate myself for how far I've come and all the challenges I've been through for many years. I'll be kind and gentle with myself and have an appreciation for all parts of me and the vulnerability as well as the strength.

This is a kind of 'Self-Love' I will see through the toughest of times.

Through my connection with 'Nature' I've learned to connect deeply with myself and the 'Divine'. When I rest, rejuvenate and feel grounded it can be a foundational period for me in the rest of the year so I am taking time to think about what I want now based on who I am in this moment.

My past is waking-up and I am replenishing and getting my mind right to take on the upcoming winter. I have been walking with the past and living it repeatedly again and again whether I wished it or not and I have reached a point now in my life I am "Letting Go" LETTING GO of this old energy and I am beginning NEW in a new beginning. Heaven is touching Earth and signifying my 'sensitive intuitiveness' guiding me on a 'SPITIRUAL Path' of growth with MAGIC, MIRACLES, and BELIEF.

-   TREE of BLISS -
-   Great tree of bliss! Your swaying braziers
-   Musk each second with Eternity!
-   I wade incessantly your sea of starflowers
-   Your trunk soars blazing from my heart. Jalal-ud-Din Rumi Poet
-   (Translated by Andrew Harvey Daily OM)

I believe I am grounding myself in the NOW and as the goal in my education through the seven great planetary transits and observing the movement of the Stars In 'Astrology,' 'Numerology,' as well as learning about the 'Tarot Cards' and 'Philosophy' concerning matters of knowledge, values and reasons, with beliefs in the divine and 'Mystical Relationships and Language.' This has been my desire since childhood and learning how to apply the results.

STUDIED RESULTS:

- NUMEROLOGY is any belief in the divine, mystical relationship between a number and one or more coinciding events. It is often associated with the paranormal, alongside astrology and similar divinatory arts.

-ASTROLOGY is the study of the movements and relative positions of celestial objects. Astrology can provide daily horoscopes with online tarot readings, psychic readings, and Chinese astrology.

- TAROT CARDS is a pack of playing cards used from the mid-15th century in various parts of Europe to play games. Many of the tarot card games are still played today. In the last 18th century it began to be used in parallel for divination in the form of teratology and Cartomancy. Cartomancy is fortune-telling or divination using a deck of cards and specialist packs were developed for the occult purpose.

- Teratology is the basis for the reading of Tarot cards, and a subset of cartomancy, which is the practice of using cards to gain insight into the past, present or future by posing a question to the cards. The reasoning behind this practice rangers from believing the result is guided by a spiritual force, and to believe that the cards are instruments used to tap into a collective unconsciousness or into the subject's own creative, brainstorming subconscious.

Cartomancy is the practice of seeking knowledge of the future or the unknown by supernatural means. The 'Celtic art of divination' can forecast using a deck of cards. Forms of Cartomancy appeared soon after playing cards were first introduced into Europe in the 14th century. Practioners of cartomancy are known as cartomancers card readers or simply readers.

The three most common decks used in esoteric tarot are the "Tarot of Marseilles" the "Rider-Waite tarot deck" and the "Thoth tarot deck." The 78-card tarot deck has two distinct parts:

The terms "major arcana" and "minor arcana" were first used in relation to Tarot card games.

* The Major Arcana (greater secrets), or trump cards, consists of 22 cards without suits:

The Magician, The High Priestess, The Empress, The Emperor, The Hierophant, The Lovers, The Chariot, Strength, The Hermit, Wheel of Fortune, Justice, The Hanged Man, Death, Temperance, The Devil, The Tower, The Star, The Moon, The Sun, Judgement, The World, and The Fool.

Cards from The Magician to The World are numbered in Roman numerals from (I to XXI), while The Fool is the only unnumbered card sometimes placed at the beginning of the deck as 0, or at the end as XXII.

* The Minor Arcana (lesser secrets) consists of 56 cards, divided into four suits of 14 cards each; ten numbered cards and four court cards. The court cards are the King, Queen, Knight and Page/Jack, in each of the four tarot suits. (The traditional Italian tarot suits are) swords, batons/wands, coins and cups; in modern occult tarot decks.

- However, the batons suit is often called wands, rods or staves; while the coins suit is often called pentacles or disks.
- There are also decks that use the elements as the names of the suits:
- 'Earth' is for Pentacles/Coins/Disks, 'AIR' is for Swords, 'FIRE' for Wands/Batons, and 'WATER' for Cups'.

NOTE: The terms "major arcana" and "minor arcana" were first used by {Jean-Baptiste Pitois also known as Paul Christian} and are never used in relation to Tarot card games. Some decks exist primarily as artwork; and such art decks sometimes contain only the 22 major arcana.

Occult tarot decks:

Etteilla was the first to issue a tarot deck specially designed for occult purposes around 1789. In keeping with the misplaced belief that such cards were derived from the "Book of Thoth", Etteilla's tarot contained themes related to ancient Egypt.

Divinatory, esoteric, and occult tarot:

The earliest evidence of a tarot deck used for cartomancy comes from an anonymous manuscript from around 1750 which documents divinatory meanings for the cards of the "Tarocco Bolognese."

The popularization of esoteric tarot started with Antoine Court and Jean-Baptiste Alliette (Etteilla) in Paris during the 1780s, using the Tarot of Marseilles.

After the French tarot players abandoned the Marseilles tarot in favor of the Tarot Nouveau around 1900, 'the Marseilles pattern' is now used mostly by cartomancers.

The tarot ('taeroo') ia a pack of playing cards, used from the mid-15th century in various parts of Europe to the playing games such as 'Italian' 'French' and 'Austrian.' Many are still played today. In the late 18th century, it began to be used in parallel for "divination" in the form of "Tarotology and Cartomancy" and specialist packs were developed for this occult purpose.

In the English-speaking countries, where these games are not played, tarot cards are used primarily for DIVINATORY purposes, and using specially designed packs. The cards are traced by some occult writers to ancient Egypt or the "Kabbalah" but there is no documented evidence of such origins or of the usage of tarot for divination before the 18th century.

The TAROT Nouveau has 78 cards and is played in France. Its genre art trumps use Arabic numerals in corner indices in a plural form of index.

ASTROLOGY and NUMEROLOGY Observing the movement of the Stars in Astrology is the study of the movements and is relative to positions of celestial objects. In the broadest sense, it is the search for human meaning. It is your 'portal' to the stars unlocking the mysteries of the universe with horoscopes, tarot, and the psychic with life's toughest questions no matter what your zodiac sign.

There are 12 zodiac signs, and each sign has its own strengths and weaknesses and its own specific traits, desires and attitude towards life and people. By analyzing the projection of the position of planets, and the Sun and the Moon on the Ecliptic now of birth Astrology can give us a glimpse of a person's basic characteristics, preferences, flaws and fears. In an intelligent and accurate life of culture, style, romance, money, and real estate it is a means of divining information about human affairs and terrestrial events. Astrology has been dated to at least the 2nd millennium BCE and has its roots in calendrical systems used to predict seasonal shifts and interpret celestial cycles as SIGNS of - 'divine communication.

Inspired by the times of history and past, present and future, I became more and more confused with the 'time and years' and listed without any letters with saying {the 'Common Era' starting from year 1}. The 'Common Era' begins with year 1 in the 'Gregorian calendar'. The Gregorian calendar is the most widely used civil calendar in the world and is named after Pope Gregory XIII and introduced in October 1582.

The calendar was developed as a refinement reforming altered lunar cycles used by the Church to calculate the date of Easter, restoring it to the time of the year as originally celebrated by the early Church.

Instead of using the traditional abbreviations AD and BC

* AD is short for Anno Domini, Latin for year of the Lord.
* BC is an abbreviation of Before Christ.

The letters CE or BCE is in conjunction with a year meaning after or before year 1.

* CE is an abbreviation for Common Era.
* BCE is short for Before Common Era.

The Common Era begins with year 1 in the Gregorian calendar.

(CE and BCE) are used in the same way as the traditional abbreviations as AD and BC.

Because AD and BC hold religious (Christian) connotations, many prefer to use the more modern and neutral CE and BCE to indicate if a year is before or after year 1.

According to the international standard for calendar dates Both Systems are acceptable and used for Centuries.

The numbering system was introduced by a Christian monk in the 6th century. The year count starts with the year 1 in the Gregorian calendar and is supposed to be the birth year of Jesus. Although, modern historians often conclude that he was born around 4 years earlier.

The expression Common Era is also no invention. It has been in use for several hundred years. In English, it is found in writing as early as 1708 and was used interchangeably with "Christian Era" as far back as in the 1600s.

Increased textbooks in the United States also use CE/BCE, as well as history tests issued by the US College Board.

Even people celebrating the beginning of the 'new millennium' on the correct date must contend with the fact that, in astronomical terms, there was nothing special about this event.

*   A year on Earth is defined as the time it takes Earth to complete an orbit around the Sun. This is called a solar or tropical year. Solar calendar systems, such as the western calendar, are designed to reflect that time span and the SEASONS it encompasses as precisely as possible, and they do so with varying levels of accuracy.

The 'Year numbers' on the other hand, are just a means of counting our planet's revolutions. While this is undoubtedly a handy feature to describe and structure long time spans, the Earth's 1999th revolution around the Sun is no different than its 2000th revolution.

It becomes clear how ambiguous year numbers are. Example: The year 2001 marked the beginning of the 3rd millennium (only in the Gregorian calendar). Other calendars, such as the Jewish calendar the Islamic calendar and the Hindu calendar use completely different year numbers. So while the Gregorian calendar is the system officially used around the world, this goes to show that our year count is nothing more than a random fabrication, which is based on the ideas and religious fervor of the 6th century monk.

Today's calendar system and based on the beginning of the year AD 1 in the Julian calendar, is the predecessor of today's calendar system. On a religious event the birth of Jesus which not only lacks astronomical relevance but is also based on religious lore and as such, is a rough estimation at best.

WOMEM PROPOSED to Their Men

According to an old Irish legend, or history. St Brigid struck a deal with St Patrick allowing women to propose to men every four years and not just the other way around.

This is believed to have been introduced to BALANCE the traditional roles of men and women like leap day and balances the calendar."

"UNLUCKY in LOVE: In Scotland, it used to be considered unlucky for someone to be born on leap day, just as Friday 13th is considered an unlucky day by many. Greeks consider it unlucky for couples to marry during a leap year, and especially on Leap Day.

NOTE: "Thinking Backwards" to a leap day in high school, we celebrated the occasion called 'Twerp' Week' much like the old Traditions and Customs.

The school class of boys were FIRST let out from school and the girls afterward so the girls could run across the school yard after the boy of choosing and upon catching the one wanted they are to be linked to them for the week. The boy of choice would be presented with a red plaid bowtie to wear around his neck as their date for the 'Twe rp Week' and followed with a dance at the end of the week. -

When you think of 'TAROT CARDS' you think of the gypsies of old with their beautiful time-honored traditions. It might surprise you to know that the 'Tarot is as modern as it is ancient, and there are many things you can learn about your personality by studying the cards. There are three main approaches when it comes to exploring the world of tarot card reading. Looking at the cards through 'numerology is the first, and you can figure out your 'life path number'.

Analyzing the suits (made up of Wands, Pentacles, Swords, and Cups) is the second approach, and the third is using the court cards (Page, Knight, Queen, and King).

TAROT & NUMEROLOGY

Do you know your life path number? THE MAJOR ARCANA:

Look at the appropriate tarot cards. The major arcana will reveal a lot about your personality. All you must do is add up your (date of birth) (day + month + year) and if it is (more than 21, you must reduce it).

EXAMPLE: If you were born on August 11, 1958, you'd add (11 + 8 + 1 + 9 + 5 + 8) to get 24, which you treat as (2 + 4 = 6), so your guiding tarot card would be (6), the Lovers. If you were born on August 5th, 1958, you'd add (5 + 8 + 1 + 9 + 5 + 8), to get (18).

THE MINOR ARCANA:

It's possible to really run with this and to get additional information about yourself! Don't forget the (minor arcana). You can reduce your birthday, in the same way, to arrive at a number from (1 10). Here's a quick way to interpret the cards in the suits of the minor arcana:

* The Aces: New beginnings, uniqueness, someone who is fresh and stands out from the crowd.
* The 2s: The peacemaker, someone who is very sensitive, and just wants everyone to get along.
* The 3s: This person is imaginative and creative, but they're prone to self -indulgence.
* The 4's: Someone who's balanced and steady, on whom you can depend.
* The 5's: Artist, entrepreneurs, and people who aren't afraid to fight for what they want.
* The 6's: Caring and compassionate individuals who tend to worry too much.
* The 7's: Unique personalities who are aloof, and don't really care much for popular opinion.
* The 8's: Hard-working, practical, and someone who will take risks to get what they want.
* The 9's: Aristocratic and sophisticated, these people are often seen as eccentric or arrogant.
* The 10's: Don't be afraid of closing the door on something that's finished so that something new can blossom.

TAROT SUITS:

Now, of course, with the minor arcana, you also have the suits. There is a different energy for each suit which will color those numbers, making each one unique. To find out how the cards are speaking to you, simply marry the number of the minor arcana with the qualities of the suit it belongs to.

* WANDS: Fiery personality, gets things started, impetuous, impulsive, assertive.
* PENTACLES: Down to earth and practical, gets things organized, can sometimes be a bit of a bore.
* SWORDS: Witty, intelligent, intellectual, pensive, and frequently blunt and abrasive.
* CUPS: Sensitive, romantic, dreamy, and prone to mistaking fantasy for reality. COURT CARDS:

Of all the cards in the tarot, it's the court cards that most often represent people. Like with the minor 'pip' cards, to really interpret what or who these cards represent, you must take into consideration both the card and the suit. The page of cups will behave very differently than the page of swords.

* PAGE: This is a young person. It may be a child, an infant, or news of a pregnancy.
* KNIGHT: A young adult, still finding out who they are, still making mistakes along the way.
* QUEEN: A matriarch, a mature woman, or a caring and compassionate man.
* KING: A patriarch, a mature man, or a disciplined and authoritative woman. WANDS:
* The element of fire
* The Sun signs of Aries, Leo and Sagittarius
* The major arcana card of Judgment
* This card says you can be very judgmental, which doesn't always suit you. Remember, everyone is different, coming into this life with their own lessons to learn and their own assets and challenges. You don't have to pass judgment just because they're different from you something fire signs often have a hard time accepting!

PENTACLES:

* The element of earth
* The Sun signs of Taurus, Virgo, and Capricorn
* The major arcana card of 'The World'
* The World card reminds you that everything comes to an end. You are great at seeing a project through to its finish of picking up the pieces that others left behind of wrapping up events and organizing your lives. Just don't get so bogged down in what you're doing that you forget to take other people's feelings and ideas into consideration.

SWORDS:

* The element of air
* The Sun signs of Gemini, Libra, and Aquarius
* The major arcana card of 'The Fool'
* The Fool has no number in the tarot because he's impetuous and playful, the trickster who is likely to appear at any moment. Like him, you're capable of coming up with new ideas, changing your mind in a heartbeat, and throwing a sabot in the works just to see how the pieces fall.

CUPS:

* The element of water
* The Sun signs of Cancer, Scorpio, and Pisces
* The major arcana card of 'The Hanged Man'
* The Hanged Man is a symbol of sacrifice, and there are times you feel you're doing that, repeatedly. No one understands the depth of your feelings. You often long for things to be different, but don't know what to do or aren't bold enough to change them.
* You may have a reputation for being cheerful and helpful, but there's also a superficiality around you that you need to work on.

By looking at the suits (above) and then delving into the individual court cards you get a good idea of someone's personality. When the court cards come up in a reading, they might not represent a person in your life, but they'll always represent that ARCHETYPE. The king of cups is a kind and compassionate man, while the queen of swords is an intelligent and assertive woman.

The 12 Common ARCHETYPES: - (By Carl Golden) -

The term "archetype' has its origins in ancient Greek. The root words are (Archean), which means "original or old"; and (typos), which means "pattern, model or type". The combined meaning is an "original pattern" of which all other similar persons, objects, or concepts are derived, copied, modeled, or emulated.

- The psychologist, Carl Gustav Jung,

Used the concept of 'archetype' in his theory of the human psyche. He believed that universal, mythic characters archetypes within the collective unconscious of people the world over. Archetypes represent fundamental human motifs of our experience as we evolved; consequentially, they evoke deep emotions.

Although there are many different archetypes, Jung defined twelve 'primary types' that symbolize basic human motivations. Each type has its own set of values, meanings and personality traits. Also, the twelve types are divided into three sets of four, namely (Ego, Soul and Self). The types in each set share a common driving source, for example types within the Ego set are driven to fulfill ego defined agendas.

Most if not all, people have several archetypes at play in their personality construct; howsoever, one archetype tends to dominate the personality in general. It can be helpful to know which archetypes are at play in oneself and in others, especially loved ones, friends and co-workers, to gain personal insight into behaviors and motivations.

The Ego Types:

1. The Innocent
   Motto: Free to be you and me Core desire: To get to paradise

   Greatest fear: To be punished for doing something bad or wrong Strategy: To do things right

   Weakness: Boring for all their naïve innocence Talent: Faith and optimism

   The Innocent is also known as: Utopian, traditionalist, naïve, mystic, saint, romantic, dreamer.

2. The Orphan/Regular Guy or Gal
   Motto: All men and women are created equal Core Desire: Connecting with others

   Goal: To belong

   Greatest fear: To be left out or to stand out from the crowd

   Strategy: Develop ordinary solid virtues, be down to earth, the common touch

   Weakness: Losing one's own self to blend in or for the sake of superficial relationships

   Talent: Realism, empathy, lack of pretense

   The Regular Person is also known as : The good old boy, everyman, the person next door, the realist, the working stiff, the solid citizen, the good neighbor, the silent majority.

3. The Hero:
   Motto: Where there's a will there's a way

   Core desire: to prove one's worth through courageous acts

   Goal: Expert mastery in a way that improves the world

   Greatest fear: Weakness, vulnerability, being a "chicken" Strategy: To be as strong and competent. Weakness: Arrogance, always needing another battle to fight. Talent: Competence and courage

   The Hero is also known as: The warrior, crusader, rescuer, superhero, the soldier, dragon slayer, the winner and the team player.

4. The Caregiver
   Motto: Love your neighbor as yourself Core desire: To protect and care for others Goal: To help others

   Greatest fear: Selfishness and ingratitude Strategy: Doing things for others Weakness: Martyrdom and being exploited Talent: Compassion, generosity

   The Caregiver is also known as: The saint, altruist, parent, helper, supporter.

The Soul Types:

5. The Explorer
   Motto: Don't fence me in

   Core desire: The freedom to find out who you are through exploring the world Goal: To experience a better, more authentic, more fulfilling life

   Biggest fear: Getting trapped, conformity and inner emptiness

   Strategy: Journey, seeking out and experiencing new things, escape from boredom Weakness: Aimless wandering, being a misfit

   Talent: Autonomy, ambition, being true to one's soul. The Explorer is also known as: The seeker, iconoclast, wanderer, individualist, pilgrim

6. The Rebel
   Motto: Rules are made to be broken Core desire: Revenge or revolution Goal: To overturn what isn't working

Greatest fear: To be powerless or ineffectual Strategy: Disrupt, destroy, or shock

Weakness: Crossing over to the dark side, crime Talent: Outrageousness, radical freedom. The Outlaw is also knowing as: the rebel, revolutionary, wild man, the misfit, or iconoclast.

7. The Lover
    Motto: You're the only one

    Core desire: Intimacy and experience

    Goal: Being in a relationship with the people, work and surroundings they love Greatest fear: Being alone, a wallflower, unwanted, unloved

    Strategy: To become increasingly physically and emotionally attractive. Weakness: outward -directed desire to please others at risk of losing own identity Talent: Passion, gratitude, appreciation, and commitment. The Lover is also known as: The partner, friend, intimate, enthusiast, sensualist, spouse, team-builder.

8. The Creator
    Motto: If you can imagine it, it can be done Core desire: To create things of enduring value Goal: To realize a vision

    Greatest fear: Mediocre vision or execution Strategy: Develop artistic control and skill Task: To create culture, express own vision Weakness: Perfectionism, bad solutions Talent: Creativity and imagination. The Creator is also known as: The artist, inventor, innovator, musician, writer or dreamer.

The Self Types:

9. The Jester
   Motto: You only live once

   Core desire: To live in the moment with full enjoyment
   Goal: To have a wonderful time and lighten up the world's
   Greatest fear: Being bored or boring others

   Strategy: Play, make jokes, be funny Weakness: Frivolity,
   wasting time Talent: Joy. The Jester is also known as: The
   fool, trickster, joker, practical joker or comedian

10. The Sage
    Motto: The truth will set you free

    Goal: To use intelligence and analysis to understand the
    world Biggest fear: Being duped, misled or ignorance

    Strategy: Seeking out information and knowledge; self-
    reflection and understanding thought processes.

    Weakness: Can study details forever and never act. Talent:
    Wisdom, intelligence. The Sage is also known as: The
    expert, scholar, detective, advisor, thinker, philosopher,
    academic, researcher, thinker, planner, professional,
    mentor, teacher, contemplative.

11. The Magician
    Motto: I make things happen.

    Core desire: Understanding the fundamental laws of the
    universe Goal: To make dreams come true

    Greatest fear: Unintended negative consequences Strategy:
    Develop a vision and live by it Weakness: Become
    manipulative

Talent: Find win-win solutions. The Magician is also known as: The visionary, catalyst, inventor, charismatic leader, shaman, healer, medicine man.

12. The Ruler
Motto: Power isn't everything, it's the only thing.

Core desire: Control

Goal: Create a prosperous, successful family or community
Strategy: Exercise power

Greatest fear: Chaos, being overthrown Weakness: Being authoritarian, unable to delegate Talent: Responsibility, leadership.

The Ruler is also known as: The boss, leader, aristocrat, king, queen, politician, role model, manager or administrator.

The Four Cardinal Orientations:

Four Groups with each group containing three types (as the wheel of archetypes) Each group is motivated by its respective orienting focus:
- Ego-fulfillment, freedom, socialness and order. -
This is a variation on the three groups of Types previously mentioned;
However, whereas all the types within the (Ego, Soul & Self) sets all share the same driving source.
The types comprising the four orienting groups have different source drives but the same motivating orientation.
EXAMPLE: The Caregiver is driven by the need to fulfill (ego) agendas through meeting the needs of others, which is a social orientation; Whereas, The Hero which is also driven by the need to fulfill (ego) agendas, does so through courageous action that proves self-worth.
Understanding the groupings will aid in understanding the motivational and self- perceptual dynamics of each type.

ZODIAC SIGNS in Astrology

ARIES Zodiac Sign (Dates: March 21 April 20)
-   Traits: Confident, Inspired, Sexy

TAURUS Zodiac Sign (Dates: April 21 May 20)
-   Traits: Loyal, Patient, Hardworking

GEMINI Zodiac Sign (Dates: May 21 June 20)
-   Traits: Eloquent, Quick, Fast

CANCER Zodiac Sign (Dates: June 21 July 22)
-   Traits: Reserved, Conservative, Family

LEO Zodiac Sign (Dates: July 23 August 22)
-   Traits: Passionate, Fun, Successful

VIRGO Zodiac Sign (Dates: August 23 September 21)
-   Traits: Organized, Diplomatic, Grounded

LIBRA Zodiac Sign (Dates: September 22 October 20)
-   Traits: Diplomacy, Tactfulness, Communication

SCORPIO Zodiac Sign (Dates: October 21 November 20)
-   Traits: Mysterious, Intelligent, Analytical

SAGITTARIUS Zodiac Sign (Dates: November 21 December 21)
-   Traits: Adventurous, Generous, Honest

CAPRICORN Zodiac Sign (Dates: December 22 January 21)
-   Traits: Organized, Responsible, Leadership

AQUARIUS Zodiac Sign (Dates: January 22 February 18)
-   Traits: Intelligent, Genius, Communicators

PISCES Zodiac Sign (Dates: February 19 March 20)
-   Traits: Dreamy, Intuitive, D

ASTROLOGY THE TWELVE SIGNS

ARIES

Cardinal, Fire (March 21st April 20th)

Key word: Assertion / Ruler: Mars Aries types like to be first; they are impulsive and easily provoked. They thrive on competition. Aries is associated with the head.

TAURUS

Fixed, Earth (April 21st May 21st)

Key word: Consolidation / Ruler: Venus This sign is very stable, immoveable almost, and yet very fruitful and bountiful. Taurus types are also said to be stubborn and materialistic. Taurus is associated with the throat and neck.

GEMINI

Mutable, Air (May 22 June 21st)

Key word: Connection / Ruler: Mercury This sign reaches out to others creating a network of communication. Gemini types are sociable, gregarious, and full of ideas. Gemini is associated with the hands and lungs.

CANCER

Cardinal, Water (June 22nd July 21st)

Key word: Protection / Ruler: The Moon This sign is motivated by family and home- building. Cancer types are emotional, and they build a protective shell. Cancer is associated with the breasts and stomach.

LEO

Fixed, Fire (July 23rd August 22)
Key word: Individuation / Ruler: The Sun The crucial area for Leo is identity building up self-esteem and confidence. Leo types are normally proud, dignified and very creative. Leo is associated with the heart and back.

VIRGO

Mutable, Earth (August 23rd September 22nd)
Key word: Discrimination / Ruler: Mercury This is the most perfectionist of signs, and Virgo types are very conscientious and helpful. They worry a lot about work and health. Virgo is associated with the intestines and digestion.

LIBRA

Cardinal, Air (September 23rd October 23rd)
Key word: Balance / Ruler: Venus Libra is gregarious and friendly and tends to compromise for the sake of peace. Libra is associated with the kidneys and balance.

SCORPIO

Fixed, Water (October 24th November 22nd)
Key word: Intensity / Ruler: Mars (Pluto) Scorpio types lead an intense emotional life. They are secretive, magnetic and powerful, and have a mysterious ability to empower others. Scorpio is associated with the genitals.

SAGITTARIUS

Mutable, Fire (November 23rd December 21st)
Key word: Insight / Ruler: Jupiter Sagittarian types are philosophical and very frank. They are great travelers and strive to gain wisdom throughout their life. Sagittarius is associated with the thighs and the liver.

CAPRICORN

Cardinal, Fire (December 22nd January 20th)
Key word: Achievement / Ruler: Saturn This is the most social of signs. Capricorn types have long-term goals, and work hard, methodically, and dynamically to achieve them. Capricorn is associated with the knees.

AQUARIUS

Fixed, Air (January 21st February 19th)
Key word: Equality / Ruler: Saturn. This is the most social of signs Aquarians have an egalitarian and humanitarian outlook. They have a magical, electric aura. Aquarius rules the angles and blood circulation.

PISCES

Mutable, Water (February 20th March 20th)
Key word: Dissolution / Ruler: Jupiter. Pisces types are sensitive and attuned to the cosmos. They are compassionate, but there is also a sense of being a victim. Pisces is associated with the feet and lymph glands.

The sun isn't a planet It's the star around which our solar system moves just as the sun is the center of our solar system, you are the center of your life. You see things through your own eyes, you understand things from your own point of view.

The sun's position on your astrology chart shows you where you need to push yourself. This is where it gets interesting. Your date, time, and place of birth places the sun in a specific sign, house, and aspect of the zodiac.

Learn About Sun Signs About Houses About Aspect

SUN SIGNS:

There are 12 signs of the zodiac, each one taking up 30 degrees in your birth chart making a complete 360-degree circle (30 degrees x 12 signs = 360 degrees). Every astrological sign has a specific set of qualities positive and negative.

ZODIAC SIGNS:

ARIES - (Adventurous, Confident, Self-Centered, Impulsive) TAURUS (Dependable, Strong, Oversensitive, Obstinate) GEMINI (Communicative, Changeable, Inconsistent, Superficial) CANCER (Devoted, Compassionate, Moody, Hesitant)

LEO (Vibrant, Assertive, Egotistical, Possessive) VIRGO (Dependable, Patient, Critical, Judgmental) LIBRA (Charming, Loving, Indecisive, Lazy)

SCORPIO (Passionate, Charismatic, Secretive, Manipulative) SAGITTARIUS (Gregarious, Sociable, Blunt, Restless) CAPRICORN (Willful, Serious, Rigid, Demanding)

AQUARIUS (Intelligent, Humanitarian, Unconventional, Noncommittal) PISCES Romantic, Imaginative, Illusional Wistful)

- ASTROLOGY HOUSES: -

There are 12 houses in a birth chart. The size of the house depends on where and when you were born. That is why astrologers need your TIME, DATE, and PLACE of birth.

A brief description for how the sun behaves in each of the astrological houses.

The sun takes the traits of your sun sign as well as the energies of the houses, which is why many people with the same sun sign may have very little in common. The house in which your 'Sun' falls and 'The Aspects' it makes to other planets combine to make you who you are: Below are some of the key traits for each zodiac sign:

FIRST HOUSE of Self: Rules your personality and your countenance. The Sun will bring you a strong personality, and a lesson in humility.

SECOND HOUSE of Finances & Resources: Rules your income and how you support yourself. The Sun will bring you a strong interest in your finances and belongings, and a lesson in not being too materialistic.

THIRD HOUSE of Communication: Rules communication and intellect. The Sun will bring you an interest in all matters of communication, and a caution against too much gossiping.

FOURTH HOUSE of Roots & Foundations: Rules family and traditions. The Sun will bring family issues both positive and negative out in your life.

FIFTH HOUSE of Pleasure & Entertainment: Rules creativity and your leisure time. The Sun brings luck, and a playful nature, but cautions against getting too egotistical.

SIXTH HOUSE of Work & Family Routine: Rules your daily routine and health matters.

SEVENTH HOUSE of Relationships & Love (Business Partnership). Rules partnership; - romantic, business, and platonic. The Sun brings you a need for that special someone but reminds you not to lose yourself in the process of finding that partner.

EIGHTH HOUSE of Shared Resources & Transformation: Rules the occult, and the support you get from other people. The Sun fills you with intrigue but cautions you - against being to manipulative.

NINTH HOUSE of Foreign Matters: Rules philosophy and higher education. The Sun can bring you a real interest in other cultures but warns you not to be too superficial and in your thirst for knowledge.

TENTH HOUSE of Career Destiny: Rules your career and social standing. The Sun is a good placement for an excellent job, but cautions you not to become a workaholic.

ELEVENTH HOUSE of Friends: Rules your wishes and your circle of friends. The Sun brings you the energy and desire to be a special butterfly, but make sure you are not using others just for your own gain.

TWELFTH HOUSE of Spirituality: This is the house of endings and hidden things. The Sun can be a hard taskmaster, for even though you are probably very interested in the unconscious mind, it can be hard to find your authentic self - because it too is hidden.

ASPECTS

Next in understanding your sun sign are the aspects (as if signs and houses weren't enough). In addition to being in a sign, (a house), your SUN also makes aspects geometrical angles to other planets in your birth chart. There are two kinds of ASPECTS

*   Easy aspects
*   Challenging aspects

You might think that the easy aspects are always positive, but it really doesn't work like that. A conjunction (where two planets are within a few degrees of the same space in your birth chart) is considered an easy aspect, yet it can get complicated if one planet's energy is competing with the other.

Similarly, you might think that an opposition is a challenging aspect, but some planets need opposition to bring out their best qualities.

Here are the most common aspects. Don't worry if it get a bit complicated; there's a lot to take in. Just remember that planets have their own energies, and those energies are influenced by the Sun sign and the House that they occupy.

CONJUNCTION:

A conjunction is just that, when another planet is next to the Sun in your chart, and it can either work with or against the Sun's energy, to enhance it, or to overshadow it.

SEXTILE:

This is when the planet makes a 30-degree angle to the Sun in your chart. It's an easy aspect, and usually indicates the potential for the energies of the planets involved to work together.

SQUARE:

This is where a planet makes a 90-degree angle to the Sun in your chart. It's a challenging aspect, and usually indicates tension. That doesn't have to be a bad thing, though, because it can force you out of your comfort zone.

TRINE:

This is where a planet makes a 120 degree angle to the Sun in your chart. It's an easy aspect, with the two (or more) planets involved working in harmony to bring out the best in each other. Because this aspect is so easy-going, it's potential is sometimes overlooked.

INCONJUNCT:

This is where a planet makes a 150-degree angle to the Sun in your chart. It's the most challenging aspect, because the two will have absolutely nothing in common with each other. The only way to deal with this aspect is to work on understanding the difficulties that it brings, and then integrating the solution into your life.

OPPOSITION:

This is where a planet is completely opposite where your Sun is in your chart. Although it's considered to be a trying aspect, it can reveal a lot about your life's lessons, and what you need to be working on. It mirrors your uncertainties back to you, so you can deal with them and rise above the challenge.

ASTROLOGICAL 'ARCHETYPE'

The origins of the archetypal hypothesis date far back as Plato's ideas were pure mental forms that were imprinted on the soul before it was born into the world. They were collective in the sense that they embodied the fundamental characteristics of a thing rather than its specific peculiarities.

ARCHETYPE:

The twelve signs of the Zodiac represent twelve different characters, like roles in a play. They can be described as archetypes, models into which human personality traits tend to group.

Seeing the Zodiac signs as 'archetypes' helps revealing their meanings in astrology.

Archetype is a concept familiar already to Ancient Greece, where it was called archetype upon and meant "first molded" like a prototype. Plato had theories about mental ideas or forms that were imprinted in the human mind before birth.

Psychoanalyst C.G. Jung Picked up the idea and developed his own meaning to the word.

He claimed that there is a fixed number of models or types that we all share, without necessarily having been taught them. They are part of what he called our 'collective unconscious' and influenced how we look at reality and what we expect from it. He also meant that we should see these archetypes as inner clues as to how we can grow into 'self-realization.

C.G. Jung's theory on archetypes:

There is some truth to the idea that certain roles or characters, as well as some inanimate objects, seem to be familiar to all mankind. They are probably resulting of what is to be human and in the life experiences we share, in a sort of dream version more or less.

This has been known and discussed since the time of the ancient Greeks, who gave birth to this art form and fixed its structural rules. Storytelling seems to need to follow on stage and the silver screen but not to the same extent in literary fiction.

EXAMPLE: There is always a 'protagonist' who is the main character of the drama. The one forcing the 'protagonist' through this process is the 'antagonist' often the villain of the drama.

'Jungian' understanding is that the former would be the central symbol of any person's struggle for 'self-realization.' Otherwise, we remain the victims of misunderstanding ourselves.

The 'antagonist' is that gnawing reminder of the necessity of self-realization for life to - be complete.

The 'twelve' signs of the Zodiac can be a system of 'archetypes' making a complete world that represents human life completely.

It is obvious in the cases, such as the warrior Mars, the lover Venus, and the grim ruler Saturn and the Sun is said to represent the father and the moon, and the mother, who are also basic archetype. So, shouldn't the planets be regarded as archetypes and even more so than the Zodiac signs?

In Astrology those heavenly bodies are regarded as active forces within us, and by which we receive the energy and momentum to get things done-well. They are the fuel that makes us alive. Patterns of the cosmos consist of twelve archetypes and that cosmos has a say too about the thoughts behind astrology and the horoscope.

Each of us play distinct roles to different people around us. Through time, we grow older as children, parents, lovers, friends, adversaries, and strangers and several roles simultaneously.

ZODIAC SIGN Archetypes:

The twelve Zodiac signs consist of the combinations of 'two attributes' 'ELEMENT' and 'QUALITY'. They asked: Of what basic substances was the universe made and found four:

Fire, Earth, Air, and Water -

Each of the Twelve Zodiac signs belongs to one of those FOUR ELEMENTS Each Zodiac sign has its unique combination of 'Element' and 'Quality' with an equal spread of three to each element and this is the essence of how the signs should be understood. The combination reveals most of its characteristics.

There are also three 'QUALITIES' - by which the Zodiac signs are sorted:

- Cardinal Fixed and Mutable -

The three Zodiac signs belonging to the same element differ in qualities.

{Three times four is twelve} so the whole Zodiac is covered. CARDINAL is the leading quality MUTABLE is the follower. The FIXED quality is neither.

Each Zodiac sign has its unique combination of 'Element and Quality' and this is the essence of how the signs should be understood. If not all, 'the combination' reveals most of its characteristics.

See what 'Element' and 'Quality' each Zodiac sign belongs to in the 'Four Elements:

ELEMENT	CARDINAL	FIXED	MUTABLE
Fire	Aris	Leo	Sagittarius
Earth	Capricorn	Taurus	Virgo
Air	Libra	Aquarius	Gemini
Water	Cancer	Scorpio	Pisces

Signs that have the same element are naturally compatible because they understand each other best, and in addition, AIR is highly compatible with FIRE, WATER is highly compatible with EARTH {The strongest attraction is expected in opposing signs and their potential is always great}.

SYNASTRY or a relationship horoscope is the branch of astrology that studies relationships by comparing natal horoscopes. A natal horoscope is a chart or map of the angles and can be a useful tool for partners who want to know the strengths and weaknesses in their relationship. Comparing signs can also help in gaining a better understanding of the partner, which will result in a better relationship.

In Astrology, each ELEMENT represents a certain main characteristic:
Fire is activity and energy
Earth is the material world Air is thought
Water is emotions.

So, the element decides the basic drive and perspective of the Zodiac sign. The quality shows how it is expressed. The archetype of each Zodiac sign is extracted from this combination and how it can be interpreted.

Each of the 12 horoscope signs belongs to one of the [four elements] Air, Fire, Water and Earth. These elements represent an essential type of energy that acts in each of us.

ASTROLOGY aims to help us focus these energies on the positive aspects and to gain a better understanding of our potential and our positive traits and deal with negative ones.

These four 'Elements' help describe the unique personality types associated with Astrological signs. The four zodiac elements exhibit profound influence on basic character traits, 'emotions' behavior and thinking

WATER SIGNS:

Water signs are exceptionally emotional and ultra-sensitive. They are highly intuitive, and they can be as mysterious as the ocean itself. Water signs love profound conversations and intimacy. They rarely do anything openly and are always there to support their loved ones. The WATER SIGNS are: Cancer, Scorpio and Pisces.

FIRE SIGNS:

Fire signs tend to be passionate, dynamic, and temperamental. They get angry quickly, but they also forgive easily. They are adventurers with immense energy. They are physically very strong and are a source of inspiration for others. Fire signs are intelligent, self-aware, creative and idealistic people, always ready for action. The FIRE SIGNS are Aries, Leo, and Sagittarius.

EARTH SIGNS:

Earth signs are "grounded" and the ones that bring us down to earth. They are mostly conservative and realistic, but they can also be very emotional. They are connected to our material reality and can be turned to material goods. They are practical, loyal and stable and they stick by their people through tough times. The EARTH SIGNS are Taurus, Virgo, and Capricorn.

AIR SIGNS:

Air signs are rational, social, and love communication and relationships with other people. They are thinkers, friendly, intellectual, communicative and analytical. They love philosophical discussions, social gatherings and good books. They enjoy giving advice, but they can also be very superficial. The AIR SIGNS are Gemini, Libra and Aquarius.

By selecting your sign from the detailed zodiac sign dates list you will discover everything on the character of your SUN sign, it's HOROSCOPE, traits, profile, history, myth and love.

WHY DO WE BELIEVE IN ASTROLOGY?

Although astrology is not a religion it offers comfort, faith and a deeper understanding of the world we live in. Interpretations often offer assurances of one's future, but more importantly, they are supposed to show us a way to resolve our issues and to improve our relationships with our partners, family, and friends and tools to meet ourselves and discover our own inner worlds in a different light.

Astrology claims that nothing in life is coincidental and everything that happens to us happens for a reason. Astrology can provide us some good answers as to why these things happen to us and it guides us on our steps forward. In this way, astrology helps people to understand themselves and the world around them much better.

Astrology can be a real lifesaver because it lets you know of the future obstacles and problems in advance. It is up to you whether you want to believe the advice and precautions suggested in a horoscope reading and save yourself from the pain without doing much. Here is your first This is the main problem with approach to chart readings and everyone must put up a strong effort to change things in their lives.

Astrology considers two major aspects our birth potential and the effects of the planets and the stars on our personal horoscope. It can help us choose the right career and education path to make a good and successful life.

Last, but not least we believe in 'astrology' because it's about us. My horoscope is like a blueprint of my life that got created precisely at the time I was born That means that my birth chart is as unique as my fingerprints. Each planet's placement in my horoscope can reveal a lot about my personality and destiny.

ASTROLOGY is both an art and a science. Astrology is art because interpretation is needed to bring the different 'ASPECTS' together and formulate an idea of the individual's character traits. However, the mathematical part of astrology is also considered to be a science because it requires an understanding of 'Astronomy and Mathematics'.

My Trips:

A few years ago, taking with taking a trip to ROATAN HONDORUS, BELIZE, and COSAMEL, Mexico, in a journey through the 'Rain Forest' and the 'Mayan Ruins

I began learning the power of the planets and God's Spiritual Resources of Miracles being the highest gift of God to the Universe with learning to accept help and guidance in the higher self and inner teacher and guiding the Soul on my path to Union with God.

In ROATAN, HONDORUS I visited the shopping area where the natives had beautiful handmade weavings, baskets, handmade carving clothing and jewelry. The Bay Islands of Honduras has the most beautiful clear blue water of any I had ever seen anywhere except for story books and an elaborate imagination. It was heaven. The History, Gift Shoppe & Snack Bar were dedicated to keeping the Culture alive including masked 'Ethnic Dancing' and tribal attire. The music so brilliant one native stood in front of where I stood inviting me to dance as I joined in with dancing their tribal beats. This was a defining highlight of the day.

I stood by the blue waters looking out over the breath-taking horizon of coastal edge and found myself in acquainted conversation with one of the community nurses. Her wish was to come to Houston, TX for a three-week medical seminar but it was defendant upon their government and if she would be allowed to go for furthering her education. My heart and love went out to her and reminding that she was being guided and to be patient and cherish the NOW moments for all that she is and has and for all that she would become in time with the will of 'God's love.

The Journey in Lamanai, BELIZE is simply magical and learning more about the MAYA people, their structures in the Mayan world and the 'Mayan' astrology and civilization.

– The 'Mayan' calendar is based as one of the most forward-thinking kinds of ASTROLOGY ever encountered. The Mayan calendar {Tzolkin calendar} consists of twenty-day signs called (solar tribes) and thirteen 'Galactic' numbers, making it a 260- day calendar year. The Ancient Mayans believed that to have peace and harmony in life you had to understand and align yourself with this universal energy. Each of these twenty signs represents a day in a Mayan calendar, allowing individuals of different months and years to share the same day sign {or glyph a shape or representation} for defining his/or her personality of a specific shape or representation.

LAMANAI Belize is one of the largest Mayan sites in Belize, expanding over a hugh expanse on the Belize 'New River' where the Lamanai Mayan Center holds over 800 structures deep in the TROPICAL FOREST.

Occupied as early as 1500 bc, the small onsite musicum is where your LAMANAI exploration begins holding precious artifacts spanning well over 2000 years of 'Mayan History.' Getting to LAMANAI is half the fun!

Arriving at the Tower Hill Bridge and boarding a spectacular boat ride upriver continues the journey to LAMANAI traveling through miles of virgin river of living things, viewing majestic trees with overhanging air plants and colorful Orchid. It's a wonderful opportunity for wildlife spotting as well with a variety of tropical birds and occasional freshwater crocodiles floating near the river's edge. Well-kept paths through ancient jungle leads to the monuments and Temples. Monkeys relax on many of the tall huge 'Ceiba Trees' a tall tropical American tree from which {kapok} a silk-cotton is obtained and 'Toucans' are ever present. The exploration took 5 hours, leading to a 'Lag Temple' in a period of where you can climb 125 feet to the top and gain an unforgettable view of the LAMANAI ruins the 'New River Lagoon' and the great extent of the LAMANAI Archeology Reserve.

NOTE: The LAMANAI Mayan Rainforest Spices are the trees where the spice 'Cinnamon' is obtained from the inner bark of several tree species used in a wide variety of sweet and savory dishes in our snack foods, tea and traditional foods.

The TULUM MAYAN RUINS of TULUM, MEXICO, is 'A View to the Past!'

It was a 6 ½ hour duration on the excursion but very well worth it. The more I walked the Mayan path, the more I understood the depth they 'TEACH.' Their greeting has become more than a simple, honorable Maya greeting. It has evolved into a moral code, and a way a positive reality for all life. It is common knowledge these days that every action we take in our lives affects ALL living things. We understand that if we act negatively, our actions impact all life negatively. When we act positively, we affect all life in a positive manner. When you live the Mayan code meaning "I AM

ANOTHER YOURSELF" it does not matter which culture you come from. When one of their sacred greetings is given, there is always an action of placing the hands over the heart. The greeting has become more than a simple, honorable Maya greeting. It has evolved into a moral code, and a way to create a positive reality for all life. When living the Mayan moral code, its action is taken out of RESPECT for all life and living and giving from their hearts. They give their hearts in a positive manner very day to each other, to the trees, to the sky, to the birds and to the stars.

You greet each sunrise by saying {Lak'ech Ala K'in} each day and is sacred with giving your heart.

Remember "When you give in this way, you are also giving to yourself!

You are not giving your energy away to something separate from yourself. You are giving to another part of yourself!"

Learning to understand the challenges in staying positive these days and where the energy is so compressed

"We can learn to breathe, by simply walking in gratefulness"

When we give, we receive. When we are energized by our giving we know we are giving from the heart. When we feel drained or exhausted, it is possible that we gave out of FEAR, LACK, OBLIGATION, EGO, or a need to be accepted or liked.

Remember, "What goes around comes around exactly the way it was sent out."

If you don't like what like is sending to you, look at what you are sending out to life.

- "We all need to be responsible for guiding humanity through a prophesied evolutionary transition or the "Shift of Ages." The ancestors, as well as men and women of wisdom are returning to usher in a new era of global harmony and a new phase of human evolution. We are at a critical crossroads and the message is simple and clear We must change the way we live NOW." -

- "To those people who have been disregarded and disrespected my message is one of Equality, Sharing and Unity."

To help in bringing in the coming age we must start by purifying ourselves and HEALING past traumas to ourselves and to the mother earth and to all those people who have been disregarded and disrespected.

Each person must take responsibility and investigate their own heart for the ways they can participate in this shift and do it your own way.

NOTE: {'Glyph' is an elemental symbol within an agreed set of symbols, intended to represent a readable character for the purposes of writing. As such, 'Glyphs' are unique marks that collectively add up to the spelling of a word or contribute to a specific meaning of what is written, and dependent on the cultural and social usage.}

I wanted to know more about the effects of shifting and the characteristics in Astrology and I began studying:

ASTROLOGY ARCHETYPES of the Twelve Signs:

– Most Astrologers will agree on what gives them their archetype. Notice also the shifting of the seasons as the sun travels through the Zodiac can tells us a lot about the characteristics of the signs.

ARIES Archetype:

ARIES is the cardinal fire sign, bursting out at the spring equinox, when nature boldly renews itself, {like the mythical bird Phoenix} rising out of its own ashes. That death- defying strength is the sign of the WARRIOR which is therefore the archetype of Aries. It's the character of seeing life as a challenge and gladly taking it on. Without it, we would crouch in our cradles all through life.

TAURUS Archetype:

TAURUS is the fixed earth sign. In the solar year, its time is that of sowing the fields, securing food for the coming year. Thus, its archetype is the FARMER who cares for the land and makes sure we have the substance essential for our survival. The farmer knows the cyclic rhythm of the year and is in no hurry to deviate from it, or from any other established pattern. He knows the risks of ignorant alterations, and the necessity of staying grounded.

GEMINI Archetype:

GEMINI is the mutable air sign, the thought flies away so quickly many will miss it. Therefore, nothing is to be taken too seriously. It's the archetype of the JESTER the one who can take any turn of fate with a laugh and makes sure we remember to enjoy ourselves. What we cannot joke about, we cannot ever get over. Without the jester, life would often be too much to bear.

CANCER Archetype:

CANCER is the cardinal water sign, the one who cares for our feelings and wants each of us to be pleased. That is the archetype of the MOTHER. She gives birth to us, as the crops ripen in the middle of summer, and nurtures us with all that plenty. This mother is our protector, not our servant. She decides what's best for us and makes it so. Make no mistake about it she is a ruler.

LEO Archetype:

LEO is the fixed fire sign, the sun at its zenith of power, right before the summer bids farewell. This proud time is one of glory, so the archetype of Leo is the KING. Majestic, resting on his throne, dazzling with subjects as well as himself with his shine. It's the personification of pride and the beauty that emanates from such self-confidence. It's the attitude by which mankind accomplishes the greatest feats and the most horrible ones.

VIRGO Archetype:

VIRGO is the mutable earth sign, the fragility of the material things necessary for our survival. It's the time of harvest, which can go this way or that depending on the whims of nature as well as the soundness of our own previous preparations. What we have neglected will surely strike us now. We are reminded of the need to take proper care of things. The archetype of Virgo is the CRAFTSMAN, paying the greatest attention to every detail, making as sure as possible to reach the intended outcome. There's no substitute for skill and challenging work.

LIBRA Archetype:

LIBRA is the cardinal air sign, the word that rules. It's the mind set on principles and logic, and the willpower to stick to sound conclusions, no matter what. This is the archetype of the JUDGE, who knows the law and the importance to respect it or chaos will emerge, soon enough. It's the conviction that what has been concluded in theory also must rule practice, even if the latter must bend and change to adapt. Firm but fair. Still confused at times, since reality doesn't always fit the model of it.

SCORPIO Archetype:

SCORPIO is the fixed water sign. Water ceases to move only in the deepest abyss of the ocean, where nothing can be soon and most of us never reach. It's that hidden realm, the mystery of which scares us when we get a taste of it in our dreams and fantasies. It seems unreal, but still works its WAYS. It's the archetype of the ACTOR, whose pretense has hidden meanings and influences us beyond our understanding of it. Pretense and innuendo there is no way of escaping them.

SAGITTARIUS Archetype:

SAGITTARIUS is the mutable fire sign, the spark that appears and then disappears far away at the speed of light. Sagittarius is as difficult to contain as flames in the wind. It will never remain where it appeared. It is the archetype of the EXPLORER, constantly searching for new world, never settling, never at peace. But without this unattached adventurer, we would remain forever at the spot where we were born, doing nothing but reproducing right there. It is what makes us go on.

CAPRICORN Archetype:

CAPRICORN is the cardinal earth sign, taking the material that can be assembled and making something out of it, something that impresses and lasts. It is the archetype of the BUILDER, the one who puts use to everything at our disposal. And it is necessary for our survival, as the emergence of this sign on the winter solstice reminds us the darkest day of the year, when only our own abilities can guarantee our existence, since nature's resources have abandoned us. It is what makes us persevere.

AQUARIUS Archetype:

AQUARIUS is the fixed 'air sign' the thought that stayed and became how we define ourselves and our world. It's the contemplation that we find time for during long and cold nights. Time for reflection. It's the archetype of the TEACHER, who makes sure that we cherish the conclusions of our predecessors and pass them on to posterity. It's the profundity that makes us dare to call our species Homo Sapiens, 'the Wise Man.' It may not make us cheerful, but it helps us come to peace with the terms of life.

PISCES Archetype:

PISCES is the mutable water sign, the restlessness of emotions. We live our lives searching for inner peace, by which we really mean lasting solace and joy. But feelings do not last, it's not in their nature. We chase them and they escape us after the briefest of embraces. That's the archetype of the MARTYR who struggles and makes countless sacrifice's in the futile attempt to find satisfaction. But every bliss is a mirage, dissolving when reached, indifferent to our devotion. On the other hand, that's why we move at all.

The ASCENDANT is the sign that rises on the {eastern horizon} at the time of birth.

ASCENDANTS in the ZODIAC signs:

ASCENDANT FIRE signs:

The fire signs of Aries, Leo and Sagittarius are noticed for their energy, enthusiasm and optimism. When a fire sign is on the ascendant the manner is friendly, but professionally competent signals which draw out a friendly and respectful response from others. Aries rising gives out a well-organized, slightly military bearing which makes them fit for any military or civil service organization. Leo rising gives a dignified and formal manner which inspires confidence. Sagittarius rising gives a cheerful, pleasant and witty outer manner which suits all kinds of teaching, training and public speaking situations.

ASCENDANT EARTH signs:

The earth signs of Taurus, Virgo and Capricorn are noted for their practicality and security. When an earth sign is on the ascendant the outer manner is shy, serious and cautious. Taurus risers gives the most sociable of the three and are often musical or artistic. Virgo risers look for mental stimulation in others.

Capricorn risers enjoy both work and social pursuits.

People with these ascendants send out signals which are pleasant and tactful suggesting that they prefer to form part of a team at least to begin with, and then to push themselves immediately to the front.

ASCENDANT AIR signs:

The air signs of Gemini, Libra and Aquarius are noted for their communication skills. When an air sign is on the ascendant they are friendly and sociable, but also independent and detached.

The Gemini riser is constantly busy, and fully engaged in a kind of juggling act with at least a dozen activities on the go at any one time.

The Libra riser occupies him or herself with business schemes which often need the air of a more earthy partner to make them come into fruition.

The Aquarius riser makes wonderful plans for himself and others and may even carry some of them out.

ASCENDANT WATER signs:

The water signs of Cancer, Scorpio and Pisces are noted for their emotions, intuition and feeling. When a water sign is on the ascendant the subject will hid their true feelings and have a strong need to prove themselves from the world around them.

What you see is often not what you get with water ascendants. In other words, the signals they send out are consciously or unconsciously chosen for effect.

Cancer risers appear chatty and helpful and they do well in any situation that requires tact. Scorpio risers can use many different forms of camouflage with people they do not know, and one of their favorites being offensiveness and an off- putting manner. Pisces risers appear soft, gentle, self-sacrificing and sometimes even helpless, but this is misleading, as they will fight strongly for what they think is right.

The ASCENDANT RISING SIGN:

It is important to know your birthplace because of the time zone.

The Ascendant is the sign that rises on the {eastern horizon} at the time of birth. The ASCENDANT Rising Sign:

The Ascendant (abbreviation AC) is the sign that rises on the eastern horizon at the time of birth and more precisely at the point of intersection on the {eastern horizon} and ecliptic. The earth's axis causes the sign's changes every 2 hours. So, within 24 hours each zodiac sign passes, it is important to address the time of the birth besides the place of birth. The term ascendant derived from the Latin origin, means 'rising'. So, this fact is significant for individual horoscope charts about the sun sign compatibility:

The sun sign dictates the personality and individual quality of thoughts.

The ascendant represents and shows the reaction of a person's environment and surroundings the interactions and exchange towards others.

THE DESCENDANT:

The axis on the horizon is precisely located opposite the 'descendant.
The Ascendant and the Descendant are situated as opponents.
Contrary to the Ascendant that defines one person's characteristic,
The Descendant points to the missing link, and the lack of what is absent. It offers a chance how to handle in situations that demand too much. It symbolizes what must be learned and improved.

The Descendant represents the outside and outside influences that impact on a person. It is a challenge to react and interact under the influence of the Descendant.

The (astrology) Descendant forms the CUSP of the of the 'Seventh' house of the horoscope and refers to partners or relationships.

The Descendant is ruled by the Seventh sign of the Zodiac, Libra, and its ruler planet, Venus. The sign of Seventh house represents for astrologers, the sign of people you are the most attracted by, and you easily get along well with. You are most likely to start a love relationship with if backed up by other zodiacal 'Aspects.'

BEGINNER'S ASTROLOGY: and 5 Things to Know First

1. THE PRIMAL TRIAD
   - Primal Triad refers to the three most influential parts of your birth chart:
   - The placements of the sun and moon and your rising sign. These are determined by the exact time and location of your birth. You can know a lot about a person just by knowing their primal triad.

Your Sun Sign is your 'Ego' the mark of the innermost structure of our character. In Western astrology the sun sign is considered primary. This sign guides your actions, like you career and skill development and how you perform in social interactions. We respond at the deepest level through the filter of our sun sign. It's a mark of our developmental needs, our core personality.

Your Moon Sign describes your emotional inner self. The moon sign also affects your romantic behavior when in love. This sign represents your physical, emotional and social needs. In {Vedic Astrology} from India the moon sign and rising sign are considered most important along with the houses. Everyone needs to understand why their moon sign will improve your relationships.

The Ascendant {also known as your Rising sign} is your exterior, and the face you give to the world, the way you appear to others. It can become the mask you wear that prevents the world from getting to know the real you. This is how we see the world and how the world sees us.

2. NORTH NODE:

This is what your soul came here to learn. It's not your comfort zone but how you must push yourself to learn. If you stay in your comfort zone {the South node) it can be to your soul's detriment and cause depression. However, aligning with your north node can lead to an extraordinary, exciting, and fulfilling life!

3. The HOUSES:

There are twelve houses and each reveal something about a different 'Aspect' -of our life. Depending on your time of birth you'll have different sign in each.

- The First house is your persona
- The Second house is your finances
- The Third house is your network
- The Fourth house is your home
- The Fifth house is your creativity
- The Sixth house is your health
- The Seventh house is your partner's
- The Eighth house is your business
- The Ninth house is your spiritual life
- The Tenth house is your career
- The Eleventh house is your community

- The Twelfth house is your soul's growth or sacrifice.

Your birth chart interpretation will reveal what each sign in each house means for you.

It's revealing of your innermost behaviors and thoughts.

4. The TRAITS of Each Zodiac Sign:

There are only twelve signs and knowing their basic theme helps you understand how they affect you when they show up in different parts of your chart. Knowing the signs will help you to better understand other people's many layers as well. Here are basic ideas of each:

AQUARIUS is a big picture person. PISCES is an artistic type. ARIES is a fast mover and thinker. TAURUS is a slow mover. GEMINI is indecisive and curious.

CANCER is nurturing and sensitive. LEO is extravagant and the center of attention. VIRGO is organized and helpful. LIBRA is intuitive and happy go lucky. SCORPIO is erotic and deep. SAGITTARIUS is evolved and adventurous. CAPRICORN is loyal and business minded.

5. The MOON CYCLES:

Every two and a half weeks is either full or new. During a new moon is when we want to retreat from the world and often feel tired. When you look in the sky, the moon is completely in shadow, invisible to the naked eye. This is when our creativity is heightened, and we can hear the whisper of our soul. We then hold that vision from the new moon to the full moon and act towards it. The full moon is when we usually see things move forwards. This is when one side of the moon is completely illuminated, a full circle in the sky. The two days before and the two days after a full moon are a window of change for most people. This is when things seem to show up unexpected and our hard work finally pays off.

CONCLUSION:

I am still learning astrology, layer by layer. It's a life-long study! When I finally got a handle on the personalities of each sign, I made a list of the symbols of the signs and yet learn how to read the birth charts, linking the zodiac signs to the planets that rule them. This isn't something to concern yourself with at first, but just know that the horoscopes you read on a website are just the tip of a huge, cosmic iceberg. Essentially, Astrology is a roadmap to your greatest fulfillment, success and strong relationships.

THE 7 CHAKRAS:

The study of 7 chakras originates in Eastern spiritual traditions that consider the seven primary chakras the basis of our human existence. Similarly, today's Western approaches place an emphasis on the seven chakras as representations of different 'aspects' of our life and describe their function in various terms encompassing the psychological, physical, energetic and spiritual.

The basic human chakra system, as it is accepted, consists of seven chakras stretching from the base of the spine to the crown of the head. Their names, locations and corresponding chakra colors are:

1. Root chakra base of the spine - Red
2. Sacral chakra just below the navel Orange
3. Solar Plexus chakra stomach area Yellow
4. Heart chakra center of the chest Green
5. Throat chakra base of the throat Blue
6. Third Eye chakra forehead, just above area between the eyes Indigo
7. Crown chakra top of the head Violet

Sometimes, a Sanskrit name is used instead of plain English because the study of the chakra system as we know it in our modern Western culture originates mostly from yogic traditions from India. You will sometimes find them referenced as:

1. "Muladhara"
2. "Svadhishthana"
3. "Manipura"
4. "Anahata"
5. "Vishuddha"
6. "Ajna"
7. "Sahasrara"

The seven chakras are associated with the following parts of the body:

* The first one the perineum (in the coccyx area)
* The second one the lower belly (below the navel in the level of ther gonads)
* The third one the solar plexus
* The fourth one the heart (center of the chest slightly to the left of the physical heart)
* The fifth one the throat (at the carotid plexus)
* The sixth one the point between the eyebrows or "third eye" (the spiritual connection)
* The seventh one the top of the cranium (the crown)

It's important to remember that the location of the seven chakras varies slightly depending on the traditions or the school of thoughts.

Even though the 7 chakras are associated with specific parts of the body, they are not "physical" entities per se, but belong to the realm of "subtle energy". The CHAKRAS are both 'biological' and the 'spiritual', and shows a connection between the body, mind, and spirit all together.

The 7 chakras are part of the most commonly known chakra system and are made of seven energy centers located along the spine and ending in the brain, from the perineum area to the top of the head.

Each chakra possessing its own color and vibrational frequency, these wheels are the catalysts of consciousness and human function. They govern various emotional issues, from our survival instincts and self-esteem to our ability to communicate and experience love.

What is CHAKRA BALANCING?

A large part of getting to know how to work with your chakras involves chakra balancing. A chakra blockage and imbalance in one or several of the 7 chakras can initiate mental, emotional, physical and/or spiritual ailments. Regardless of whether you use chakra stones, crystals, reiki, or another form of vibrational healing to restore chakra balance, being well-versed about chakra systems, their function, and the areas they govern can be invaluable.

When properly balanced each of your 7 Chakras work together to create an optimal life. If you are like most of us your energetic ecosystem could use some help.

Balancing chakras and healing with the chakra energy system requires a working knowledge of chakras and their functions. While a basic chakra chart illustrates the foundational seven chakras, did you know there are additional chakras to consider?

Beyond the SEVEN CHAKRA System:

It is important to understand we are all made of pure energy and we share it with the Earth which gives and sustains life. The more intricate 12 chakra system illustrates just how closely we are "tied" to the planet. Stretching from an estimated three feet below the earth's surface too deep into space is a cord of energy that links each human being to the planet and the universe.

Included are the following CHAKRA Mantra's to 'Unleash Blockages' and to be repeated daily during meditation.

MANTRA'S to Unleash Blockage
ROOT Chakra Planet Mars
MARS Mantra: {I am who I am I am able and will accomplish my desires.}
SACREL Chakra Planet Venus
VENUS Mantra: {I feel I feel it all deep within me.}
- {I feel myself of inhibition and I embrace my true self.} SOLAR PLEXUS Chakra Planet Sun

SUN Mantra: {I do I will be the force of positivity in my life.}
- {I act and therefore I receive rewards for what I create.}

HEART Chakra
- HEART Mantra: {I love, I love you as I love my self
- and can see that we are all connected.} -
- {I love you and will always be loved.} -
- THROAT Chakra Planet Mercury

MERCURY Mantra: {I speak. I speak with intent and purpose.} {I share my ideas and listen to what others say to me.}

THIRD EYE Chakra Planet Saturn
- SATURN Mantra: {I see. I see the world around me.}
- {I see that there is more to me than meets the eye.} CROWN Chakra Planet Jupiter

JUPITER Mantra: {I understand. I understand my self
- and I understand my purpose in this life.} -
- {I endeavor to always reach beyond -
- so that I live the life I was destined for.}

After moving through the energy of Astrology, Numerology, and the Chakras and learning the belief in the divine and spiritual knowledge of 'endings' and 'new beginnings' I found my 'Humanitarian' side concerned with seeking human welfare.

– I have an active belief in the values of human life with order and to better humanity for 'moral' of right and wrong 'altruistic' or disinterest and 'logical' thinking and reason. It is a 'PHILOSOPHICAL' BELIEF in movement toward the improvement of the human race in a variety of areas and teaching whether it be in technology advances or sharing their geo-technology with people in need and threatened in terms of health, safety, with violation of human rights. This means that all humankind shall be treated humanely and equally in all circumstances.

SPIRITUALITY has developed and expanded over time. Contemporary New Age Spirituality is a term applied to a range of spiritual or religious beliefs that developed in Western nations during the 1970s,. Definitions of the New Age differ in their emphasis. Analytically often considered to be religious, those involved in it typically prefer the designation of spiritual or Mind.

SPIRITUAL PHILOSOPHIES:

PHILOSOPHY: Is to teach reasoning and argumentative skills.
SPIRITUAL PHILOSOPHY: Is a generic term for any philosophy

or teaching that pertains to spirituality. It may incorporate 'religious or esoteric' theme by learning the Tarot.

Esoteric Themes) and especially those from THEOSOPHY {the Master, and the 'Ancient Wisdom'} and ANTHROPOSOPHY {to nurture the life of the soul, both in the individual and in human society, based on a true knowledge of the spiritual world}. Esotericism can be described as a Western form of spirituality that stresses the importance of the individual effort to gain spiritual knowledge. NOTE: THE MAGICIAN a tarot card displaying the Hermetic concept connects this concept to 'Correspondences' defining the characteristic of esotericism.

"Correspondences": This is the idea that there are both 'real' and 'symbolic'

Correspondences existing between all things within the universe

- As an Examples: Pointing to the 'Esoteric Concept' points to the 'astrological

Idea' of the planets having a direct corresponding influence on the behavior of - human beings. -

MYSTICISM: It is the practice of RELIGIOUS ECSTASIES {of rapture, transport, and exaltation in a feeling of extreme happiness sharing a sense of being taken or moved out of one's self or one's normal state}. Religious Ecstasies is an alternate state of consciousness, together with whatever ideology of beliefs whether it be ethics, rites, myths, legends, and magic related to them. It may also refer to the attainment of 'INSIGHTS' in ultimate or hidden truths', and human transformation supported by various practices and experiences valued as a key element of 'mysticism.

Broadly defined, mysticism can be found in all religious traditions, and folk religions like 'SHAMANISM' to organized religions like the Abrahamic faiths, Indian religions, and modern spirituality New Age and New Religious Movements.

These are all asking relevant questions and I pondered as the Moon ponders in the different Chakra Houses. We have forgotten the significance of permitting ourselves time to do the things that nourish us and replenish our energy reserves like relaxing with your partner at home and still enjoying yourself just as much as if you were to go out and do something fun. Distractions in our life today we have forgotten how to converse in communication. Allow yourself to experience the pleasure in doing the simple yet meaningful things and treat yourself to the things that feed your soul like taking a bubble bath, cooking yourself a yummy meal, watching a movie or even cuddle up and read a good book. These are practices allowing you to remain in touch with your inner world and emotions.

Feelings I didn't expect are blooming up inside me and I am keeping in touch with what the soul feels most and is calling me towards. It is a sense of a higher calling. We all incarnate into this life with destiny that feels very natural to us and allows us to connect to the larger world beyond our personal life, and through curiosity and exploring what that unique thing is for me to fulfill myself I pursued the reality and to find meaning. Without it, it's difficult to find fulfillment. Unconsciously I had sabotaged my ability to create what I have wished for in my life and I began exploring all parts of myself including the ones I didn't want to look at. Becoming aware of them and taking practical steps to change the ways in those areas of life you must go to the deepest darkest place within yourself to find the answers. You must experience the heartache, pain and grief to experience Love. Before you and deeply love another, you must learn to love yourself first. By doing this I began finding the strength and courage with assertiveness and found the leader side of me that works from a place of 'integrity.' The quality of being honest and having strong moral principles and values with trust in myself I found honor in the quality of hanging strong and choosing to hold myself in consistent standards of the values and ethics of Integrity and I'm leading with it!

Reflecting on the ways I communicate my mind is opening to the thrilling journey of learning something new. We may well be dead if we give up on the path of being a constant student of life, and so much of the newness occurs. So this is also a fun time to reflect on the way I communicate dedicating my life to the practice of being honest, open and clear about my thoughts and feelings in a diplomatic way of course, and the 'divinatory' meaning of discovering hidden knowledge.

Every day, I am reminding myself that getting to where I desire takes discipline, challenging work and dedication. I have a lot of energy to roll through some changes, to tie up some loose ends on the domestic front, and may also help clear the air and bring some matters full circle including Love. I am following my intuition and emotions that could send some brilliant ideas. Also, it's an appropriate time to finish some home projects and beautify my home. I may just be bringing more love into the home! I may see some dreams come true along the way through innovative ideas and new ways.

I am taking responsibility for that {ASPECT} of my psyche. I am devoted to undo the suffering that has been passed down from lineages before me and recognize the unconscious patterns I've inherited from my 'Ancestors'. It has been connected to my upbringing and I am healing my own personal unhealthy patterns of self-sabotaging and I am healing others and their wounds that came before me and those who come after me. I am not projecting my issues onto the world and all those who come into connection with.

While writing my thought reminded me of a poem with a lesson:
"Alive in You"
"How many hooks He has threaded my throat with?"

- Gasped the fish, as he struggled and died.
- 0 Fisherman, I bless You, though You killed and ate me!
- My passion was always to be alive in You.
- Poet 'Jalal-un-Din Rumi'

I am a nomadic Sagittarius, wandering with a passion for writing and trying to help others grow. I enjoy the studies of astrology and metaphysical, spiritual, and esoteric subjects mystic and magical to be understood We have all had people in our lives, whether family, friends, or colleagues, that are a drain on our energy. In many circumstances, we are not able to distance ourselves from these people and seem to take and take, giving nothing in return. Unfortunately, we don't always have the option of removing these people from our lives.

I found myself asking exactly what is an 'energy vampire'? 'Energy Vampires' are known as a 'psychic vampire' and is anyone who feeds off the energy of others, either knowingly or subconsciously and when you've been around someone who's wearing you down, your psychic shield can weaken, allowing the vampire to get under your skin and into your head.

For instance, I have text messages phone calls and internet emails I don't ask for all demanding to sell me something whether it be a piece of information, or something they want to do for me but with a price or wanting to give me a bunch of details they say I'm supposed to know or not know So who knows? Craziness! They seem to wear down my psychic shield. Your psychic shield is what protects you from negative and draining energies and gives you the strength and intuition to defer hostile vibrations. But, when you have been around someone who's wearing you down for a while, your psychic shield can weaken, allowing the VAMPIRE (and anyone else, for that matter) to get under your skin and into your head.

Fortunately, there are useful metaphysical tools you can use to keep your psychic shield protected from negative and draining energies giving you the strength and intuition to defer hostile vibrations.

CRYSTALS are an outstanding tool for battling many of life's challenges, as well as manifesting the things you want out of life. Crystals have many different purposes, and each crystal holds a unique charge of energy that can assist you in diverse ways along your journey. Many of these crystals have protective qualities that build your immunity to the negative energies of those around you.

The best gemstones and crystals for strengthening your psychic shield!

FLUORITE If you do find yourself in a situation where someone is actively trying to drain your energy or harm you Fluorite works well for this type of protection.

ROSE QUARTZ may not be the first crystal one thinks of when speaking of protection, but it has a unique effect that will help you in unexpected ways. Rose-quartz helps you build up your self-confidence and self-assurance so that when people throw those negative cure-balls your way, you can easily deflect them. This stone reminds you to be gentler with yourself and practice self-love as often as possible. It's incredibly difficult to remain strong and centered in the face of energy vampires when we are not telling ourselves that we are worthy of love and respect. You are awesome and rose quartz will ensure you never forget it!

GARNET IS ANOTHER STONE THAT ASSISTS AGAINST ENERGY VAMPIRES IN AN UNUSUAL WAY.

This stone is typically a deep, crimson hue that is reminiscent of the blood coursing through our veins. This stone boosts your energy when you have been drained, giving you a little extra pep in your step when you need it most. The other interesting feature of garnet is that it deflects the intentions of negative energies. While protected by garnet, anyone attempting to drain your energy will drain the energy of the stone itself, leaving your psychic shield strong and impossible to pass through or enter.

Life can be hard enough without having to worry about keeping your aura safe and protected from harmful energies around you. These crystals may not protect you from every negative aspect or person in life, but they will certainly assist you in keeping yourself and your energy safer in this world of busy, busy, busy, go, go, go, it's easy to forget the simplest things in life and this always has a direct impact on our relationships no matter what we are stressed about.

One of my favorite HEALING CRYSTALS is the 'rose quartz.' The rose quartz will GROUND YOU and remind you that in this busy world, the only thing that matters is sweet love.

There is a lot of mythology surrounding the 'love stone and healing crystal known as the 'ROSE QUARTZ.' Rose quartz is a pink stone, used in the 'New Age' world for love and healing in relationships, and it's said to attract love as well as heal it.

Legend: The 'ROSE QUARTZ' was the first gem ever shared between lovers, when 'CUPID', {the ancient Roman god of love and son of Mercury, the messenger god} and 'EROS', {the ancient Greek god of love, identified by the Romans, as the goddess of sexual love and beauty, and as the counterpart that fits another perfectly the 'ROSE QUARTZ' stone was brought to Earth to restore love to all mankind, and within each other. Their hope was that its pink hues would inspire love in humans everywhere.

'Aphrodite' {an ancient Greek goddess associated with love, beauty, pleasure and procreation}, - 'Adonis' {was the mortal lover of the goddess Aphrodite in Greek mythology} are also part of the legend of the rose quartz. One day, 'Adonis' was attacked by a wild animal, and Aphrodite ran to him but caught herself on a briar patch. When they united, their blood intermingled upon a white stone, and the resulting color was pink. This stone became the 'Rose Quartz' used for love and healing.

The Egyptian love goddess, 'Isis' also used 'rose quartz' but to attract love rather than heal relationships. 'Isis' the renowned mother goddess of Egypt, reportedly used 'rose quartz' to make facial masks that would help her retain her beauty and youth. It worked. Rose Quartz masks have been found in the ancient tombs of Egypt centuries later.

Today, 'rose quartz' is found in India, Brazil, Japan, South Africa, and

Madagascar, {an island country off the coast of East Africa} and in South Dakota, in the United States. It is used for many purposes of healing, but also to attract love, and it works! It's like having a little love spell or portion in your pocket, wherever you go.

BLACK TOURMALINE the-powerful-protective-gemstone helps to clear electromagnetic radiation that can come from electronics as well as cell and radio towers. Black tourmaline transforms negative energy into lighter vibrations, so it is a great purifier to have about anywhere. It's a powerful energy cleanser that aids your energy and helps protect your aura from being infiltrated by negative thoughts. If you think negatively, it also helps that negative energy from building up and causing psychic pressure in your aura which can cause physical symptoms like tension and anxiety. Instead of getting into nasty emotional states when you're around people spewing toxic words and energy, you can more easily keep your mind in a positive state. In practical terms, it can allow you to live and feel light, carefree, and in touch with your spiritual truth. It's a beautiful crystal that can be an energetic anchor in your lifestyle. If you feel like you have trouble focusing or feeling like you are safe, this crystal will help you feel secure and slow down your rapid thoughts. The Root chakra is linked to our ability to provide for ourselves and feel like we belong in the world. If you want to follow-through on your projects and create a life where you aren't struggling financially, this crystal can help shift your thoughts to the right frequency to manifest those things. Black tourmaline is well known for its grounding properties. Meditate with black tourmaline and ask what negative energy it's time to let go of and gently heal your thoughts so you can be free of fear. You may also find you sleep easier and open up to people without anxiety.

BLACK TOURMALINE is one of the best stones for protecting yourself from unintentionally negatives energies. While this stone may not protect you from those who wish to do you harm, it will protect you from those who do not realize they are getting to you. This stone acts as a goalkeeper for the mind, rejecting harmful energies and providing a barrier for those frequencies that tend to bring us down. This crystal's force extends to your aura, blocking bad vibes and allowing you to remain positive in the face of negativity.

CITRINE is a wonderful stone for promoting the naturally occurring positive energy of the Libra personality. Citrine is also a stone of fortune, bringing opportunity and abundance to those who work with it.

AVENTURINE is a stone that brings fortunate events and circumstances it's known as the Stone of Opportunity. This stone can be translucent or opaque and comes in shades of green, peach, blue, and brown. It's known for its ability to attract luck and fortune, but it also boosts confidence and reduces stress. It is also excellent for increasing intellectual thought, imagination, and perception. This crystal is perfect for increasing opportunity.

TIGER'S EYE is a beautiful stone with a glowing effect that is known as the cat's eye effect, which gives it an illuminating shimmer that is quite a remarkable sight. This stone brings balance between the Libra's external and internal realities, aligning both parts of the self.

After studies of 'Astrology' 'Numerology' and the 'Tarot,' I found my interest in the spiritual and esoteric subjects consisting of "Western Esotericism."

WESTERN ESOTERICISM: Known as the Western mystery tradition and a wide range of loosely related ideas and distant from the orthodox Judeo-Christian religion and from rationalism. Esotericism has pervaded in forms of Western philosophy, religion, pseudoscience, art, literature and music, and continues to affect intellectual ideas and popular culture. The Esoteric ideas have also exerted an influence in popular culture, art, literature, film, and music.

ESOTERICISM as an enchanted world view:

1. Western esotericism is an artificial category in retrospect to a range of current ideas - and known by others prior to the end of the eighteenth century.

In short: 'Western esotericism' is a modern scholarly concept found in moral, political, and controversial ethical issues and are emerging from new situations and possibilities brought about by advances in biology and medicine. Ethics, Genetic engineering, aim at improving the quality of a human population. The study of improving the qualities through moral philosophies do not have the freedom to govern itself and control its own affairs from external authority.

2. Conceptual development is a modern scholarly construct rather than a pre- existing, self-defined tradition of thought and is defined as connecting philosophies and recognizing that these ideas are linked back to earlier philosophies from late antiquity which is the ancient past. Many spiritual teachings were reserved for a specific elite and hidden from the masses.

MYSTICAL BELIEFS a historical interpretation of esotericism became a popular approach within several esoteric movements and Traditionalism. The Western esoteric all shared a core characteristic "a claim to 'gnosis,' or a direct spiritual insight into cosmology or spiritual insight" and referred to as "Western gnostic" being just as much as "Western esoteric."

Examining the means of accessing higher knowledge, it was believed that esotericism

- and mediation through contact with non-human entities and individual experiences could be found and understood as "a structural element of Western culture."
- Esotericism can be described as a Western form of spirituality that stresses the
- importance of the individual effort to gain spiritual knowledge -
- Gnosis - is the 'Greek noun for knowledge of spiritual mysteries - where man
- is confronted with the divine 'aspect' of existence.

NOTE: THE MAGICIAN a tarot card displaying the Hermetic concept connected this concept to 'Correspondences' defining the characteristic of esotericism.

"Correspondences": This is the idea that there are both 'real' and 'symbolic' correspondences existing between all things within the universe

- As an Examples: Pointing to the 'Esoteric Concept' points to the 'astrological idea' of the planets having a direct corresponding influence on the behavior of human beings.

ESOTERICISM and History:

Late Antiquity and the origins of Western esotericism are in the origins of Greek civilization belonging to a period of the 9ᵗʰ century to the 12ᵗʰ century to the end of antiquity in the Greek Dark Ages a period which encompassed a mix of religion and intellectual traditions from Babylon and Persia which globalization, urbanization, and multiculturalism brought about socio cultural change - and I thought about WHY I felt so connected to history.

At the age of four or five years of age, I was enrolled in a 'dramatic class' featuring a children's play of GREEK MYTHOLOGY. Some of the children in the class were elected to be angels and fairy's dancing to music However, I was elected to play the part of a legendary Egyptian wise man named "Hermes" {Trismegistus.} The lines I spoke were to portray the true nature of 'GOD' emphasizing 'spiritual divinity.' I had no idea what any of this meant to me but in a robotic way I was to merely learn my lines and speak battling it out with "Hades" the Greek god of the underworld.

This resonated so deeply with me I began to think and wonder "Who Am I Today?"

"Who Will I Be Tomorrow?" "What Was I Yesterday?"

When we're born it isn't the freest expression of what we can become. If we pay attention to the THOUGHTS that shape our ACTIONS and the actions that shape our HABITS and the habits that shape our CHARACTER we will find that character is what shapes our DESTINY.

In my life as a child, I drifted to things in a graceful manner and bowed down to ACCEPTING. Out of some sort of FEAR I would turn flush and red hot with the result of strong emotion and feel embarrassment. The thought of having to sit still long enough to hear an entire question or statement and I stopped listening and felt allergic to being questioned and saying "I don't understand."

Having FAITH without questioning is just being 'Fundamentally Blind."

There is no FAITH without questioning. This is HOW I learned to sit upright and be willing to be the questioned person. FAITH is to be willing to QUESTION ourselves. The people who are weird or odd and who are always walking questions may be the most INSPIRING. These people allow us the opportunity to see our own 'unwillingness' to a question so they can INSPIRE FAITH.

Our hearts ache deeply when things CHANGE into a natural TRANSFORMATION of the Divine and the beauty is of letting go of the frozen images of who we think we were. Feeling reluctance and unwilling for a long time was whether I had the right to question FAITH and to question myself. As I began striking out on my own from the people, I sensed the most weird or odd and began walking away with many questions. I allowed myself the opportunity to see my own reluctance to questioning

Faith helped me to relax into the 'Grace of Nature' and the naturalness and beauty of 'letting go' of the frozen images of who I thought I was.

Long since passed I began learning that CHARACTER is my Only Life Raft... and I understood what it takes to be me.

In the morning light of days floating and changing facing the strange changes of getting older with insights I felt it was WISER to see it as the Soul's passionate expression of the emotional 'grief and sorrow' of weeping. WHY did I still mourn losing my friend, my lover, my teacher and my soulmate of fifty-six years husband for thirty-five years with a total of sixty-seven years "Loving Him". Why do I care so much about him still after his death or is it wiser to see it as yet another one of my transformations?

Who am I today? Who will I be tomorrow? What was I yesterday? Still puckering up and filling with dread, I remain playful rather than feel fearful but I deny the 'Impermanence' every day. (Early Buddhism dealt with the problem of impermanence in a very rational manner. This concept is known as 'Anicca' in Buddhism, according to which, impermanence is an undeniable and inescapable fact of human existence from which nothing that belongs to this earth is ever free.

How easy is it to accept these changes from one state to another? How accepting are we when a relationship changes from the state of a 'true love' to friends to strangers? Why have I accepted the law of gravity but not the law of Impermanence? Am I stupid? Or Scared? If I am scared, then what?

Have I fallen into the trap of 'Suck-cess?' When we are born it isn't the freest expression of what we can become. The best definition of SUCCESS has nothing to do with money or fame. Success is the ability to deliberately change one's CHARACTER. Having 'Ambivalence' is a state of having mixed conflicting feelings, belief, or feelings towards another. It's the experience of having an attitude reflected in behavior and enough to hear an entire question or statement or statement and I stopped listening and felt allergic to being questioned and saying "I don't understand."

Paying attention to THOUGHTS can shape you actions and my actions then shape my habits and my habits then shape my CHARACTER. I then found my character that shaped my DESTINY.

A Person's CHARACTER is their DESTINY!

When life sucks we tar and feather in a form of public torture and humiliation used to enforce our justice or revenge and we buy into the purpose of distractions with worthless garbage and reckless behavior. Instead, without ever thinking about if we created this disgust and anger through our own circumstances we try to tease and make light of a situation by deceiving another with exclamations. This begins to resonate so deeply it makes the reality of 'discussion' seem natural and colorful and fun!

RELUCTRANCE

The hesitant 'Unwillingness' in our action or non-actions shows distrust, doubt, and suspicion with a reluctance to commit ourselves. Disallowing our willingness to cooperate stops every proposal made. ETHICS or moral philosophies enter and are even more pressing than refusing responsivity.

ETHICS vs. MORALS: Is there a difference?

Ethics refers broadly to moral principles, and is often applied to questions of correct behavior in the relation to a narrow area of activity: Ethics tends to suggest aspects of universal fairness and the question of whether an action is responsible:

Morals usually implies and suggests an idea or feeling and they are understood as a cultural or emotional association of inherited characteristics of essential traits.

NOTE: For me These are reminders of my very favorite story "PRIDE & PREJUDICE" and "The Living Sculptures of Pemberley."

NOTE: Ambivalence is the state of having opposing attitudes or feelings contrary about ideas or something or someone. It is about unsureness, doubt and indecision.

The HISTORY and SIGN of 'SAGITTARIUS'

Sagittarius in Greek Mythology is a mythological creature with the upper body of a human and the lower body and legs of a horse.

Sagittarius is a mutable sign that represents the change of seasons from autumn to winter. It also represents everything that comes after a cycle of life that has ended. This links it to heaven and places our Souls visit after our physical body is gone.

The constellation of Sagittarius was identified as the god 'Nergal' in ancient Babylonia, a centaur-life creature firing an arrow from a bow. This speaks well of the two natures of Sagittarius one animalistic and one human. The later division of the sign, and the constellation and stories linked to them is something that didn't fade in centuries.

Later, it was connected to 'CHIRON' in Greek mythology held to be the superlative centaur amongst his brethren, as he was called the "wisest" with justness of all the centaurs" and is represented by a horse with human torso and head again pointing at a connection of animalistic with human nature.

It was one of the 48 constellations listed by the astronomer 'Ptolemy' of the 2nd century. The Latin name for the constellation is "Archer." Its Sumerian name was "Pabilsag" and it was composed of two words 'Pabil,' meaning "elder paternal kinsman" and 'Sag' meaning "chief, head" In other words, it was translated as "Forefather" or "Chief Ancestor" and symbolically representing the moment when people turned from animals to 'aware beings.'

'Sag,' meaning "chief, head". - In other words, it was translated as "Forefather" or "Chief Ancestor", representing the moment when people turned from animals to 'aware' beings.

The constellation of Sagittarius is full of stars, clusters and nebulae, {an interstellar cloud of dust, hydrogen, helium and other ionized gases} for the center of our galaxy lies in it. The current position of the center of the 'MILKY WAY' is still the sign of Sagittarius, on its 27th degree.

The arrow of this constellation points towards the star 'Antares', the "heart of the Scorpion", speaking of the necessity for CHANGE and strangely, the direction of life towards death.

The MYTH of SAGITTARIUS

There's a dilemma regarding the myth of this constellation. By one interpretation,

Sagittarius is a centaur shooting an arrow, but the constellation does not show a creature with four legs. Because of this it is viewed either as the satyr CROTUS {the son of Pan} or as CHIRON {the son of Saturn}.

Greek credited CROTUS with the invention of archery. He was considered a great huntsman and a better musician, raised and lived with the Muses, {Muses were the Greek goddesses of poetic inspiration, the adored deities of song, dance, and memory, on whose creativity, wisdom and insight of all artists and thinkers depended}. Because of his talent for music, the Muses requests ZEUS, {the Olympian god of the sky and the thunder, the king of all other gods and men, and consequently, the chief figure in Greek mythology. This is when ZEUS gave CROTUS two horse feet, a tail and a bow with an arrow because of his archery skills. His music inspires the Muses to applaud to him, and this was the mythological explanation on how applause came to existence.

CHIRON on the other hand, was the first ASTROLOGER and the only centaur that did not give in to his animalistic tendencies. He was a TEACHER and a HEALER, who was also immortal and badly hurt by his friend, HERCULES. Hercules was chasing other centaurs who stole his wine, shooting at them with poisonous arrows and by mistake, he shot CHIRON in the thigh, inflicting an incurable would upon him. CHIRON'S pain was unbearable, and he begged ZEUS to give his IMMORTALITY to PROMETHEUS, to take his place in the UNDERWORLD. In his wish he finally died and stopped feeling the pain. CHIRON gave his immortality away and saved someone's life -

THE CONNECTION BETWEEN THE SAGITTARIUS MYTH AND THE SAGITTARIUS ZODIAC SIGN:

The main concept of the sign of Sagittarius is the human need to overcome animalistic instincts and become increasingly human. This involves learning, teaching, healing, and traveling, widening one's SOUL to set apart from the primal forces that weigh us down. The entire sign is split in two halves, one that belongs to the animals and the other that belongs to the human mind. Sagittarius represents everything from hunting, weaponry and persecution, to healing, learning, the divine spirit and one's focus to learn theology or philosophy.

The strongest impact of the myth of CHIRON is shown by accidental betrayal of a friend and wounds that cannot heal, while the most intense need is given to an individual through preparedness to give their life for someone who is in pain, out of a need to set free from their own. From a certain point, this is a win-win situation in which a person manages to die, or metaphorically make a deep CHANGE, only to help someone unselfishly, saving their life. This explains the tendency of each Sagittarius to give, rescue and save those around them.

In Greek Mythology CHIRON was called the "Wisest & Justice of all centaurs" and notable throughout Greek mythology for his youth-nurturing nature:

His skills matched those of {Apollo}, his foster father and sometimes along with {Artemis}. CHIRON was the Master of the Healing Arts: He was placed in the sky among the stars to be honored by his brother, ZEUS and become a trainer of "demi- gods" and lives on today as a constellation and an Inspiration.

CHIRON was also known for Medicine, Music, Archery, Hunting, Gymnastics, and the Art of Prophecy. He was credited with the discovery of botany and pharmacy, the science of herbs and medicine and known as a great HEALER ASTROLOGER, and respected ORACLE. His pupils were by contrast Cultured. CHIRON by contrast of all 'centaurs' was intelligent, civilized and kind, and highly revered as a teacher and tutor. His weapons were only used for hunting and there was no savage behavior. CHIRON created a status as a loving father, and a strict and wise teacher disassociated with the aspects of 'centaurs.'

SAGITTARIUS & GEMINI & INTIMACY COMPATIBILITY

Sagittarius and Gemini have this strange approach to sex, childish, and light, as if they don't really care about it. When they get together, they usually get strangely involved in emotions none of them really understands. Their sex life is something to cherish, easy, open and with no pressure at any side. They will both enjoy their sexual relations, followed by laughter, creativity and joy. As two children in bodies of grown-ups, they could go through the feeling of shame together if they don't have much experience.

When they meet a bit older, there is a slim chance that both didn't have enough sexual experiences and partners to understand their personal needs and desires. This can make them both a bit selfish, but if their communication keeps going, there is no reason this would be a turn off for anyone.

It is a strange thing, but sex is not that important to these partners. They are looking for someone to complete their mental personalities, someone to talk to and give of purpose. Therefore, they could decide to stay friends after a breakup, for their starting premise was in building a strong relationship founded on their personalities, rather than their sexual or emotional natures.

TRUST If anyone can understand the need of their partner to not be faithful, it is these two. Strangely enough, this can lead to ultimate faithfulness, for there will be no more excitement in the secrecy and mystery of "parallel relationships." SAGITTARIUS is not someone who can tell a lie and keep a straight face, and they are usually really disturbed by the lies of other people. GEMINI can tell a lie with such ease that they sometimes don't even know they're lying. When they get together, this all becomes something to have fun with and they could play a game of TRUST until they build it on "strong foundations of mutual RESPECT.

WOW! This kind of understanding is truly something to cherish. A problem can surface when they are both preoccupied with chasing their personal values and don't see what they have with each other. As OPPOSING SIGNS they complement each other in general, but this is strongly sensed in this segment of their relationship. With GEMINI'S ideas and mind flow, there is nothing SAGITTARIUS can't learn or share, being a student and a teacher at the same time. The curiosity goes both ways and they will spend days just learning about each other and absorbing shared experiences.

The only thing that can interfere with the quality of their mental connection is the possible fear of intimacy that builds in the meantime. That strength of personal exchange stops being mental and starts being emotional at some point, and as two signs that aren't exactly emotional to begin with, they can be frightened by the intensity of EMOTIONS that are surfacing when they are together.

In general, this is a couple you want to hang out with, every day. They will share happiness with one another and with those around them. They can INSPIRE anyone to love and to smile, because when in love, they will laugh so sincerely and have so much fun together.

The "here-and-there" nature of Gemini will get new meaning and purpose through the eyes of their SAGITTARIUS, while the search for the ultimate Truth can be so much easier for a SAGITTARIUS with the mind of a Gemini. Their optimism and their eloquence will multiply, day after day until one of them gets scared and decides to take-off or death do them part.

EMOTIONS

It is strange to think about the emotional side of the relationship between a Sagittarius and a Gemini. Both signs have a non-emotional feel to them, but their contact develops so much emotion that maybe neither one of them will be able to cope with it. They are not used to feeling that much, and when they "CLICK" SAGITTARIUS could discover the new meaning of life and Gemini, a Synthesis {the synthesis of intellect and emotion in his work and often contrasted with analysis} that they have never had a chance to experience. This can be a fascinating "LOVE STORY" if we don't run away from all that emotion.

VALUES

There is this important thing they both value and they are the THINGS that make sense. As opposing signs it might signify that GEMINI is scattered and superficial, while SAGITTARIUS is collected and deep, but in fact, they have the same core in the fact that everything needs to make sense. Usually, we would connect this with SAGITTARIUS, but GEMINI has it in their approach to words and everyday actions.

Gemini's 'Mercury' deals with senseless words, stories without meaning and purpose, whatever that purpose may be. SHARED ACTIVITIES

Not only will they share every activity that any of them thinks of, but they will also laugh all the way whatever they decide to do together. This positive emotion and pure joy they can share, becomes something like a happy drug to both and they no longer want to be apart. As two mutable signs, they understand each other's changeability and flexibility, and they are perfectly capable to find all the right reasons why everything they do makes perfect sense. There is a point when they will get irritating to their surroundings, like two spoiled children without a care in the world, but while they are this happy why would they care?

SAGITTARIUS Archetype:

SAGITTARIUS is the mutable fire sign, the spark that appears and then disappears far away at the speed of light. Sagittarius is as difficult to contain as flames in the wind. It will never remain where it appeared. It is the archetype of the EXPLORER, constantly searching for new world, never settling, never at peace. But without this unattached adventurer, we would remain forever at the spot where we were born, doing nothing but reproducing right there. It is what makes us go on.

ASCENDANT FIRE SIGN for SAGITTARIUS is noticed for their energy, enthusiasm and optimism. When a fire sign is on the ascendant the manner is friendly, but professionally competent signals which draw out a friendly and respectful response from others.

SUMMARY;

GEMINI and SAGITTARIUS make an incredible couple, being the most innocent one of all oppositions in the zodiac. They don't often find each other right away, but at some point, in life, it is almost certain that a Gemini will find their Sagittarius and vice versa. Our relationship has a strong intellectual connection, in which we will gradually find deep emotions. There is no real prognosis how things will end though, because the emotions of how we feel could easily scare them away and their relationship could end only because of FEAR. If we would decide to give in and find out what we could share together with GEMINI'S ideas and SAGITTARIUS' beliefs, the sky is the limit. Or is it beyond?

- I'm calling in my Soulmate

My prayers are calling in my Soulmate with Affirmations and my visualizations help bring us together.

I have an 'Air' Sign that's being a bit difficult so wherever my Soulmate is I need to call you in and have A Heart to Heart Conversation and discuss our feelings with each other.

I must admit the TRUTH Sometimes I need to take a step back and say, OKAY

'We need to try it your way and discuss our feelings with each other.

I've been defending myself my rights and defending my beliefs but was I really right? Was that path right for me and did I really make the right decision? I think maybe I need to say to you, my partner (I was wrong!) Let's try it again! -

- Let's change the past! LET'S WORK ON THINGS!

I really want this to work. I can turn things around but, I must admit the TRUTH to myself I'm Not Always right and I'm as STUBBORN as the rest of us

My 'Co-dependency' Addiction is affecting me and my romantic life. I don't want to be dependent on anyone else but myself. I am FORGIVING and LEARNING with each heartache of experience to release and experience more love in my present moments. It's a HARD LESSON for me to learn but these lessons are always coming about for a reason and to become more Rounded & Balanced with more Love in the present moment here and to help us develop our INNER SOUL and to become more Rounded & Balanced before going on to heaven Right?

* A Message from the Archangels in a form of clarity saying "We have TRUTH"

Look for a SIGN in this situation and pray to 'Archangel Michael', the Divine Guardian Angel of the Divine and ask him to offer assistance:

* Archangel Michael: "Am I on the right path or not?" "Can I change that path?"

Archangel Michael's answer: "ABUNDANCE there is Abundance waiting for you."

* Archangel Michael, I asked: "What is the most important thing?"

Archangel Michael's answer: "Maybe it's not about relying on somebody else and relying on support from others but to find out the HONESTY of relying on yourself and standing on your own two feet and not to be dependent on anyone else. I suddenly felt a NEW expression of interpretation and independence and I enrolled in a dance class expressing my creative feelings and I began looking backward to when I first began a whole new experience of me.

It was 1957 after attending Ball State Teacher's College and having just taken a job at the home office of an Insurance company in Ft. Wayne, Indiana, I was offered a new position with a move to Dallas, Texas, along with two others and an office manager for opening a new branch office in downtown Dallas. This was the true adjustment of independence from what I had ever known before and I responded with an overwhelming "YES" with acceptance and off to Dallas I went.

I remember an experience I had one evening taking the bus home from downtown Dallas on a forty-five-minute drive from work. Upon entering the bus, I found a seat in the center of the bus next to a little black lady with saying 'Hello' in a friendly manner as I sat down for a long quiet and restful ride home from work. The little lady I sat next to has a bearing resemblance of "Rose Parks." If you remember 'Rosa Parks' was an American activist in the civil rights movement in the Montgomery Bus Boycott and she was best known for her pivotal role in the segregation movement on the public transit system in 1955.

I remember this so well as {1955 was also the same year I was graduating from high school with a business and history major}.

'Rosa Parks' was best known when she 'refused' to give up her seat to a white male on a Montgomery, Alabama bus and was a courageous woman who was not afraid to stand up for an unpopular cause and helped to end public segregation. I believe "Rose Parks" was the first lady of 'civil rights' and went down in history as 'the mother of the freedom movement. Suddenly, I was finding myself in 'Déjà vu and in a place of reliving history without realizing my determined feelings of actions at the time. A few short moments later I heard the bus driver announce over his microphone that someone on the bus needed to relinquish their seat and find a different seat to sit. Well, not really paying any attention to what the bus driver was saying or what that was all about I knew it had nothing to do with me. However, the bus driver continued to announce the same message repeatedly and began referring to someone on the bus in particular and to get up and change seats. Still trying to rest comfortably with not paying attention to what any of this meant, suddenly the little black lady sitting next to me began gathering up the little plastic bags sitting at her feet and stated to me that she would move from her seat and that I could remain sitting there. I asked, "Why should you do that?" You were sitting here before me so please stay where you are sitting." "I don't understand what the problem is here." Coming from a northern state to a southern state and being in unfamiliar territory - it still didn't dawn on me what this was all about. All the passengers began turning around and looking directly at me as the bus driver began describing my full attire over his microphone with urgent and continued persistence and suddenly a well-dressed white business man holding a briefcase was standing in the isle next to my seat asking me to get up and take his seat up front and he would sit in my seat. Well, besides feeling man-handled and embarrassed by their actions towards me I stood my ground and didn't budge. I said calmly, I'm quite comfortable sitting here so WHY SHOULD I MOVE TO ANOTHER SEAT?" The businessman said again, "You are asked to move from this seat so you should do it." Well suddenly it dawned on me IT DAWNED ON ME THESE PEOPLE WERE STILL FIGHTING THE WAR OF CIVIL RIGHTS!!!

Oh my God, I thought! Public segregation ended with 'Rosa Parks' in the civil rights movement in 1955 It is now 1957 two years later since the segregation movement law came into effect and this little lady sitting next to had every right to sit wherever she pleased and so did I. Having been raised in the North we didn't have such outward discrimination as these people. The businessman continued to stand there in the isle next to me during that forty-five minute bus ride with the bus driver harassing and bully me with his microphone. T

Through my intuition I felt this little lady sitting next to me was on her way home from a hard day of work in someone's home as their maid cleaning up after them. The little plastic bags she was holding on to so tightly looked to have someone's old pair of shoes or a piece of clothing which may have been given to her. I felt her embarrassment and humiliation as she sat there quietly with a mild and gentle temperament.

It was not until the end of that bus ride did I even think of "Rosa Parks" and how her people must have felt during those days of being 'Bullied' and 'Tormented' with such unjust discrimination. Laws had been passed and the South didn't seem to have any regard for the rule of law that was made two years before. I felt I had been passing through some sort of a time warp and it was not until the bus stopped did I begin to feel for my safety of being followed home! FEAR was upon me once I left that bus with two to three blocks to go to my home I say: When in doubt don't just walk But RUN!

My Life turned into a new chapter surrounding me with feelings in a moral manner of human behavior. I thought of "Les Misérables" the French historical novel of [1862] by 'Victor Hugo' and being considered one of the greatest novels of the 19th century. "Hugo" explained his ambitions for the 'Novel' and the overarching structure of works saying: "I don't know whether it will be read by everyone but it is meant for everyone."

- The book "Les Misérables" - Is Progress in work "From evil to good, Injustice to justice,

From falsehood to truth, From night to day,

From appetite to conscience, From corruption to life, From bestiality to duty, From hell to heaven,

From nothingness to God."

The starting point: The Matter, Destination, The soul.

The 'hydra' at the beginning: The Angel at 'The End".

[NOTE:] "The Hydra" was a serpentine water monster in Greek and Roman mythology.

Remembering another day, a beautiful day in Dallas with the sun shining brightly and a tornado funnel cloud bigger than life appeared at a very fast-moving speed. The sky looked like a painter's brush had drawn the perfectly fine line across a white canvas dividing the two sides one side being white and the other side black. Suddenly in a mixture of rain and hail stones falling the thunderous cracking sounded like a train roaring through and blowing its horn as a warning… I could hear debris twisting and turning with the sounding of scattered pieces as if a bomb was hitting with blasting force and blazing bolts flashing throughout the darkness of night. Complete loss of all electricity my bedroom phone began ringing I was shocked! How could that be ? Looking to my wind-up alarm clock for the correct time it was 3:00 AM exact! Amazed I picked-up the phone receiver and heard a long-distance operator say to someone at the other end of the line "You are now connected." I wondered if this could be my parents from Indiana calling me in some way?" The voice on the other end of the line said "Pat this is Jim Are you Okay?" I was completely speechless, and my heart took a few leaps before I could even speak not knowing which was the loudest my heart pounding or the cracking thunder? "Jim, is that really you or is it my imagination playing tricks?" "Yes, he said, and I had to know if you are Okay?" "How did you find me?" "I left instructions for everyone to NOT let you know if you came back looking for me since you had last walked away. " "I have my sources but what is important is knowing that you are safe from the storm." Jim always knew my fear of storms and always seemed to find me no matter where. I had left Indiana coming to Dallas and to try and get over my 'feelings' for Jim but everyone I met and dated was still not Jim!

Everyone's phone was down that night, and it was just so amazing to me how Jim was able to get through to me through all this lightening and still able to make a connection to my phone without electricity. It was Magical! Then through the static I heard Jim telling me how much he loved me missed me and asking me again to marry him and that he would always be in love with me. He said he was afraid before but now everything was clearer, and he wanted to marry me. I so wanted to believe it could be true and next he was driving to Dallas to pick me up. I had signed papers with a contract that I would be staying with the company for at least a certain amount of time and the next thing I knew I was breaking my contract.

Jim came for me in Dallas and everything was beautiful again and no blue thing. He is the man who could always make me feel safe, protected and deeply loved. Always, when I didn't know which way to turn or go he would hold my hand inside his hand always showing me the way and saying I love you I love you I love you without a word and inspiring me to a clarity I could float in and trust. His smile would always fill my heart with his presence, and in the smile of strangers for today tomorrow and forever. I knew Jim would always be in my heart my friend and True Love.

Upon my arrival back to my parent's home in Indiana I received a long-distance phone call from an attorney named 'Russel Wise' asking me to come for a job interview. I was advanced in business but had only one law course in college. In my reluctance I was convinced to interview for the job. Upon arrival I felt I was walking into 'Perry Mason's' law office like seen in the old TV Series of the 50's and 60's with episodes of a defense lawyer and his legal assistant-secretary named 'Girl Friday.' I did take the job with Attorney Mr. Wise and he was a great mentor in law as well as becoming a good friend. High respected, Attorney R. Wise was also a Bank President, a Business Owner of several Newspapers, City & State Attorney, and highly regarded in politics with dignitaries flying in from Washington D.C. to attend cocktail parties with my help to host. I loved working with Mr. Wise and remained with him and the law firm for six years until after his passing death and staying another four months with the law firm with the distribution of files to the perspective clients and before the new owners took over the practice.

That summer, with Jim on summer break from college he was staying at his mother's place in northern Indiana. A glass and mold company asked Jim to deliver a huge 1000-pound steel mold by truck, from Indiana to Michigan. After the mold was delivered, he would meet me at my parents for the weekend.

It was a beautiful summer morning that weekend as I sat in my parents backyard waiting for Jim's arrival after delivering the mold and returning from Michigan. As the early morning began, I thought of Jim's arrival as I watched the power of time. I began having uneasy feelings 'Clairvoyant' thoughts deep within and I wondered if 'Fate' was becoming a real actuality in our lives. Destiny is sometimes referred to as fate having a predetermined course of events often referred to as 'The Fate of Destiny.' My feeling grew stronger and stronger with each moment and I knew something was terribly wrong concerning Jim. I sat in the sun's reflections and I began silently praying throughout the rest of that morning, asking "God" for his help to keep Jim safe.

A little kitchen window was open to where I sat in the backyard in the sunshine. Being a Saturday morning, mother was in her beauty shop doing a customer's hair. The only telephone in our home was stationed in mother's beauty shop for her business calls and appointments. As I sat intensely in the backyard, I thought deeply to NOT to let the telephone ring. I didn't want to hear news that something terrible had happened to Jim. My emotions were peak high but then I heard the telephone ring and I knew that Jim had been in an accident and was terribly hurt. I asked again Dear God, "Please let Jim be alive."

I heard Mother's footsteps suddenly approach the little kitchen window and my heart stood still, and paralyzed. Mother's words began saying, "Jim's mother just called to say that Jim had a terrible accident and was critical in a hospital in Michigan.

There was not a bus going that way, so I thought my only alternative was to hitchhike. I had never done that before and the next thing I knew, mother was dismissing the customer and sending her home and we hurried into the car with mother driving me until we reached the Michigan hospital in the unique way of 3:00 AM on the dot! I knew 'Fate' was playing its role again with Destiny. Mother waited for me in the car.

I ran into the hospital and found the owners of the mold company silently peering at Jim from the foot of his bed but quickly turned and left without a work upon my arrival. Jim lay subconsciously with stitches, a brain concussion, and with a Hematoma on his hip. When Jim heard my voice he slightly opened his eyes and knew that I was with him. I felt a PEACE of mind with reassurance removing any fears or doubt and knew Jim would soon be on his way to recovery. I 'Thanked God' and all the Angels with the highest Gratitude for their Blessings in Jim's Life Recovery. It was a promise being fulfilled. After 20-30 minutes, I left Jim's hospital room thanking all the nurses and staff members for Jim's care and for allowing me to be with him in those wee hours.

Mother and I stayed the rest of the night in a motel getting up at daybreak to leave for home with the long drive back. My poor mother, and what I must have put her through all my growing years.

Jim and I were together during his recovery that summer. Most memorable was on Angola's Lake James, in Indiana, at the most beautiful and delightfully FUN place called Blitzos located on the water's edge dancing to 'Tommy and Jimmy Dorsey' on their trombone and trumpet and their essential collection of music. We could have danced all night under the open skies with the clearest bright stars shinning down upon us from above and the loveliest summer breeze softly speaking of Love all around in a night of romance. It was Heavenly!

At summer's end Jim was back in school at Purdue and began having dizzy spells and blackouts. Lost in the dissolution of heartache and tears with fear and the uncertainty of his life ahead, Jim broke-off our longtime loving relationship which forced us to change course and go separate ways. The grief and loneliness took hold on us both for we had learned early and loved deeply. Always there for the other we held one another tightly with saying our last 'goodbye.' Still I didn't know how this could be a last step in our lives together.

It was during a time of the Draft and many young men were being drafted into the army. Jim quickly took the Air Force test to avoid the army passing the test with the highest score every made on any of the Air Force testing. Staying at his mother's place while waiting for military orders to arrive, Jim wrote to keep me informed of his whereabouts and I immediately replied with a letter back. However, I didn't hear back from Jim, but I did hear from his mother instead with this statement. "Jim had received his military orders and had left and for me to "stay away' from Jim and to leave him alone." I never heard back from Jim again after that. I learned in later years that Jim had never received my letter I wrote to him. His mother had kept my letter and never gave it to him or ever mentioned that I had written him back. I am sure Jim felt that I did not want to hear from him again by my not writing him back. What else could he have thought?

Having not heard again from Jim I married a man named 'Bob' later becoming the mother of two beautiful children my son, Eric and daughter, Renee both whom I love very much. Early in our marriage of twelve years, issues were developing with doubts, distrust, lies, and cheating as well as heavy gambling debts prevailing,

My identity and faith had been stripped away by the controlling and deceitful actions and non-truths of another. I felt helpless protecting my children's values and emotional securities and I set out on a different course of action seeking a divorce in marriage by filling a trifold briefcase of evidence for the divorce attorney.

Christmas holidays were approaching with a deferred appointment with my divorce attorney until after the holidays. Son Eric was close to age nine and daughter Renee close to age four so I was certainly busy preparing for their Christmas along with family dinners and holiday parties. Also, in this same frame of time an internal link began leading me into something of a real urgency like it was requiring my immediate attention, but I could not put my mind to it. The urgency became so strong, so real with each day and never letting up that it was driving me a little coo-coo. Walking in a constant daze I couldn't concentrate or react to what my heart might be trying to tell me. All I wanted in my life was to go forward with my children as a family but life was standing still in TIME and things didn't happen all at once.

- "In other words, I can sum up everything I've learned about life: It goes on" -

Dedicated to Poet: Robert Frost

Directly after the New Year in 1972, I found myself standing in front of a closet door I had not opened since moving to this home and I really didn't remember how I found myself standing there. It was like I was being directed and guided by something or someone with a force of gravity pulling me toward something urgent. I did remember however, that Jim's past letters of twelve or thirteen years before had been stored in this closet, but it was not something I had been thinking about. As I stood at the front of this door I debated whether to open the door which could bring my heart and mind to a place of sad memories again. Jim and I had struggles with a lot of conflicts before and all I wanted now was to live in a quiet and peaceful way with my two children.

It would be impossible to detail every step of an instance through those in-between years but with just walking down a street sometimes I would suddenly see or sense a figure in the distance ahead and with an irresistible force I would run to catch-up from behind shouting out and saying "Jim it's me" but then only to see a complete stranger standing there. I always remembered Jim saying "We were like two ships passing in the night." I have always felt a powerful spiritual course of love with Jim and a bonding connection of happiness always knowing he was my one 'True Love so deeply embedded in my heart and mind.

I sat quietly holding the box of Jim's letters while gathering my senses inside with a last glance beyond my consciousness somewhere in time and found my convictions at the world's extreme bringing periods of time as a guide to truth. The complicated emotions of being overly emotional with loving are sometimes the nostalgic sadness of illusion and I was trying to be practical and realistic and bring things down-to-earth. There was nothing for me to do but to continue loving him with another look at my heart. Love can bring innocent dreaming or it can be put on a shelf forever.

I acted in silence clearing the space in a mind of shadows and psychic visions with my emotions spilling over granting an absolution with a release from all consequences in a profound way I could see myself standing on the bridge between the past and the present re-connecting to Jim in a mysterious and magically way.

Atmospheric protection could only consist in my own predominating brain and heart with a fantastical unrestrained imagination. Through the tragic sadness of pain and hurt hopeful words were now challenging me and I could see the bigger picture with such stimulating optimism. I saw our future fates at parallel and I knew the 'fates' were not only intellectual but of the mind and heart and I knew I was living and learning from my 'intuitiveness' once again.

Awakened I knew Jim was sensing my feeling of unhappiness and it was Jim who was driving me into a coo-coo daze of urgency through the Christmas Holidays with urgent messages through ESP {Extra-Sensory Perception} and hoping I would receive them and be back in touch. Through the sub-consciousness of our two brains acting in the same wave length of vibration I sat in a separate splendor at my kitchen bar resting my elbows on the tabletop and held my head in my hands with eyes closed and clearing my mind in the silence of empty space. Suddenly I began laughing and could hardly believe in my own 'awareness.' I suddenly knew in thought that Jim was in Midland, Texas. Immediately making a long-distance telephone call to the operator, I asked, "Is there a James C.

Harbour living in Midland, Texas?" "Yes" said the operator with giving me his postal address.

I made the choice to immediately write a note to Jim with asking the questions: "Do you remember me?" "Did you ever find your 'NITCH' in life?" "Jim if you would like to write back to me please write at this address." At that time I did not know if Jim was married with a half dozen kids but something inside kept nudging and guiding me with purpose. I sensed the 'Spirit' firing messages of 'Love (Le Petit) from the bright stars within us both and I could hardly believe my own psychic abilities and awareness of Intuition. I could see Jim smiling at me in memories filling my heart and soul with his song once again.

It was a few days later that I received a letter back from Jim. "Of course, I remember you" he said, "What took you so long?" Then Jim telephoned saying he had been working in Midland, Texas for a geophysical service company and he was entitled 'The Computer' being very mathematical in the higher realms of math and equations. After talking a few minutes re-introducing ourselves once again we could not wait to see one another.

Through Jim sensing my thoughts telepathically he transmitted a message through 'Transcendental Meditation' of 'Extra-Sensory Perception' which I received. After asking mother if she had ever had an experience like what I had just experienced she quietly nodded her head "Yes" and I could see a slight tear come to the corner of her eye and knew my 'Intuition' was 'gifted.'

Jim sent a plane ticket for me to fly to Dallas, Texas where we would meet.

That following evening, Mother telephoned saying she was taking me shopping for an evening at our good friends Jo' s Dress Shoppe. Jo' and mother were so in agreement saying that Jim and I should have been together long ago as everyone knew us as a couple through school together. I felt like a princess and could not remember having more fun as I was having that evening with my dear mother and 'Jo.' We laughed and giggled while 'Jo' presented special outfits she had put back for my private viewing. Toward the end of a beautiful gala evening of excitement 'Jo' presented the most elegant sensual two-piece black lace pajama set combined with a touch 'chic' extravagance' and a graceful feminine svelte of sophistication.

My head was spinning with excitement and thoughts of 'WOW!' What a 'character boost' from modesty!

My parents drove me to the Indianapolis airport with plans to keep my children the two weeks I would be in Texas with Jim getting re-acquainted. Upon kissing my parents 'Good-Bye' and 'Thanking them' I boarded the plane dressed in a mini-skirt and white 'go go' boots five-foot two-inches and weighing one hundred eight pounds, and looking like a tree-twig. When the plane landed on the tarmac of 'Love Field' in Dallas I bounced down the flight steps with eyes quickly looking over the crowd of people and I spotted Jim and running through the crowd I jumped into his arms the arms of my 'Big Teddy Bear' just like I use to do and I felt truly safe and at home again.

It was such a beautiful encounter transcending into a 'Healing' zone of knowing Love again. I never fall in love with the same guy over and over because we change through our experiences and failures and it's good because this it's how we learn through our soul experiences.

After thirteen years in a river of dreams and now sitting in a Dallas hotel room making small talk for a few quiet moments there was triumph into the breathlessness of 'our love' and TIME had completely stopped in the harmony of having no beginning and no ending but only our love and there was only us.

Having remained a bachelor Jim said, "He was waiting on me" and we began discussing marriage. I pointed out how life can be drastically different when raising children than when you are single and the ways in which children's needs must be met and always come first in a loving family. I will never forget Jim's words that still ring with love and reassurance in my heart and mind when he said, "Any children of yours Pat will also be my children and I will love and raise them as my own." We came together in moments of 'grace' with a deep calm in our relationship with the understanding of finally being married. I knew Jim would be a great father to the children.

We made a quick trip to Midland where we would be spending the rest of our remaining two weeks together counterbalancing our personality strengths to avoid pitfalls in the future from being repeated and we never faltered or changed our minds as to where we would be living later as a family.

Upon returning to Indiana, I immediately followed through with the suite of a divorce from my husband Bob. I soon received a phone call from Jim's older sister, stating that Jim had a nervous breakdown in the meantime and was in the hospital for a period of two or three months. I was told that I should not jump from the fire into the frying pan with my decision to marry Jim, but I still held true to my trust in love, regardless of the circumstances that I might need to go through. The fact remained we are especially attached and enjoy being with one another.

I continued with the divorce proceedings I had started, and it took a good three months to finalize before completion.

After Jim's release from the hospital he called to quietly reconnect our conversation with a wonderful mind-merge and Jim asked, "What do you want to do?" I said, "Jim, I have always been deeply in love with you and all I have ever wanted was to marry you and be with one another like we are meant to be." Jim said, "Okay, then let's do it."

I began packing up the kids things and our belongings with making the final arrangements for our move to Midland, Texas and to our new home with Jim.

Mother and Dad drove me to the Indianapolis Airport where I would board the plane taking me to Dallas. However, before leaving my parents to board the plane I began giving my 'farewell' to them with kissing and hugging my parents back and forth from one and then to the other holding them tightly and trying to ignore and deny the unconscious 'stuff' lying outside of my focused attention that was catching me off guard in my heart and conscious mind. My intuition was trying to tell me that I would never see one or both of my parents again. Not facing this subtle fact I told myself it was just my imagination.

- "The Eternal body of man is the 'Imagination' that is God himself" - Poet, William Blake

Upon my arrival in Dallas, Jim and I drove home to Midland where he had made all arrangements for our Wedding. We were Married July 29th, 1972 in the Presbyterian Church, Midland, Texas. It was the church in which Jim sang in choir and I became a member also of the church. We had a late afternoon wedding and went directly to the minister's home where guests were waiting to help celebrate us with homemade peach ice cream, cake and cookies. Later Jim and I had a beautiful dinner at the "Blue Moon" with a quiet celebration and just the two of us.

After a few days in our marriage, we drove to Houston to pick up Eric and Renee and to get acquainted with Jim. Jim's sister and husband who live in Houston were in Indiana visiting and flew the children back with them to Houston. Eric and Renee learned to love Jim as everyone in the family does.

> - "One merit of poetry few persons will deny: It says more in fewer words than prose" -
>
> - Voltaire. Poet

In those first three or four months of our marriage Jim suggested taking the kids on an educational trip to the Caverns in Carlsbad, New Mexico but first stopping in West Texas between the Permian Basin and taking the kid to "Six Flags" A Texas Amusement Part which the kids really enjoyed. After traveling a few days into the Southwestern Region of 'White plains' New Mexico meeting Indians visiting reservations we dusted ourselves off and came back home to Midland.

Immediately, calling for a hair appointment for a quick perm and tint at the hair salon I changed my appearance from a redhead to a 'platinum blond' WOOPS! Looking deeper into the large vanity mirror I began thinking backward with a vision of mother standing there and doing my hair in her home beauty parlor and in the same way having mother and daughter talks looking at the other's reflection in the mirror and laughing and giggling together.

Suddenly, this didn't feel like it was a very pink and fluffy thing. I was having an 'awareness' or Intuition with a real urgency to get home quickly and to call mother and dad. I was sensing a 'timing' of life and death and remembering the life and death awareness I had when mother and dad drove me to the Indianapolis Airport when boarding a plane to re-unite with Jim in Texas for our marriage. Those feelings I had four months ago of not ever seeing one or both of my parents again had not left me. What could I have said or done without scaring my parents of why I felt what I did without any explanation? This time, I felt it to be conclusive.

"Intuition is the awareness of subtle things in the unconscious mind and heart that alerts us to the slow conscious mind. Our Intuition is to keep us in touch with those things outside the mind and to rule it out is to miss the WISE things we could have done."

December 9, 1972 shortly after arriving home from the beauty salon the telephone rang. It was my sister Frances calling from Indiana. I felt hesitant and nervous picking up the receiver not wanting to hear what the phone call would be about. I started talking rapidly about our trip we just came back from with the kids and my sister interrupted. I knew it was not a social call and knew what she was going to say. Death is a real SHOCKER but I still was NOT prepared to hear the words. Sister Fran spoke in a quiet tone saying my name 'Pat' and that told me to be brave and brace myself I stopped breathing as Fran began talking and knew exactly what she was about to tell me.

December 9, 1972

"Mother died in an automobile accident as the EMS worked on her first. She had been thrown halfway from the car and Daddy has kidney failure and broken ribs and was taken to the hospital. The graphic's I'll leave out. They were on their way to their lake house up north for the weekend and as usual, mother was driving crossing a 'duel' highway containing many speed bumps and large STOP and GO LIGHTS giving mother the right of way to proceed cross the highway. Their car was hit broadside with high impact. All I can say I don't remember much after that. Body, heart and mind were numb 'adrift' somewhere in the STICKY parts of Love, Sadness, and Grief all connected beyond any dreams. Still denying death I wanted to believe this dream was not real and was only my Imagination.

- "The Eternal body of man is 'The imagination' that is God himself" -

Dedicated to Poet 'William Blake'

Numb in SHOCK and heartbreak I boarded a plane in Dallas for Indianapolis lacking words and deeply lost in an extended daze of grief and sadness. A source of words were saying, MOTHER WAS KILLED IN A CAR ACCIDENT and my father has BROKEN RIBS and NON-FUNCTIONING KIDNEYS critical in a hospital. A glass of wine appeared in my hand and I don't know how or by whom? I didn't feel anything as I sat blinded in the infinite reflection of my parents. When the plane landed in Indianapolis, I was completely unaware and I don't remember anything. A miracle of life had taken my hand leading me to the destination to where I was to meet my sister waiting for my arrival. Saying 'hello' to my sister I turned to look back to whoever had led me there, but there was no one. I asked my sister if she saw anyone lead me to her? She said "no, one was with you "I walked by myself." I knew then that I had just experienced the guidance of an angel leading me in a rescue during a time of 'grief.' 'Thank You' God and to my 'Guardian Angel' and 'Spirt Guides' for bringing me strength and guidance in a strong and courageous way.

- INTUITIVELY - "mother always 'knew' her death would be from a car accident."

Psychic since a little girl, Mother always knew her death would be in an automobile accident. Mother asked me to promise her if her life was taken by a car accident to make sure her casket would be closed at the viewing. When I arrived at the funeral home Mother's Wish was being broken and other arrangements were being made for mother's casket to be open for viewing to satisfy a church congregation's viewing. Trying to hold-up mother's wishes, I was told to apologize to the funeral director for the displeasure and my actions. My sister Frances and I immediately went to our family friend's Dress Shoppe and found a long piece of white lace to place across mother's shoulders.

Upon arrival to mother and dad's home, their bed unmade looking warm as if they had just gotten up. I could visualize the morning with seeing mother and dad hurrying around and getting things together for their trip to the lake-house and taking the dog with them for their long weekend at the lake. Parting with mother under this type of family circumstances was very emotional for me. Her every presence was around me with every movement being mirrored in every wavering form, color and texture and with every sound, smell and taste in the perception of my heart and mind. Through mother's individualization she had looked after the families every need including the realities and I knew in my heart that mother was not in the unwavering light but she is truly 'the Light' the glorious eternal unwavering light to the light of day. -

Mother's burial was held December 12, 1972 the day of my thirty-sixth birthday. Conversation strayed and might not be considered an exhilarating topic at a cemetery of burial. Everyone had someone with them while the wind blew cold. The following day I went to visit daddy in the hospital one last time before leaving for the Indianapolis airport. I loved my dad with many hugs and kisses as we said our 'farewells' until he could improve enough for a visit to Texas. Later he was able to come for a visit with us in Midland, Tx.

Jim and children were waiting in Dallas for my return from Indiana and for our long drive home to Midland. I wore a heavy heart with not many words but walked into a glorious "Homecoming of Christmas Love." Never had I experienced such bliss and beautiful 'love' as the closeness of Jim, Eric and Renee together with their combined effort and thought tackling their first Christmas together and bringing into our home the loveliest of all gifts. A delightful Christmas tree perfectly sculped and truly dignified and stood leaning with a bit of space between the sparse branches that were thinly scattered. The three of them together had adorned the tree with 'deep love' decorated from the Roots to the top of its own Nature showing all the glory of memorializing our first family Christmas together. I could not have felt more grateful then that moment bursting in Love and Joy with family. 'Thinking Backwards' I began remembering all the other Christmas trees shared from the past with loved ones, and I knew this 'God 'sent tree of 'Life' was by far the loveliest and most connected with the 'Soul ' and our Family and I knew dear mother was watching from above.

Six weeks after mother's death I was still feeling solemn and heartache did not allow me to sleep well. One night I woke at 3:00 am as I so often did and rubbing my eyes while propping myself up on one elbow to think I looked around in the dark night sensing an 'awareness' around me. To my surprise and disbelief of what I was seeing in front of my eyes was a mystic form of light vacillating and waver between different actions with an array of 'Light' colors unbroken in rhythmic formed and into a singular moving dance developing a 'sphere' and enlivened in a physical form - SHAZAM!

A body composed solely of 'Light' was standing before me at my bedside. It was Mother showing pleasure of Joy and happiness with her face looking serene and angelic. I twisted myself around to have a better view of her and there above mother's head was a white light a 'HALO' of illumination reaching around her.

Mother began showing picture scenes of snapshots and expressions she knew I would remember. It was like a mystical, magical fairy tale like in a story book but this was for REAL!

Mother continued with so much 'Love' and I felt breathless as if in a stepping-off point on Earth. Leaning higher on my elbow I wanted to touch Mother and her beautiful blue eyes widened a glistening twinkle throwing kisses like shooting stars. She then backed away in the direction of the bedroom door as I sat straight-up in bed watching mother with the white 'halo' of light continuing around her she was almost floating on air l our bedroom. I knew the gown she was wearing is a gown I had given her, and she was wearing the last time we were together at the lake house. Remembering that special morning I was with mother and dad at the Lake House bringing her a first cup of morning coffee to her bedroom she was sitting leisurely in that same beautiful filmy gown. I said, "Mother, it is your time to be pampered and waited on" while you relax this beautiful morning.

Being part of the experience I suddenly knew "Heaven was having its own way of 'Healing Love's Hurt.'"

After Jim awakened I couldn't wait to tell him of the mystery drama and Mother's 'spirit' appearing from the dark of night into a mystical illumination of light eternally flowing in timeless scenes with the glorious love of remembering. Jim asked, "Why didn't I wake him so he could see mother also?" "Of course, I said I wanted too but was afraid if I took my eyes away from mother for a split second she would leave and not be there when I looked back again." I know mother had come to help me through the 'Grief' and 'Healing' letting me know that she would always be my mother as she often said to me. She had brought with her the 'Gift' of Believing' in 'miracles from God'.

In 1977 we moved from Midland, TX to Katy, TX a sub-division from Houston. Jim had already completed his physics degree in "Nuclear Physics with a high standard. His professor said Jim lost him in applied mathematics dealing with the motion and forces producing motion in Quantum Physics and in 'The Speed of Light' like in Einstein's 'Theory of Relativity.'

The year 1996 I began noticing an alarming appearance around the same area of a mastectomy I had in 1984 but now twelve years later I knew I had to find a doctor quickly. We did not have health insurance at that moment and I had just taken a job for ensuring our family with health insurance for any unforeseen health problems.

At this same moment I received a call from family in Indiana that my dad was very ill and close to death.

My health concerns were taken out of my hands for that time being and I caught a plane immediately. The siblings and their children were already there with daddy and surrounding him with deep family feelings of love and compassion giving peace of mind. After my arrival I knew those few precious days I spent with daddy were for re-assuring him with my love but I also knew it was urgent to justify quickly the needs for me to quickly get back home for protecting my new job I had just taken for family health insurance and benefits.

I did not let the family or daddy know that I also had urgent needs for my own health. I remained silent not wanting to upset my dad or give him any cause to worry. Shortly thereafter, I gave daddy a big, big, hug reassuring him I would be back with him just as quick as a wink. We said our 'farewells' for that minute and I caught the next plane out for Texas. My 'psychic intuition' never let me forget for an instant that it was imperative for me to reach a doctor as soon as possible.

Upon arriving home Jim had already checked-out the doctors on my new insurance program and found the right surgeon making an appointment. Time was of the essence and I felt so grateful to Jim for making things easier for me. I was immediately seen by the surgeon and an immediate operation ordered. Cancer was found again for the second time and in the very same place of having the mastectomy twelve years before in 1984. It was at 'Stage 4'.

A psychic vision appears before me and it was like in the enchanted garden of when I was but five years old. I could see the 'weeping willow tree' bowing down to me with a mountain of 'miracles' and the large oak leaves were falling on the scene of nightfall feeding the birds… in the sounds of a night song with music descending from 'the darkness' bringing new emotions of affection and love and I did not turn away feeling new life.

Influenced by the soul's inspiration enhanced with shadows of 'Fairy Wings' I wrote the following piece of poetry giving back a gift of light from my heart to my surgeon giving new life for all that I will be. I am so 'grateful with gratitude and satisfaction' with all my love and blessings.

- THE ANGEL'S REED -

You ... hold all life in the eye, with gift of life

- From ancient scribers ... You bear all the gifts
- From all the heights, other heights, in other lives ...
- Yet gifts should prove their use you own the past profuse.

Let the breast be opened ... piece out earthy fright

- Where the tumid reed lies upon me with weight,
- Heavy as rebounding hail deep as life ...
- You wait close by those mends for the birth of fate
- Created one angel borne, a victim of grace

See, on my breast!

- There two soul-sides meted by the angel's reed:
- One with to face the world . . . Ah, speak as you please
- And one to turn a new side you smile indeed!
- And yet I hardly dare ... yet only you to see
- Is whether I'm not grateful but more pleased.
- The pride of my soul was in sight, so it seems
- As if the hollow hole fell into shape ...
- Where the angel plays ...
- And there I found and fixed its wandering star
- Heaven's Gift, It lay at the bottom of my heart.
- Patricia A Harbour Poet

Within my recovery from breast cancer the second time around daddy had passed before I could get back to being with him but I was able to fly back for daddy's 'Life Celebration' and Blessings.

The following year of 1977 Jim's began having 'Esophageal cancer' with symptoms of difficulty in swallowing and weight loss found with having a routine chest x-ray. I took Jim to the same surgeon I had the year before with my second 'breast cancer.' The surgeon was well informed with this type of operation as he had perfected many operations for 'Esophageal cancer' having lived in Africa. Many African natives came down with cancer of the 'Esophageal' from cooking their meals over open fires in large iron kettles leaving the smoke cortisones remaining in the kettles and never cleaning them after cooking. Therefor the cortisones kept building-up in their kettles which caused the natives to have Esophageal cancer. The survivor rate from the operation was not good and with only half or less surviving. There weren't many doctors in the United States at the time who knew how to perform this type of operation for lack of knowledge and experience.

A good three weeks Jim was in the hospital learning to eat again with a feeding tube. 'Filipino Nurses' were hired at that time and kept bringing large pitchers of water to Jim for he was so thirsty. Instructions were that Jim could only have small chips of ice since the stomach was pulled-up to the throat and no longer had an Esophagus. I remember going to the head of the hospital to stop the nurses from bringing pitchers of water and risking Jim's life. It was a 'Miracle' that Jim did not drown.

Soon after this time, my health problems began which I thought was a sinus problem but learned that I had old 'calcifications' in the lung that caused a blood clot from a childhood infection.

Knowing I should be in a hospital late one evening I soon checked myself into a Houston hospital in the medical center without a doctor. After being taken to a waiting room I laid on a table for six days while shadowy heads appeared occasionally looking down through glaring bright lights as I drifted in and out of consciousness. Later awakening from a dream state of 'healing' and not knowing I just had a 'Lobectomy' of the Third Lobe of the right lung, there sitting on the edge of my bed was the surgeon holding my hand and asking, "Do you know who I am?" In a stuttering disjointed weak voice sounding like a speech disorder of repetitious sounds, I answered "th-e Do'-Do'Doct-orr' rrrr" and a ray of light beamed shinning down from his face like a diamond in the sky gleaming with the brightness of luminous stars appearing out from his eye. He squeezed my hand affectionately with a calming silence of reassurance and I knew I had been touched by the Angel of God. My eyes closed once again to while away the soundlessness in another hour and knowing the peacefulness of being 'okay.' I will never forget 'Dr. OTT' world acclaimed, and most renowned pulmonary doctor known worldwide and distinguished above 'ALL' was the 'Lucky Star Angel' who had saved my life with his luminous plasma of 'Stardust.'

Jim and I have already encountered many rough spots in our health and intimate relationship that could usually smooth over things. We are the same at the base and always quite able to provide one another with adventure and still have that quality of independence we both require in a close relationship. We both like the same people and pursuits with similar tastes and has gone a long way to ensure a lasting interest and harmony between us. We have fun creating together encouraging our joint artistic efforts as a pair emotionally and intellectually.

2002

It was 6:00 o'clock one evening It was a doctor I never heard of before calling about testing I had done with a sinus x-ray and telling me that my sinus's were clear but I had a very large brain tumor and needed to see a brain surgeon immediately. I really thought they had me mixed up with someone else as I didn't have headaches or dizziness or any symptoms representing a 'brain tumor.' However, after squeezing and wringing my hands a few minutes - I did call MD Anderson for an immediate appointment to have myself checked out in case it could be brain cancer.

After being shown the conclusive results of an 'MRI' of the brain I began laughing and saying "Oh Look what the Easter Bunny left for Me" since it was close to the Easter holiday. I don't know if anyone else enjoyed my sense of humor at that moment, because the X-ray showed a huge 'white egg' sitting upright in my brain. Sometimes a bit of laughter is a better 'healer' than crying. Soon after, I was having a 'Brain Tumor' operation and "Thanking God" for being a benign tumor that lacked the ability to invade or metastasize. The surgeon in a straight-forward manner said "The tumor was in the 'silent part of the brain' and did not affect any functions." I didn't know what to say - "I only knew if that was the case my brain has been still and silent most of the time, and - could be part of my 'Secret Intelligence!' My 'Ego' was showing-off!

I do believe my 'Ego' has been there since growing-up in my mother's beauty salon of younger years that provided a perceptual experience of pleasure in social psychology. It's like the childhood 'fairy tale' 'Beauty and the Beast.' I could only see the things worth seeing and I was handed a small hand mirror to view my head from the back as mother finished doing my hair. Today the mirror for me holds the values and philosophy by 'Pythagoras'

'Pythagoras' meaning 'the love of wisdom' or 'friend of wisdom.'

'Pythagoras' was the Greek Philosopher and Mathematician and a philosopher before 'Socrates, Aristotle, and Plato. His life teachings in music and Ancient Greek Ideas were in harmony of the Western philosophy of the Metaphysics of numbers.

Music is something Jim and I both enjoy together and his writing music on the piano from the heartstrings of Heaven with healing refreshing sounds of the deepest love and compassion. It was his way of chilling out and my way of writing poetic verse as I danced my dreams. We always had so much fun together in the sound of music.

In actual reality my 'Beast to Love' was standing next to me in our front yard of Katy, Texas, and Jim suddenly turned to me saying "Pat, have you ever thought about our moving from here and why are we still here?" "No" I replied, "but I'll think about it!" "If we do move, where would we move?" Jim asked. "I can only think of two solutions of where to move" "One would be to move across the street from the 'Houston Medical Center' and wait to die or move to 'Rockport, TX and be on the gulf coast close to water and close to our daughter Renee which is where she just moved too!" Jim said, "I vote for Rockport, TX" and so be It.

Jim and I were finding that we were open to new endeavors together after thirty some years of marriage and raising a family. We were ready to move on together to those glorious 'golden years. Our children were now settled in their lives and are very proud parents of both Eric & Renee. Eric had become a CFO and Vice-President in companies and landed in his dream job of Banking and Financial Advisor also giving us two very beautiful grandsons 'Sami & Wally.' - Our daughter, Renee attended the Houston Art Institute in 'Photography' as well as becoming a career 'Veterinary manager in Specialized 'Pet Veterinary Medicine hiring specialty doctors after having been a Physician's Assistant with laboratory studies of specialized medicine. However she still maintains time to keep up with her photography as well as her new endeavor producing artful and beautiful paintings.

Jim a 'Nuclear Physicist most of his life had been teaching 'Geophysics' in many other countries in exploring for oil in the deepest depths of ocean and land. After working in India and then Tobago and Trinidad he came home in an ailment of 'Diabetes' deciding to retire his Geophysical Consulting jobs' of teaching oil exploration.

So after thirty years of a very busy life we needed to refresh the deep love Jim and I had always experienced in our relationship. I was off to 'Rockport, Tx' and found the perfect place for us to enjoy our life together. I felt a new beginning for us together and so perfectly timed in our lives.

I flew ahead to Rockport, TX to find the perfect little community for us to live. When we walked into this beautiful little community to view a unique patio home with a loft and with the sweet grounds of a beautiful stone patio accompanied with a small iron gate at the entrance Jim turned to me saying, "Oh Pat this is it!" And as it turned out it was the very one, I had also fell in love with as being the place for our new life to begin. After moving, I scooted around to make our new home lovely and beautiful for Jim and to be proud and enjoy. I do have a bent in decorating all was falling into place with our new home. We soon found our favorite eating places close to the water and with watching the fishing boats come in with their loads for the day we would sit at dinner with beautiful scenic views making new friends and experiences together.

There had been some feelings of disillusionment with our being apart so much with Jim's traveling and our illnesses and now it would be our time doing things together we enjoyed and communicate once again in our very deep special love.

However soon I noticed that life was running its course and we were failing in our heart with one another. I noticed a pulling away from me and gradually it led into the highs and lows of neglect. I never knew exactly what my spouse was thinking at that point as he withdrew into a non-existence of communication with me as well as in our deepest kind of love and things became different almost overnight and I didn't know WHY?

I tried my heartiest asking Jim to take a walk with the dog and me each morning to the beach or just take a drive or just get out and talk with others around and enjoying the same things. Instead, he suddenly found a separate way of behavior towards me and trust and truthfulness began eroding with trivial things. I tried to tell myself it was just my 'imagination' and over-thinking but it felt we had eroded into a murky 'swamp' of mud.

With so much illness's just before we had moved from Katy, TX to Rockport, I began looking backward and could only see selfish sparks of respect and caring. Swept away in wonderment I sometimes go back through my mind in conversations to feel the deepest kind of love with Jim but now things began to feel completely different. I felt a bittersweet of heartbreak as if we were oceans apart from one another... We had encountered many rough spots in our health and at age seventy intimacy had deteriorated with no communication between us. Jim suddenly needed more space and wanted to move into the spare bedroom. He began flirting with different waitresses at dinner which told me that I was nonexistent and left out in the cold.

All these consequences I began thinking I had an over-active imagination. However, still waters run deep and I began taking smaller steps deeper into myself with fears and isolation. I saw nothing of him through most of the day as he kept his distant. When some small matter appeared, he would mention it and then dart back into his pure silent treatment. It was embarrassing when out for dinner in the evenings around other people who knew us and had admired us as a couple but it was a falseness with a perversion of truth. Anyone with an adequate understanding of English would notice the falseness of such behavior. I wore my own mask to the point of protection from the damage I felt and hiding my hurt.

Feeling depressed and Numb I didn't feel self-respect but I still loved him and missed the man I had married. Finding the courage - one day I asked to NOT be shut out and to communicate with me as to what was wrong but still there was nothing only the hollow silence of my words bouncing back from the walls. Those next months I waited for some form of reaction, but none ever came. Then one day while hurrying into the kitchen my husband was coming from the opposite direction, our eyes met magically, and we fell into one another arms holding so tightly and almost stopped breathing. Without a word he leaned down to kiss me but I paused and he pushed me backwards and darted back to his bedroom. His Leukemia Oncologist had advised that Jim had three diverse types of infections highly contagious and transmittable through close contact of INTIMACY. I remember at the time of hearing this I was too stunned and shocked and embarrassed to ask questions. Jim was sitting there beside me when the doctor made this announcement, but he never responded.

Jim had developed "Acute Leukemia" resulting in high numbers of abnormal white blood cells which is a cancer of the blood cells of the bone marrow causing bleeding and bruising problems with a short mortality rate.

He had been seeing an Oncologist in Corpus Christi and having to wait longer than ten days for a blood report. My daughter, Renee and I quickly sat Jim in the car and took him to MD Anderson in Houston. After arriving at MD Anderson Jim went through all the testing again for Leukemia and was not a happy camper.

The next morning, he was sent to see the new Oncologist at MD Anderson who was so gentle, so kind and took great pains with Jim. After Jim was told that he only had Two to Six Months to Live Life and would need constant blood-transfusions beginning with one per week and up to three transfusions per week for the next six months. MD Anderson's great Oncologists and nurses urged Jim to stay there as they could make him more comfortable and with the fact that I could stay close by and see him daily. However, it was his personal decision.

Jim chose to come home and go for treatments on a weekly basis at the Corpus Christi Cancer Clinic with all blood-transfusions and Oncology appointments being there. He was already in a wheelchair most of the time and I made the arrangements for each day's appointment including transportation there and back to the 'Corpus Christi Cancer Clinic.' I was his 'Caregiver' for medical transportation and for his daily medications alongside (a once a week) nurse coming in to check medications and take Jim's vital signs. The humor seemed to be between the nurse and myself re-checking each other as Jim's medications kept changing daily.

I did finally take a small break and go shopping for three 'ORANGE' straw baskets to hold all of Jim's medications. 'ORANGE' had become his favorite color he said and just after I had previously painted the spare bedroom 'Orange.' He loved the color ORANGE and wanted to move into the spare bedroom.

All I could do was to have an intercession of prayer during this time walking through the 'dark night of my soul' in a space of emptiness without moonglow or sunshine. "Thinking Backwards" to our once happy times I knew my heart no longer held qualifications of love with Jim. I continued to drive him to and from his primary care doctor in Rockport and always to dinner in the evening as he seemed to want to go. I did fix a few meals a home but then he would sit at the table in silence barely speaking a word as I served. I performed like a 'robot' carrying out daily duties while witnessing the brilliance of our lives together disappear into the light of Death.

Knowing and feeling Jim to be my true primary 'soul mate' since that first moment we met on that sacred day of Halloween in 1951 and married 'Thirty-Five' years of the sixty-seven years we have known one another Jim's death has become 'A SIGN' of Life

AFTER DEATH for me.

I began thinking about the blending and of the best of our "SUN SIGNS" and the qualities that would have been the best goal to aim for. Depending upon our emotional harmony and reasonable communication by our other interactions I found other disillusionments not dealt with a bit like sunshine sparkling on and off the surface of water and when nightfall came the mirage evaporated and the real and vulnerable person remained. What we both thought, was a 'shinning knight' or a 'damsel in distress' was pathetic about us. We had both tried to bluff our way out of this uncomfortable situation and then the real trouble began. One of us took on the role of {the one in charge} making the other's life feeling miserable like a slave or a fall guy. Both of us had seek solace in the form of escaping oppression like and addiction to alcohol, drugs or work and eventually from out of the relationship altogether. Jim and I both had been ADDICTED to our own illusions of STRENGTH and WEAKNESS.

Consequently, all manners of deception crept into the cracks that this interaction opened!

- Our relationship became a leaky vessel with only one fate. -

Jim felt in a superior position and I only had my point of view to offer and confront him with whereas he had his whole WILL and LIFESTYLE to either overwhelm, ignore, or offer to approve of me. If I had been very sure of myself mentally and if Jim's WILL had not been so developed, it would be a different story but even then, it still would not be a balanced or a very satisfying relationship.

THEREFORE bearing all this in mind if this interaction had become more about Jim taking on board what I had to say and not just disapprove out of a wounded and threatened pride and if I could have seen myself as some sort of an ADVISOR to a DIGNITARY and not have presumed upon my mental connections or skills of expertise we would have learned a great deal from one another but instead, it led nowhere.

- Jim and I had hit 'A COMMUNICATION BLOC -

Often when putting forth thoughts or ideas I had to go through an examination under Jim and this became a PUPIL/TEACHER relationship. In an emotional relationship it makes for an Inferior/superior relationship with resentments and feelings of being unworthy of consideration.

If I could have been allowed to put my ideas into practice then I could have seen that my ideas did need to be made more practical and that Jim had a point. This would have made a 'negative' quite fruitful. I needed to use my intellect less and my feelings more.

I began seeing Jim appear dull and slow, unimaginative and overly conservative. If he could have seriously considered (his forte) and considered whether I had a point or not and with saying whatever he had to say that didn't make me feel stupid or inferior and taking these points into a mutual learning experience we could have had an intellectual and a serious learning relationship instead of a cold and dry one. I I might not have gotten so fed-up with having my ideas squashed and finding a new teacher!

These things were valuable learning experiences called upon repeatedly to overcome the strong clashes that occurred between 'Jim's ego and lifestyle' and 'my philosophy and beliefs' with troubles persisting. Even though we are inclined to be bright and playful there was a good-natured atmosphere between us.

However, Jim regarded me as a hypocritical know-it-all, preachy and serious. At the other end of the mat I saw Jim as being 'too proud for his own good and unable to view things from what I regarded as a superior mental overview. The fact remained, we were poles apart in these significant differences and it would have been wise to take in the benefit of getting a clearer picture of our individual standpoints. We each could have become surer of that standpoint together and not have wasted so much time and energy trying to depend on it and proving it!

We needed to be reminded that there are three ways of teaching:

- By Example By Example By Example -

Jim may have needed to be subtly reminded of how enlightening my view could be when they are no longer so readily offered or available to him at all. He saw me as impractical and overindulgent in spending and I regarded him as lacking insights and understanding. He was too reliant upon status and rules somewhat of a stick-in-the-mud. This difficult interaction is an aid for teaching us both that creating a BALANCE between two sides are namely {Growth & Limitation} and are highly important.

As 'Lao-Tzu' the Chinese philosopher said:

"If you wish to contract something you must first let it fully expand"

This counsel that Jim should have let me go off on my flights of fancy and fall flat on my face and come back the 'Wiser.' Out of Jim's own 'fear' of taking chances and 'thinking big' stopped him from doing this.

On the other hand Jim could have learned a lesson or two from me by having more 'faith in life.' Underlying all of this could be a fundamental difference in our socio- cultural backgrounds and VALUES. {I am looser and fancy free while Jim was structured and more formal}.

Our standards were deeply ingrained with opinions and forced to the surface by the very conflict itself. If we could have chosen, the best of each other and discorded the constricting and outmoded uselessness of whatever we had inherited in beliefs we would have seen the things we had to offer one another.

We have always had 'efficient teamwork.' Jim could have shown me new ways of looking at life that would clarify the difficult issues and impartially point out where I am being my own worst enemy. On the other hand, I'm able to affirm what is unique about Jim and able to at least make him constructively 'aware' of how he could and should fit better into the status quo. There is a mutual problem-solving element here and which would be useful to one degree or another.

Our relationship has always been a contact of sound and sincere friendship and with working on specific projects together. Our relationship had always an emotionally intimate one and we could draw upon this sense of 'Unconditional Comradeship' to get us through the rocky patches. However, if we could have taken it still further and as pair or part of a team it could have been instrumental in helping the way for others through difficulties.

- "Faith is a passionate Intuition" Dedicated to Poet: William Wordsworth

The ability to understand something immediately and without the need for conscious reasoning is to allow the 'intuition' and the 'Sixth' sense of clairvoyance to guide you. It's the ability to acquire knowledge without proof, evidence, or conscious reasoning. It's being unconscious in patterned-recognition and such as instinct, truth, and belief and meant in the realms of greater knowledge. On the face of all this the subconscious describes something that is just below the awareness, and in time, the awareness will surface, and Jim and I could find the root of why we would get so nervous in the first place. The subconscious is a dark place and it hits beautifully with what the dark 'Mojo' side is trying to explore.

Both of us being mutable signs and the 'Realist' versus the 'Dreamer' Jim and I could have stabilized our fears and secured our solidity and strength with steadiness and with 'self-honesty' owning-up to our projecting and mirroring with putting everything onto the other. It would have been the best exercise to do because in time this 'muddy pool' turned into a swamp.

In a call for the NEW as individuals it would be a generational interaction if we were still willing to do the work of these interactions as these such qualities are central to our being together later. On a purely generational level we were both born and grew-up in a time that we saw the same technological advances and changes in social and political values.

Ideally if we both did evolve 'spiritually' then we could use the 'Spiritual' energy to achieve greater good. Compassion and good will are the basic ingredients of this basic compatibility.

Jim and I have always had a very 'Close' Cultural Compatibility. We are the same age and therefore we are subject to similar cultural, spiritual and musical influences in our lives and they are the general underlay of compatibility and trashed out through sexual forms that made up our relationship. This interaction made it clear that giving into our passions lead to reckoning and eventually ethical standards would have to prove themselves to be more than just opinions.

As perceived we could have had a business-like arrangement which is an extremely down-to-earth interaction with Jim helping me to find my place in the world and giving stability to my insights or feelings of loneliness. My part of the 'deal' would be to allow our relationship to conform and intensify Jim's sense of authority at a DEEP LEVEL.

The possibility of accusations in response is strong in my emotional urges or convictions and clashed with Jim's beliefs but the contrast between us could have served to make us both more aware of where we stood with respect to these issues. Jim and I were both after some form of philosophy that goes deep enough to enable us both to understand what it is about human nature that can draw us downward and inwards despite our best intentions or sense of what is right and what is wrong. However, both of us being stubborn we were not always willing to reach agreements and make confessions and failed to reckon with the reality of human nature. You might say that we were 'egocentric' and our world revolved around us.

Jim and I had always had the intensity of a 'Close generational contact with having similar psychological, political and global changes in our lives, with a number of passionate, obsessive contacts between the two of us with making it more so because our social environment encouraged the same.

We have had a definite layer of emotional responsibility and physical fidelity between the two of us through highs and lows acting as a steadying influence always returning us to balance with "A Close Love and Duty" of being close friends as well as lovers.

Through HEAD HEART and HARMONY Jim and I had always had an interest involving metaphysical subjects, and the frontiers of science and the understanding of human nature. This interaction could contribute to our progress, individually or together. Jim offers the Scientific explanations and formulas to my 'psychic impressions' while I introduce a vision of myth to inspire Jim's models or theories. With our other creative inter generation's between the two of us together we could make a very original and innovative duo.

The materialist age has nothing but 'ego' to fall back on, and 'ego' is just not enough to have

A happy and fulfilled life. The ego fears what it cannot understand and when we remain unconscious the 'Ego' only sees what is immediately ahead. 'Ego' is blind to opening possibilities and wants to be in control with attention always wanting more.

I had allowed myself to be obsessed and preoccupied in distractions and with the desire to create forms that would have my attention in the mind excluding others and their thoughts and my 'Ego' understood this as being its reality. Unconsciously, the 'Ego' was telling me how to maintain the structure known and my 'Ego' was telling me that I wasn't bad and I was in 'limbo.

In "Relationship Strengths"

Jim and I found we are friends as well as lovers. We both like the same people and pursuits with similar tastes. This will go a long way to ensure a lasting interest and harmony between the two of us. We have fun and are creative together. This encourages our joint artistic efforts as a pair We are in tune with one another and our emotional and intellectual accord enables us to see our way through to harmony and agreement even after the severest of conflicts.

Our "Love and Duty is 'Close'

We have a definite layer of emotional responsibility and physical fidelity between the two of us. Through high's and low's this acts as a steadying influence returning us to balance. The personal interchange of Jim validating my worth in a sober understated way is more than a sensational display of appreciation. I appreciate Jim's quiet and less sensational side and thereby establishes a very personal bond. It could be our mainstay of marriage.

We are well able to assist one another in getting things done and off the ground and it can also counteract any 'wooly' or overly romantic notions that are so common in relationships.

Through our creative love we have a wonderful interaction for making music and being creative together in any way. It is a subtle and persist gentle attraction that could be a 'healing influence' upon those around us. Whatever the outcome of our relationship there will always be a wistful connection and sweetness between the two of us.

Because of instinctively and physically picking-up on each other's feeling and desires we can exquisitely intertwin emotionally and sexually or we would avoid having much to do with each other at all. This is because we really do sense what is best for each other despite lesser thoughts and feelings. This is actual a {healing variety} with an ability to tune into areas of trouble and then lance or cleanse them. If one or both of us are inclined with this ability it is a HEALING RAY that may be used effectively upon others as well. -

Then I could see that my ideas did need to be made more practical and that Jim had a point. This would have made a 'negative' 'quite fruitful.' I needed to use my intellect less and my feelings more.

Jim needed to find a way of saying what he had to say that did not make me feel stupid or inferior I began seeing Jim appear dull and slow, unimaginative and overly conservative.

Jim should have seriously considered (his forte) and whether I had a point here because one day I might get so fed-up having my ideas squashed that I might find a new teacher! If we could take these points seriously into a mutual learning experience, then we could have had an intellectual and a serious learning relationship instead of a cold and dry one.

There are valuable learning experiences here called upon repeatedly to overcome the strong classes that occur between 'Jim's ego and lifestyle' of 'my philosophy and beliefs.' Even though we are inclined to be bright and playful there is a good-natured atmosphere between us. However, Jim regarded me as a hypocritical know-it-all preachy and serious. At the other end of the mat I saw Jim as being 'too proud for his own good and unable to view things from what I regarded as my superior mental overview. The fact remained, we are poles apart in these significant differences and it would have been wise to take in the benefit of getting a clearer picture of our individual standpoints. We could have become surer of our standpoints and not wasted so much time and energy trying to depend on it and proving it! (I needed to be reminded that there are three ways of teaching:

By example, by example, and by example. -

Jim may need to be subtly reminded of how enlightening my views can be when it is no longer so readily offered or available to him at all.

Jim saw me as impractical and overindulgent.

I regarded Jim as purblind and lacking understanding. He was too reliant upon status and rules and a stick-in-the-mud. In truth however this difficult interaction is an aid of teaching both of us that creating a balance between our two sides namely {growth and limitation} are highly indulgent.

This counsels Jim to let me go off on my flights of fancy and fall flat on my face and then come back the Wiser. Out of Jim's own 'fear' of taking chances and 'thinking big 'stopped him from doing this.

On the other hand Jim could learn a lesson or two from me by having more 'faith in life.' Underlying all of this can be a fundamental difference in our socio-cultural backgrounds and values. {I am looser and fancy free while Jim is structured and more formal}.

We both have something to offer one another but standards are deeply ingrained, and opinions forced to the surface by the very conflict itself. Hopefully both of us will consciously choose the best of each and discord whatever inherited beliefs or conditions are constricting outmoded and useless.

We have 'efficient teamwork' and I can affirm what is unique about Jim or at least make him constructively aware of how he should and could fit better into the status quo. On the other hand, Jim can show me new ways of looking at life that clarify difficult issues and impartially point out where I am being my own worst enemy. There is a mutual problem-solving element here and which is useful to one degree or another.

Our relationship is a contact of sound and sincere friendship or with working on some specific project together. If ours is an emotionally intimate relationship we could draw upon this sense of 'Unconditional Comradeship' to get us through rocky patches. But if we took it still further and as a pair or a part of a team then it would be instrumental in helping the way for others through difficulties.

- "Faith is a passionate Intuition" Dedicated to William Wordsworth, Poet

The ability to understand something immediately, and without the need for conscious reasoning is to allow the 'intuition' and the 'Sixth sense of clairvoyance to guide me.

It's the ability to acquire knowledge without proof, evidence, or conscious reasoning. It's being unconscious in patterned-recognition such as instinct, truth, belief and mean in the realms of greater knowledge: Whereas, others contend that the word 'intuition' is often misunderstood and that it means the instinct and true belief's and greater realms are the inherent mental and physical powers of instinct, beliefs, and intuition and are all factually related.

On the face of all this the subconscious describes something that is just below the awareness, but in time, Jim's and my awareness will surface and might get to the root of why we get so nervous in the first place. "The subconscious" is also a dark place and hits beautifully with what the Dark 'Mojo' is trying to explore.

If Jim and I could stabilize our fears and secure solidity and steadiness and own-up to the projection of putting everything onto each other as the 'Realist' versus the Dreamer' and have "self-honesty" it would be the best exercise to do because in time the 'muddy pool' will turn into a swamp."

Is this a call of the NEW? Is it a generational interaction for us as individuals? If so, then this interaction is saying that such qualities are central to our being together. On a purely generational level we were both born and grew up in a time and we saw the same technological advances and changes in social and political values.

Friends and associates have always noticed our harmonious vibrations and liked to be around us and even seek our help and sympathy in time of trouble. However much we make of this or don't is the question.

Ideally if we both evolved of 'spiritually' then 'we could use' the spiritual energy to achieve greater good. (Compassion and good will are the basic ingredients of this basic compatibility.

Jim and I have a very 'Close' Cultural Compatibility. We are the same age and therefore we are subject to similar cultural, spiritual and musical influences in our lives and they are the general underlay of compatibility and thrashed out through sexual forms that make up our relationship. This interaction makes it clear that giving into our passions leads to reckoning sooner or later and ethical standards would have to prove themselves to be more than just opinions.

As perceived we could have a business-like arrangement which is an extremely down-to-earth interaction allowing Jim to help me to find my place in the world and giving stability to my insights or feelings of loneliness. My part of the 'deal' would be to allow our relationship to conform and intensify Jim's sense of authority at a DEEP LEVEL.

The possibility of blame and recrimination is strong in my emotional urges or convictions and clashed with Jim's beliefs but the contrast between us could serve to make us both more aware of where we stand with respect to these issues. Jim and I are both after some form of philosophy that goes deep enough to enable us both to understand what it is about human nature that can draw us downward and inwards despite our best intentions or sense of what is right and what is wrong.

We have the intensity of a 'Close' generational contact. Having similar psychological, political and global changes in our lives, and several passionate, contacts between the two of us and this makes it more so because our social environment would encourage the same.

Through 'Head' 'Heart' and 'Harmony' Jim and I are interested and involved with metaphysical subjects, and the frontiers of science and the 'understanding' of human nature. This interaction could contribute to our progress, individually or together. Jim offers Scientific explanations and formulas to my 'psychic impressions' while I introduce a vision or myth to inspire Jim's models or theories. With our other creative interactions between the two of us together we can make a very original and innovative duo.

Allowing myself to be obsessed and preoccupied in distraction of structure and the desire to create form I was engrossed in the mind with other things to the exclusion of others and their thoughts and portrayed an image of what my 'Ego' understood as being its reality. "Unconsciously, the Ego was telling me how to maintain the structure known. It was busy telling me I am not that bad. "Was I in a place of limbo?" Confusion is good if you have lived many years in confusion as to 'who you are' - 'what you are - and meant to be' - and 'what you are supposed to do in life.'

Jim continued being increasingly distant walking away and completely ignoring.

I didn't know what he was thinking until one day he stopped me as I was walking down the hallway and announced he thought we should 'separate' - not get a divorce but just 'separate.' This was the time I felt knives plunged through my heart feeling the deepest heartbreak and anxiety and resistant to 'Believing' in myself.

Five months later, was the peaceful passing of my husband in the day just after our thirty-fifth wedding anniversary. In that following morning I grabbed the pruning shears went outside and began chopping and whacking all the beautiful shrubs with quick penetrating blows to sever and separate myself from the attachment and importance I always had with plant life. There was no rhyme or reason and had no idea what I was doing but just doing it! A neighbor came up to me putting her arms around me and allowed me to break into tears and cry on her shoulder saying, that when her husband died, she began scrubbing all her floors on her hands and knees all night. People work off 'GRIEF' and sorrow in diverse ways. I then was up every night until 4:00 AM for three months hand crafting a stunning flower arrangement five-foot-long with pheasant feathers of showy plumage and colors to go with the fireplace wall. Never having done anything like this before, you might say it was a process for 'Healing' Grief.

Later, I began exploring new ways and beginnings for myself and trying to identify with who I really am? Later after working as a 'Docent' {a guide} and giving tours with the history of a family and their home the lovely Fulton Mansion in Rockport, TX and I began finding my way back with people. Later I joined a Line Dancing group which was highly active and much like the tap dancing I had always enjoyed with interpretative skills. It was creative and much like exploring.

Through this time I began exploration through SPIRITUALITY making calls to heaven through different psychic MEDIUMS for contacting my husband, Jim, parents, and family and friends in spirit. I learned the word VALIDATION meaning {the action of checking or proving the validity and accuracy of controlled traits} and to know precisely who it is you are speaking with in spirit. 'Intuition' can help bring out all truth as only you would know it. Having experiences as a seeker of the afterlife is better than listening to lectures or watching a documentary or just reading about it and other people's experiences. It is involving all the senses and when you are actively involving yourself in personal experiences is where most of us begin our spiritual journey and by learning about the experiences of others as well as yourself.

Through my SOUL experiences it is a matter of perspective. We do not tend to have "happily ever after" romantic relationships with the same soul, life after life. I don't believe there is one soul with whom we are meant to be romantic with lifetime after lifetime. But, if you think of a soul mate as a human being and whose connection you feels so strong with that you must know this person in the spirit world, you then recognize your soul-to-soul relationship. If so, then I do believe this is possible. It doesn't mean that your human relationship is meant to be romantic. It is clearer our soul's relationship with other souls do not translate into the same relationships here in the physical dimension. The soul mate to me would be equivalent of a close friend in the spirit world. It can be a bunch of close friends as souls who make up what is called our {soul group.} And these are the souls with whom we share many lifetimes, although in varying relationships. This is where if anyone would like to have further information please read author, "Bob Olson" and his book named {ANSWERS ABOUT THE AFTERLIFE) and you can draw your own conclusion of what you believe. There are many similar books on this subject.

I found for myself and what I know and do believe through my own experiences. Often what many people don't know is that learning about

The Afterlife teaches us about life being less about the intellectual and more about the experiential and finding the awareness of 'an internal wisdom.'

> Quote: "Yes, pray for those who have passed on. This is part of thy consciousness.
>
> It is well. For, God is God of the living. Those who have passed through God's other door is oft listening, listening for the voice of those they have loved in the earth" - "Edgar Cayce Reading" American self-professed clairvoyant & Channeler

Sometimes it may be impossible to discern between the outward appearance of a soul mate relationship and the coming together of twin souls. Soulmates and Twin souls entail an ongoing connection between two individuals. Both kinds of relationships occur at the soul level, and both can be instrumental in assisting an individual in her or his spiritual growth. The primary distinction between soul mates and twin souls is that soul mates are brought together as a means of assisting both individuals in soul growth and 'twin souls' and often come together to achieve a joint task or a united work.

Personal Love is love between two people, and it is the type of love I am focusing on in this book with expressing thoughts. You can love yourself by being kind to yourself, by nurturing yourself and by liking yourself, and forgiving yourself. Accept yourself as you are now and allow yourself to become your own best friend.

We all carry around a mountain of baggage from the past. This resentment of unresolved and ancient wrongs, we should have done or said so long time ago.

So, do this simple exercise and "LET GO" of all the rubbish from the past and this is something that my soulmate love told me a long time ago in one of our readings after he had already passed on to the other side and asking me to get my 'third eye' open so we could communicate between ourselves without an acting 'Medium.' He told me to do the following with this message.

"Sit back in a comfortable chair or lie down. Close your eyes and take ten deep breaths. As you exhale, say to yourself "Relax, relax, relax." Allow all the muscles of your body to relax. You may need to pay attention to your shoulders, as tension and stress often gather there. ONCE RELAXED visualize yourself in the most peaceful place you can imagine. It could be on a beautiful beach, listening to the waves or you might prefer to place yourself in a little sacred garden in the middle of a forest. It makes no difference where you go but try to see this picture as clearly as you can in your mind. Then imagine that your body is turning into a large ball and extending from this ball are countless threads leading outwards to all the unwanted baggage that you are still holding onto. See it as clearly as you can in your mind and take a pair of imaginary scissors cutting off all the threads until the ball is smooth and round again. Enjoy the sight of this perfect ball and watch it turn back into you again. (Note 'The person you return to is different from the person you were before'). Now you are free of all the unnecessary baggage you have been carrying around for years, or even decades And then open your eyes and you will feel an incredible sense of release and freedom afterwards. (Remember to do this exercise every now and then as we all pick up unwanted baggage as we go through life.) By doing this exercise regularly will allow you to 'LET GO' of the baggage sooner than later.

From our past to where we are presently in life, "the eyes" are romantically called the windows to the soul and the lovers through history have held each other's gazes from across the room speaking volumes without saying a word. This is a way of alerting you to the information they carry.

Life can go by quickly in a moment and it is important to appreciate and 'Remember' all of life through our experiences with the pain, the grief and the disappointments as well as the moments of love and joy.

I've learned to appreciate all the good times the tough times and the in-between times in life creative within a whirlwind of experiences. My computer blew-up with the book I was writing and having the last word. I don't give up re-writing this book with a dedicated 'legacy' to my family to the love of my life to the children we raised, and to Divine Universal LOVE.

December 2018, I began re-writing the book saving 'The First and The Last Part' for being 'The Best' in this Journey and New Beginning!

"It is like saving the 'Very Best Last Piece of Chocolate' from a sack of Candy for your 'True Love' and Best Friend!" Patricia Harbour

I began writing through the natural reflections of my soul and the country walk in the love of nature like when I was a child. Nature is the best healer of life. It's like learning to sit down or stand up, or learning how to pick yourself up after falling from your bicycle. We learn repeatedly through enjoyment and the pains of life as we become what we think.

"THINKING BACKWARDS' through time is how I came to write this book. The word 're-incarnated' had leaped into the heart and mind and it wasn't s a word I had ever heard before until remembering that first country walk, I took as a small child. For me, it led me into the 'Lullaby of a Sacred Place' and into someone's backyard garden. I sat next to a pond of golden fish swimming with the sound of water flowing and inviting me to sit and rest. Only great passions within the soul can lift and elevate us in this way and this is when I first found myself in meditation with God. In a childlike way, I told God that I had been re- incarnated here to Earth to meet my very good friend. Someway I knew automatically this was the plan which had been worked-out by others in heaven before my arrival here to Earth. My friend and I had come to re-capture life in a new journey together for our spirits to grow and learn. Through new experiences, we were on the same vibrations as 'Friends' and finding 'Divine Love' together.

Through my experiences in life I learned that I needed to learn to love myself first before I could truly love another. It is the way to grow strong and learn to 'FORGIVE' and move-on but we first must learn to be in a more positive way with loving our self and learn to forgive to reach the higher levels of 'Unconditional Love.'

I FOCUSED upon what I have lived and learned having a 'positive' outcome to my own private 'Love Story.' A deep inseparable kind of love carried through many lifetimes from the heart is meant to be told. Sometimes in the same breath of life we know when it happens through a glancing gaze with an exchange of the deepest kind exchanging thoughts and ideas with one look and feelings only the two of you would know with a likeness of the deepest kind.

Finding the right person in life can seem like the hardest thing in the world, but it can happen instantly and unexpectedly with a whole new way of loving. Keep your mind 'OPEN' and be 'POSITIVE.' Everyone will be with that 'special someone' when the time is right, and when it's meant to be. Some call it Fate 'BELIEVE'

Determined I set apart each day re-creating a collection of memories and observations, organizing my thoughts for developing this compelling story from a lifetime of memoirs, and understand the uniqueness based on a profound and 'Truthful' collection of my own personal and intimate experiences. Knowledge is coming under the microscope for me with issues that I have dealt with for several years and many transits are now working in favor on these themes. I already feel some of this energy from the plants, the Sun and Full Moon and it's going to be an emotional one.

Closures and endings are high at the top of my mind and endings with bringing a powerful change. I am keeping calm and trying to roll with the changes. Maybe I will not recognize it immediately, but it's overall going to be favorable and a healthy way as the planets get closer to collecting in my sign of Sagittarius and into my personal Birthday month of December. I have many Full Moon wishes and I am making them count for the ending and the start of a new beginning.

It is my pleasure to bring and share with you 'THE LETTER' from my beloved husband, Jim who passed on July 30th, 2007 and now in spirit in Heaven. It is one of the most outstanding and beautiful experiences I've had through a reading from the favorite Psychic Medium who has channeled for my husband and me, living in Brisbane, Australia.

''THE LETTER" and 'Channeled Reading' is how things took place a self-explanatory celebration of our forty-third (43rd) WEDDING ANNIVERSARY.

Jim has been in spirit (on the other side) for twelve years now and I a mortal here on earth. Each October on the 31st (The Sacred day of Halloween for All Saints and spirits is when we first met sixty-seven years ago) and I have carried through with the traditional readings of communicating with my husband Jim through a Spiritual Medium. Our Medium "K" is the conduit and channel for conveying our hourly conversation to one another in each reading and she is truly wonderful. Aside from the day of Halloween on October 31st I would have a reading for our Very Special Day

July 29th each year and being our Wedding Anniversary. I have always felt so 'Grateful and Blessed' for having "K" as the conduit for our readings.

Daughter Renee urged me to wear my beautiful long Red lace gown with shoes and accessories for Jim to see what I would be wearing upon my arrival when it is my time for the finalization of 'Passing.'

Once

THE LETTER - (from Jim)

"IN HONOR of our 43rd WEDDING ANNIVERSARY"

"Welcome my beloved, this is our day, dear Patricia. Yes, it is our anniversary where life began in a simple moment of 'I Do' and that was all we needed.

I send you much love and all the flowers from the heavens to brighten your day.

I see you, I hear you, our loss is still not meant to be mourned. I am you and you are me and together we will write and sing the song.

If you feel I have left you, not so. You have been busy, so busy and when you take that moment I know you can feel me, even though it is less, I am still here watching over you.

Patricia my love, the heavens are so beautiful and when I am down, God is here for me as I cry on his shoulder, "I miss her God I miss her more as she misses me".

His comfort is soothing as yours was to me. There is a long chair here waiting for you and me, under the tree where we will sit and hold each other the way we used to and just be. I will show you the beauty here and you will see with eyes wide open, your world is just for a moment, my world holds more and when it is time we will be together again, you will see.

For now, make me proud, as only you can. You have pushed doors open and had faith that the manuscript must be available for all to see.

Jim says, The next door opens to you, please make the world a better place by being you, who you are and what you are meant to be. Your life has not stopped short as mine was but through you I still live for eternity, always waiting for you, loving you more and more. Your mission is set, don't stop now, remember what I asked… finish everything because I know you can for me.

Repeat this when you are weary …

"We only get what we ask for. First, we have to ask.

- Second, we must believe that we deserve it, and
- Third, we must be willing to accept it."
- "Today I am willing to accept that I have requested
- In the light, with gratitude and satisfaction".
- (Touching the Light Day by Day Meg Blackburn Losey.)

My love to hold you again, to look into your eyes to show you how much I love you, that kiss, that first kiss, again to say hello, please to meet you, then we can hold each other, laugh with a tear and know we are together, complete.

It is time to plant a tree for me, under it you will plant some coins, a note, to begin the prosperity I know is there for you to help others before you leave. Say a little prayer over the little tree and find a student that needs help when the tree prospers, you are then able to leave a legacy.

Share with this soul who I am. Tell them of the good luck that will come to them for the blessing we have bestowed upon them. A perfect stranger, but not. God will help you pick them, you will see. Education is imperative now more than ever in your world,

I want the world to slow down and listen to what they are saying and believing for. The mind must be connected to the heart and the heart connected to the mind. It is then the soul will live the path it is meant to be.

Right now, in this moment I share with you, nothing matters more than you and me. My friend my love, my wife, my teacher, my soul mate of many lives, the next one that comes is more than we could ever imagine it to be.

Love, Jim. X0x0x0x0x0x0x0x0x0x0x0x0x0x0x0x0x0x0x0x0x0x0x0

I knew his deep sorrow to not be able to guide me in my days as he would have if he was here. Some people have helped me and others not, but I have continued and for that he is grateful. He paces while chatting to me, telling me of the little tree and the legacy I would leave. The tree had tiny little white flowers on it, a symbol of purity. The leaves are shinny green. A pretty bush. He is disconnected with this world at times, and for that he finds it hard to connect. He is born and wants his girl.

At no know time do I know when I am to join him. He is waiting on God's time.

Jim said, "You have the 'Yin and the Yang' keep that energy balanced and it will keep you on track always.

- LION spirit animal, is a symbol of Personal Strength and Courage -

The lion spirit animal is associated with a representation of personal strength. If the lion appears powerful to you, its presence as a spirit guide can be interpreted as a positive representation of your self-confidence of personal power. As such, lions point to qualities of strength, courage, assertiveness.

Lions are also animals who dominate other animals in nature. Remember as an example the expression "the lion, king of the jungle". When a lion appears as your power animal, it could reflect your ability to lead others or tendency to dominate in relationships.

From this point on I began looking at pictures of 'Lions' sitting in their natural habitat home with their family and babies and tears came to my eyes as I looked eye to eye.

Earlier in the day, it came upon a TV news station when I saw that our current president had just raised the protection band against killing 'Lions & Elephants' in Africa as his two sons had killed a beautiful king Lion as a 'Trophy' of their specific Tusk' importing the ivory for personal profit. It has been noted that this United States President has broken every Law he can for his personal profit and friends. Other countries are now laughing at us in the United States for being so Weak!

Six weeks later not thinking any longer about Lions

I Had A DREAMED A Lion was sitting at my front door and I could see him in full view. He sat so stately with such large sad eyes as we looked at one another deeply together into the eyes eye so beautifully so sweetly and he looked so sad and I reached out to pet him. Next seeing my family, he wanted to chase them as we all ran to the car and climbed in with me in the driver's seat and the Lion sitting on the top of the car. I felt he was there possible for protection but then began scratching at the car and trying to get in. I quickly then drove the car away in panic to protect my family and myself. Next the Lion was in the backyard and wanting to come in. At the end of dream I asked myself, "Did the Lion want to be friends?"

I couldn't get the Lion's sad eyes out of my mind remembering the Lion is 'a spirit animal' and symbol of personal strength and courage. I began searching everywhere for a Lion which the look like the one in my dream with the same sad eyes and colorings. Finally, I found a canvas reproduction and now have the Lion canvas hanging directly over my bed with one-inch separation of five panels and he is beautiful! In a full-length mirror at the opposite end of my bedroom I can see my special friend in the mirror's reflection as I sit and meditate and write. I love the fact that the 'Lion' is my Second Animal Spirit Guide with the first animal spirit guide being 'The Hulk' with a watchful eye.

'The Hawk' and 'The Lion' are also the spirit animal guides for my past husband! -

When Jim pushes up against my Soul I feel him when I pick up and begin to write remembering the glorious times we had together and how I felt. However, I don't want this book to be mainstream for it stipulates the things I need to have in it. I have felt him saying "Okay what do we write?" That's where we design our mental desires.

- My Message to 'God' -

"My mission in life is set: And I'm not stopping now. I will finish everything because I know I can with helping to make the world a better place by being myself who I am and what I'm meant to be. I live for eternity always waiting loving more and more and when it's time, I know we will be together.

"We only get what we ask for First, I am asking and Second, I believe that I deserve it and Third, I am willing today to accept that I have made this request in the light, with gratitude and satisfaction" and by Touching the Light Day by day." -

I will do all that is asked of me and try to keep my energy balanced and on track. I do have the 'Yin and the Yang' as a positive representation. My self-confidence and personal power are to help others with strength, courage and assertiveness with mind, heart, and soul and for living the path meant to be.

"The 'Legacy' must to be with everybody who lives in the home because this will not be just for me myself but for daughter 'Renee' as well and her partner. Jim asked that the three of us look for the right nursery and the right tree. It is all about PROSPERITY and LEARNING and the student that I will find and I will also give them a gift. It doesn't have to be big but with something to say from this Legacy so that it may be taken forward and worked with in this way".

The last time Jim and I talked he was going in one direction and then decided to go in another direction after a lot of thought. Jim is "A Philosophy Leader" 'On the Other Side' and the one who teaches the new Souls about Earth before they come into Earth. He teaches them about 'WORDS' and he is teaching them 'MUSIC' and about 'LOVE' This is the format he loves currently that is in the above written letter.

I have noticed something strange going on this year of 2018 more than any other time ever before. Countless people all over the planet have reported seeing the 11:11 code repeatedly appear in their daily lives and intensifies as we approach the 11th day, of the 11th month, of an 11 Universal year (2+0+1+8=11) ... 11:11:11 this year (November 11th) is more magical than you ever could've imagined and it's the most powerful manifesting day of the decade. Waking up to make a trip to the bathroom one night and glancing at the clock, it was exactly 11:11.

The 11 is the Master Number of heightened intuitions, occurring through divine or supernatural interventions, and creation. In sacred geometry, the Number 11 represents two pillars, a gateway which opens a direct portal between divine inspiration and physical materialization.

On November 11th, 2018 the 11:11:11 the portal flies wide open just days after tomorrow's Scorpio New Moon darkens the skies and opens limitless possibilities.

After having 3 eclipses in July & August with Mars & Mercury in retrograde with feelings stuck & frustrated and trying to push me out of my comfort zone the dust settles with 'reinvesting' my life in a new direction.

NOVEMBER 2018 and watching the SIGNS is the turning point of amazing predictions of bringing in a whole NEW CHAPTER and new directions in my personal life and wants to open with two big reasons with positive aspects in the coming months and much more personal as stated by an Astrologer.

Jupiter will enter the sign of Sagittarius for 1 year and rules Sagittarius for the first time in 12 years and in the 1st House of {Confidence & Visibility) feeling lucky with new adventures and attracting new opportunities. Just being a Sagittarius, Mercury's Sign of Gemini is what is on my mind.

The "NORTH NODE" is in my birth sign and is calling for my ongoing DESTINY which moves through all 12 zodiac signs for 1 ½ years each ONCE every 19 years and moves into Cancer in my 8th HOUSE of Shared Resources & Transformation until April 2020. So, there is a lot of mystery since it is naturally ruled by planet SCORPIO. It just shows up like it's part of my Destiny {with financial obligation, business partnership settlements, inheritances, and taxes.}

The 8th HOUSE also deals with DEATH latterly and figuratively with a feeling of Destiny which there is nothing I can do about it if someone close to me passes away or there is a break-up with a partner. The "NORTH NODE" is NOT about being Negative and that is why I'm drawn to Psychology and Astrology and to re-invent and explore my Inner life. It's about this big Transformation in the 8th HOUSE of Endings & New Beginnings. So certainly, for me as a Sagittarius this next 1 ½ years with planet Jupiter giving me growth, protection, and luck, there are really some substantial changes on going.

The SOUTH NODE is my opposite! The SOUTH NODE is what I need to let go of and detach so I can move into the NORTH NODE of my Destiny. There could be more frustrations, fears, and delays with cash flow but forces me to be more pro-active. The Sagittarius's {moon & sun rising} in year 2019 and into 2020 will start making a lot more money because of everything I had to take care of to make sure I didn't run out of money. However now, the SOUTH NODE of what I need to let go of is entering my 2nd House of Income.

What does this all mean mixed with the protective lucky Jupiter in Sagittarius?

I think it is going to be an opportunity and could be with a 'Business Contract Partnership' and maybe it is just coming into unexpected monies. It is time to leave this limited way of making money and 'let go!' "So, what comes first the chicken or the egg?"

Now getting more specific I am really thinking bigger and more 'out-of-the-box' in the last couple of weeks of November and doing a lot of 'soul searching' and 'where I am going' and 'what should I do?' There are more of these better optimistic opportunities to choose now when the planet Mercury goes 'retrograde' in Sagittarius and I started to do all the 're-assessing' of my life. It is also when planet Venus 'retrogrades' backward into my 11th House of FRIENDS & BIG DREAMS & HIGHEST IDEALS with social events. I feel either that I don't have time or I'm feeling disconnected.

On the positive side with Venus 'retrograde' in my 11th House I may be reconnecting and hearing from friendships that I had disconnected with a long time ago and hearing from them unexpectedly.

I am calm and I trust! When there is something, I'm still worried about and in the wellbeing of others, I adopt the 'Buddhist' prayer mantra and let it inspire my coming manifestations.

-The Buddhist mantra: "May I act for the benefit of all sentient beings."-

I have been instructed from birth in the equality of all sentient life forms and capable of feeling the connection. I am alive, aware and listening. There is going to be some closed chapters for me, and these are excellent transits of feeling good. I will be the BALANCED objectiveness of a person or their judgment and not be influenced by personal feelings or opinions. I will be the BALANCING PARTY with communicating my philosophical intelligence and I will be the master of 'my fate.' It is important to have a keen sense of friendship between my soulmate and myself from the past and I will make sure all lines of communication are kept open between my partner and myself.

I am curious about what stands in the way of myself and my partner as I am receiving all of the inspiration of what I need to say and exactly how I need to say it with some lucky magic, drive, beauty and love on the domestic scene and to express things that I generally tend to hide or keep to myself. I need to be transparent and honest and TRUST in an intimate partnership. True intimacy is built on feelings that we can share with our deepest and darkest secrets with one another and without fear of judgment or disconnection. It is time to practice sharing more of what makes me uncomfortable with my ex-partner and with our minds thinking of how the world will see the new plans we are working on or those we are trying to make work according to how they are. HONESTY is the only way to win this one. There is past karma between myself and my ex-partner and it is a wonderful time to share more of what makes me uncomfortable with my past love partner.

There is a planetary configuration emphasizing the beauty and the magic that can occur when we are able to find a balance between the fun, the light-hearted and the romantic aspects of our relationships and with the higher spiritual and philosophical ones.

I believe while it is crucial that my friend and I experience a spiritual connection with having similar life views and beliefs it is just as important also to have a strong sexual connection. We are all physical beings and that is an important aspect of our intimate partnership and life. Having that connection with someone makes the partnership more fulfilling and in reality the connection between spirit and sex are not that separate.

To make things work cannot be made only in our own favor. Luck comes only if we are playing an honest game and keeping the mind on the big picture but doing it with kindness. TRUTH and HONESTY are the only way to win this one and it would be wise to channel restless energy. For my friend and love partner planet Mars is now working in the 10th House of career destiny and public image for the next few months with maintaining a good image under this karma driven transit and to lead with LOVE and nothing else. Following this kindness through the new year we will see the magic happen by starting to think about this compassionate drive today.

It is important in this journey to tend to the bigger 'spiritual aspects' of our intimate partnership and take care of the more mundane parts of it. Getting caught-up in the demanding work only we can risk losing touch with the meaning that this relationship can provide our life and then we become resentful with it. On the other hand, getting caught in just the larger spiritual parts the relationship is bound to fail as we neglect the daily reality and that is a major component of any healthy relationship.

EXAMPLE: The Sun's in Sagittarius and the Moon's in Sagittarius and saying "This is all so Funny" and the Jupiter is in Sagittarius and saying "They are all so 'Blunt & Honest'" and the Scorpio is in Sagittarius and saying "It's So Deep" and they all talk STRAIGHT, and they don't play 'Superficial' and the Scorpio loves to just say 'Funny Things' and 'be

Disruptive' with talking about 'FACIAL HAIR' and anything eerie or weird and with nerve to say DEEP THINGS like [Tell me about what you really are feeling] [And Tell me about your Goals and your Ambitions [Tell me about your SEX LIFE]

The MOON is talking about BLUNT and SCORPIO is talking about DEEP and if you are a SCORPIO you would be Uninhibited

So being a SAGITTARIUS I let myself stand apart from the group and especially since MARS is in Aquarius and is just watching rather than participating.

-Being a SAGITTARIUS I rise-up and say [You smell funny] or [Ugh, you look funny] and then I realize that was the wrong thing to say. -

With all these planets in my sign of SAGITTARIUS I would say [I don't know] or something like [SOMESTIMES I MUST REST]. -

It's about 'Human Nature' and all its assorted colors. It doesn't matter what I think It should be because 'Human Nature' displays itself in its own 'Authenticity' and when its RAW and when you have a SCORPIO & SAGITTARIUS Authenticity And with a SCORPIO and a SAGITTARIUS there is no holding back. Naught! So, I go ahead and be the 'Role Model' and 'Be MYSELF' and let the laughter Roar. "That is why people like being around me and when I'm being myself without being Filtered."

> Many people try to play at being NORMAL but not if you are a SCORPIO or a SAGITTARIUS! Hah! This is a huge lesson here for me and to just be Myself!

> By: Debra Silverman Astrology Lesson

My energy will pick-up and be more focused on my Appearance and on Health, and I will be more pro-active.

The NORTH NODE moving into the 8th HOUSE of [SHARED RESOURCES & TRANSFORMATION] there certainly could be joint partnerships showing-up like it is meant to be or it's all part of getting me out of this smaller job with starting a new business or going into a 'Business Partnership.' So here is a lot of opportunity that is really starting to open-up for me and with also making more money or seeing a more 'Expansive Shift.

It is known that Sagittarius dreams big and takes fearless risks while Gemini communicates and collaborates and flies full mast.

THIS IS THE STORY OF MY LIFE

- It's all unfolding with the single things I can CHANGE into EVERYTHING. -

* If I transform any DOUBTS in my mind Into TRUST It's a Hugh Difference!
* If I transform any WORRY into PEACE It's a Hugh Difference!
* Then my ALCHEMIST is DONE and it is a Beautiful ALCHEMY!

CHANGE I am making a Change or be at the mercy of Change.
I am asking if the desired outcome is assured? It is and so be it!
This is what it wants me to know and to remember. [That just from a 'Seed' this beautiful TREE can grow and it's an indicator of a person because it's just like me I Am An ALCHEMIST!

* I can CHANGE any DOUBTS into CONFIDENCE
- [If there's any Hurts & Feelings that need to take place.]

* I can CHANGE any HURTS into COMPASSION
- [And all that beautiful experience can come into WISDOM.]

* WISDOM Is one of the most valuable things
- [I can take and SHARE with everyone.]

* I just know I am making a powerful CHANGE and finding PEACE.
- [In the WORLD around me and then the WORLD finds PEACE in me.]

This is what it is that I want most in this moment and I want this

TRANSFORMATION to be complete and I want to TRANSFORM. This is saying that it is coming and this is so Beautiful and so Great!

What this is saying The FEAR is a TAPISTRY - and it is about HEALING

HEALING the Present and my Past, Present & Future and the UNIVERSE wants to help me out with this.

* Beneath the layers of UNCERTAINTY and Beneath the layers of PAIN & DISAPPOINTMENTS there is PEACE in the Highest Wisdom.

* I Am Radiant and I Am Healthy and I Am Blessed and the Inner Sacred Flame is Constant and Unites Me with All and The Greatest LOVE of All.

What it wants me to do for the HEALING that I've really confronted is to really concentrate on it and find HOPE in the future since a complex situation is really going to require a concentrated type of approach. So, tackling 'One Big Issue' is going to take care of a lot of little issues and this is quite beautiful.

My STRENGTH is by the strands of the past and their sacred threads of TRUTH & WISDOM that intertwine 'within me' and everyone around me.

I can determine my future by just one stitch at a time because I Am the 'Weaver' of this Tapestry. I Am the 'Weaver' of this Strong Enriching Tapestry and it is quite a Joy to behold.

This really wants me to be FOCUSED on filling 'My Heart' with 'Creative Powers' and 'accept the Past' and decorate 'the Present' and it can certainly... certainly 'Transform' the Future.

SO, Talking about what is going on for me 'Oh my gosh,' if I go through 'A RELEASE' then I'm going into HEALING and then I'm going into TRANSFORMATION and start to color in 'My Tapestry' by the WISDOM that is going through me that I have there. The layers of UNCERTAINTY of the Past, Present & Future and DISAPPOINTMENT is letting me find PEACE and I am getting HIGHER WISDOM bubbling-up from that. So, there is a Positive outcome for me on what is going on. This is a fabulous thing to have and through the clouds I can see 'The Light' and then 'The Flowers' are blossoming below' so with just 'a little smile' just like a song 'The greatest things don't cost a lot but they are worth more when they are shared with someone else.' Aren't they?"

It's great to sing in the car but if you sing in the car with someone else it's way so fun! Right? It's so fun, you know … but it's good both ways and just so much more beautiful when its shared with an act of kindness that you do for yourself and you feel wonderful!

The insights needed for me as a Sagittarius are interesting because it is the end of the year 2018 and it's about a lot of REFLECTION. I am at a point talking about an overwhelming or 'Unexpected' emotion. There is a lack of concentration and it's going to be important for me to use that [3rd Eye] and it's like there is 'a past trauma' or 'a sadness' that is triggered and coming. It's a very 'raw expression' from a safe and loving environment telling me to put my 'Pain' aside and release all the chaos. I am called upon with the poised, graceful and elegant bearing in me and to really focus on positioning myself watching my actions and being careful with my words.

There has been some sort of a keen and highly developed focus because it is saying whatever has happened before [is to know that the STORM is over] and it wants me to know that I am completely LOVED and that I am SAFE and to RELEASE any fears that I have and then to set my Heart FREE.

"I can't avoid peace by avoiding life"

This is from "Virginia Woolf" talking about to succumb to these struggles and then be 'Renewed' and to just know that the UNIVERSE has me in its protection. So whatever it is that I need to RELEASE it is saying that I need to do it 'FIERCELY' because what I'm going to put underneath will bring me closer to my Intuition and the 3rd Eye in my Heart and will bring a lot of enlightenment here as well. The underlying energies might be something that I am 'RELEASING' and it shivers up from within and brings some Light.

I AM THE LIGHT and I AM THE TREE with the roots as my foundation and my outer being. So obviously it's like someone is saying [It's like the Crown Chakra the 3rd Eye and the Heart Chakra all being the STAR as the powerhouse of my 'Solar Plexus']. If I have any sort of RELEASE to do whether it's a relationship, a career situation or a situation of a loved one the underlying energy is telling me to RELEASE and I am going through this process at this point.

How do I feel about myself right now?

I'm going through some sort of HEALING at this moment and it brings a lot of illumination of 'Healing and Peace.' It is here for me to take as a beautiful and intelligent multi-dimensional force and to see the world as everything has a REASON a SEASON and a PURPOSE.

It feels SAD but when life throws lemons and makes it meaningful I am saying YES, for I can make lemonade and make it meaningful by taking those lemons and really creating my world. If a past hurt has resurfaced I will color my world and hear someone out to the last word.

It's time for me to restore health and strengthen and the feeling of well-being. It's also time for someone else to help heal the wound as well as a little bit of play and pain is going to lead to a lot of empathy. It's as if I'm letting things bubble up as I am healing. Certain things are resurfacing and becoming clearer. The sky is a little clearer and I just don't feel as clogged as before. Therefore, it's important to go through the healing and just rest and let it just take me where it needs to go.

I am saying "On the other side of hurt there is also FREEDOM" and "On the other side of pain there is PEACE"

So just know that as we go through RELEASING We go through the ACCEPTANCE

And then we go through the COMPASSION

And then we go through the FORGIVENESS making sure that it works through ourselves. -

Personally, I am RELEASING my tears that are an ocean of JOY and I know that as I express it I am HEALED.

I am going to have a lot of greater EMPATHY by going through some of this pain.

TRANSFORMATION is what I want most from this moment. Obviously, it makes sense because if I go through some sort of RELEASE there also brings some sort of HEALING in that process and it brings TRANSFORMATION.

I can see now how this TREE is TRANSFORMED and what I am to be aware of. We are all transforming and there are all these SEASONS that we transform through. It's like this 'timeless earth' knowing that I am forever TRANSFORMED. There is a moment in time when I could stop but I am 'Not' doing that! I am aware and I really 'Embrace it' and 'Treasure it' and really 'Focus on it' even at the very smallest 'Change' and the way I see myself in the world. The part that I play is all unfolding. It is THE STORY OF MY LIFE and it can create powerful waves of TRANSFORMATION. Just one simple thing that I change can change everything.

For Instance: If I transform Any DOUBTS in my mind into TRUST
- It's an enormous difference.

If I transform Any WORRY into PEACE
- It's a huge change.

And then the ALCHEMY is done.

Remember just from 'A Seed' it can grow into this huge beautiful tree and it is indicative to people because it's just like me. I am the ALCHEMIST

I can change any DOUBT into CONFIDENCE if there's been any Hurt

I know through some 'Healing' what needs to take place and be sustained.

I can turn that HURT into COMPASSION and then all that beautiful EXPERIENCE can come into WISDOM

This is letting me know that WISDOM is one of the most valuable things that I can take and share with everyone.

I'm making a powerful CHANGE and I'm finding PEACE in the world around me and then the world will find PEACE in me. I want this TRANSFORMATION to be complete.

My FEAR is the 'Tapestry' and I Know I am about to HEAL my 'Present' and the Universe wants to help me out with the Past, Present and the Future.

So, beneath the layers of "Uncertainty and Believe" and the layers of "Pain and Disappointment" there is PEACE in the highest WISDOM.

I Am Radiant and I Am Healthy and I Am Blessed with 'The Greatest LOVE of All.

What I need to do for this Healing is to confront it concentrate on it and find HOPE in the Future to see that a complex situation is going to really require a concentrated type of approach. By tackling [One Big Issue] is going to take care of a lot of little issues. I know I am strengthened by the [Strands of the Past] and there are 'Sacred Threads' of TRUTH and WISDOM that intertwine within me and everyone around me. I can determine my future 'Just One Stitch at a Time' because I am 'The Weaver of this Tapestry.' So, I really Focus on 'Filling my Heart' with 'Creative Powers' and accept 'the past' and decorate 'the present' and this can certainly TRANSFORM 'my future.'

The 'TREE TAPESTRY' represent the Solar Plexus Powerhouse of 'THE STAR' and my THIRD EYE and the CROWN with a RELEASE. It then goes into HEALING and then into TRANSFORMATION, and I've started to color in my Tapestry by the WISDOM that is going through me and the layers of Uncertainty of the 'Past' 'Present' and 'Future.' I know the Disappointments and it is letting me find PEACE and get higher WISDOM. It is in me 'Knowing' and it's bubbling up and saying "There is a positive outcome for me on what is going on for me."

This is a fabulous thing to have and through the clouds, I understand something clearly at last. I see the light, THE FLOWERS ARE BLOSSOMING BELOW just like 'a smile' just like 'a song.' The greatest things don't cost a lot but they are worth more when they are shared with someone aren't they?

It's great to sing in the car but if I am singing in the car with someone else it's so much more beautiful when it is shared. When there is kindness or an act of kindness that I do for myself I smile and feel wonderful and just as beautiful as if I were to share it with another.

So, I'm being sure to share that 'Smile' with another even when I don't want to smile - because I could be walking down the street and smiling and really influence someone - - else and I think about that. My results in a relationship could be helped or a - secretaries dream could come to fruition and its beautiful.

Spirit wants me to enjoy my success and have a positive outcome and its letting me know that it's here for me. I may be experiencing this now or I may experience it in the future. It is saying that I can know and enjoy my success and to rest and ready myself for the next stage of my journey. It's like history has a lot to teach me. I have gone through those movements and those learnings and they have brought courage and inspiration for me. My heart, my mind, and my hands are aligned in PURPOSE and that is what I want to affirm. It's an Affirmation that I want to focus on and strive together 'in LOVE' and 'of SERVICE.'

I am moving forward, and I'll accept PEACE, and LOVE and mutual RESPECT.

A little bit of love does go a heck of a long way. A little bit of giving brings success on the way and that is what I want to talk about now. -

It's about 'Abundance' so I'm making sure that I am 'SUPER THANKFUL.' For some reason, I am supposed to say this because it can work against you, so really focus on that cherished abundance and be humbly accepting the 'Abundance' when receiving because [Conflict brings Famine and Hunger and Dreams are Flightless].

'Investing in PEACE' abundance will follow. I continue to want PEACE as I move through in the direction of whether it's a relationship and I'm focused on PEACE in 'a relationship' with a lot of abundance."

"Spirit wants me to tend to 'the 'Seeds of my Heart' because I will reap a prosperous harvest moving through by planting the seeds like planting the scenes of flowers.

They will multiply and this time will shine as well. If I have any challenges I've got support through the challenges and act decisively in my abundance as I move through the future and don't pay attention to worry. I want to focus on a brighter future, and I want to stand-up and look to that brighter future, so this is what I keep in mind. There is more than enough that the Universe has and there is more than enough for everyone in my heart. It is endless and my mind is boundless with 'new Ideas' solutions, opportunities, creativity, and all of that I know. They are pieces of me, and all 'Abundance' is abounding for me."

The Universe is limitless, and it is on its way. It's what happens when I do the challenging work and I find the WISDOM that this positive constant outcome brings?

Now what is my future outcome? I have 'a new beginning' and it just blossoms into the most beautiful 'Brand New Beginning.'

So obviously, I have gone through a 'Major Change' for myself and this 'New Beginning' is A TREE 'Blooming of Hearts' and these hearts could be 'A NEW RELATIONSHIP' HANGING ON THIS TREE as if it is in the shape of a heart. It is about so much potential that is available now for me and there is so much PASSION that I have moving forward for this 'New Beginning.' I know the world is abound and abundance is there for me wanting me to keep focus and to know that in every new chapter there is definitely 'A New Beginning.' That I can have a 'New Beginning' at every second of the day, let alone every minute, every hour, every day of every week and every year. So, every month, every year is what is seen here I have created that for myself.

There is a 'Brand New Beginning' for me and it could be a fresh start in 'A New Relationship' that could be an 'Existing Relationship' and taking it to the next level. It could be an 'Exciting Project at Work' but it is up to me to get things moving so I am not waiting. I will 'Instigate' with all the abundance in this position, so I won't wait. YES, I will make mistakes, but YES, I will persist, and I'll bring PEACE today. I hold myself with STRENGTH and I'll begin with a vision today with New Beginning's and that is what I want to take into 'Heart'. I am acting on 'My Dreams' today.

Every dream must start somewhere at some time, so I don't wait I instigate and this is what I am saying to get this PEACE. I am here and I'm ready 'to catch and support and guide' and the Universe is here to do that for me so I must do what I must do to make 'My Start.' I'm ready to begin and there is no time like the present to begin. The Calendar is doing that for me in the month of December 2018 before I go into the New Year of 2019. So, what is it that I might need to know through this process that is going to be extremely important for me as I move through this?

'Physical Activity' is going to help get the juices flowing and help to move that energy internally in my body and that is going to be very helpful and the foundation for 'The New Beginning. 'Physical Activity' is going to be extremely important for me as a Sagittarius. Keeping this is mind, I am making sure that I get out there and exercise being careful of the holiday with [SWEETS] and just good enough that I keep this in mind and making sure I get some 'Physical Activity' because it's going to move the energy after I've gone through some stern peeling with a shift that is happening inside me. Therefore, I must have PATIENCE with myself as I move forward in my relationship and have patience with more PEACE and ABUNDANCE. The more Peace I bring into my life I will have greater abundance in that relationship. I know this about myself so I will really have greater PATIENCE with others in this relationship and whatever it is that I am working on that is coming to the surface.

The things that are happening now are in 'Synchronicity' and the time that they should be happening and that I am going to feel a 'Big Shift of Energy' from the Universe.

Planet SCORPIO is the last sign or the {shadow sector} for Sagittarius.

This time becomes transitional and low key and just wants to be left alone and is a bit tired but with a Breath of Light to make my Intentions clear and that I want to speak to my beloved Soul Mate I Meditate to My Soul Mate

-"I Am here I'm finding my way as I've been swimming in a lovely sea of you and I am pouring my emotions out to let you know that I am ready and willing to accept anything you may want to say to me. I am ready to have an honest communication and I am willing to do the work together with you." - "I have asked for you to come back into my life and for long-term. It's the Ending and the Beginning of a brand-new cycle and it's not that you need to agree with me but just that I want you to listen to me." "I believe we can teach and learn from each other and grow with an honest commitment to something 'Spiritual' and with friendship and love giving back to the world with something bigger than ourselves. It would be nice to have quality time together and reflect with honest, open clear lines with our Hearts Open and find BALANCE between our essential traits. Love transcends space and time Nothing is missing, and I wait to hear back from you." 'Poppy'

Right! Nothing was missing but from hearing back from my Soulmate.

Christmas Holidays arrived and left moving on into January 2019 and still without hearing anything back from the letter of offer I had made to my Beloved Soulmate

It is known that Sagittarius dreams big and takes fearless risks while 'Gemini's communicate and collaborate and flies full mast. So, what happened to my 'Gemini Jim' soulmate and his non-communication with me?

IN SEPARATION Soulmate Twin Flame

I began surrendering to the change the Soul was guiding me to do and feeling free emotionally and spiritually from the past and the things I had been holding onto in separation. Big Issues were coming back from the past with thoughts and emotions and spiritually going within with an internal shift of awareness. It has been a slow and steady process through months and months and into the summertime with growth and patience of a new beginning and working towards some stability. A new change is something I've put a lot of time and energy working through and I'm now beginning to benefit from it.

There has been a lack of growth in connections and I've decided to move forward with the NEW BEGINNINGS and LETTING GO of those burdens that I have been holding onto for so long. Some of what I was holding onto I felt was not my own energy, but because I was attached to someone and going through a cycle with them I was entangled with their Karmic thoughts and emotions and it tripped-me-up on my path. It doesn't mean the other person is Karmic because everything is Karmic in what we think about and our energy and our intent in that moment and when everything is playing out. So, everything is Karmic.

There is an awareness as to what I am willing to take on and what I am not willing to take on, so there is this division from an attachment to energy. An awareness of this energy has been blocking my manifestation and growth and I have an awareness of this with a new beginning that I am leading into with a period of Balance and from a period of Imbalance. I was getting pulled back into that old thought process and old experiences that I had in the past that triggered those up and down and back and forth thoughts I had been having for quite a while. Now I find that I must begin Releasing the causes that made massive changes in my life with separation with either a loved one, a soulmate or someone who has been a huge part of my past.

I've had A KARMIC ATTACHMENT to someone in thought and something I kept going back too and couldn't let go of. It came up in my awareness and has been blocking me in my past. I had to tune-in emotionally in how my emotions are clouding my thoughts and affecting my energy by pulling me back and forth blocking my energy from a new beginning with a manifestation and needed to be put to healing.

Any Soul Contracts we have with people will need to be reset internally and it will become known with the things I was not trusting, intuitively or emotionally. Guidance came through God, Source, and the Universe with a change in Happiness. I have been standing on my own for a few years in the physical separation since my husband Jim had passed. There is a focus on Home and Stability. I saw the foundation for myself after going through the 'Eternal' battle in thought with this person from my past.

Everyone in life has different Karma and different lives we move into with different intensions and we all have 'Free Will.' Through my realization someone I've been dealing with has their own timeline and their own Karmic path that they have to go through and have to experience, and it's not up to me to take on their Karma and their energy along with their thoughts and their fears. It has block me from moving forward. This is something I didn't realize in the past and that it was blocking me in some way. But now, I have gained a lot of psychic ability of what I've been dealing with in my awareness and thoughts.

There is a lot of movement forward and I'm directing my energy in the way I want it to go. A change is coming in with initiating and guiding this action with making and getting an offer to my worth and how I create resources for myself and my stability, my homelife and foundation. Creatively at times, I felt lost lost in dreams and lost energetically and I tried to force things too hard in what had been clouding my thoughts in the past.

It feels like Healing and Balance that has been slowly progressing and there has been a lot of inner work and reflection at the root cause of my emotions, and the causes that have been coming up with reactions and triggers. I want to move forward, and I have been trying to leave the past patterns behind, redirecting my energy and consciously being aware of what I'm directing. My emotions are directing my awareness consciously from the past and the patterns I have fallen into because of my past experiences, and especially with a certain person that I've not been in contact with or in communication with and one that I've had this difficult experience with. I'm guarding my feminine energy and especially sexually.

The other person is now seeing my worth and the energy of our connection in the past, and how it has affected the past in my life. There is something unfolding in 'Divine Timing' and it feels like a 'Power Moment' and I am meant to put myself out there in some way. There is a change and it could be a creative project that I'm putting myself out there in and for a positive moment in changes with the TRUTH in some way. I'm sharing my TRUTH and something that I'm interested in that I haven't moved forward with. There is someone initiating a positive and momentous CHANGE for me that I can create and move forward with.

There is a Reunion here A SPIRITUAL REUNION like 'WAKING-UP'! I have psychically and telepathically linked-up with someone and re-connecting, but instead of being a burden it's with someone in control who understands this connection in the non-physical place and redirecting the energy in my path in the 3rd dimensional, and remaining grounded. So this has been a huge development from the psychic what I am going through Psychically.

"Synchronicity" this is saying that the things that are happening are in the time that they should be happening in and that I'm going to notice something that the Universe has in an order of events that takes place especially during hopelessness and uncertainty. Who would have thought the positive outcome of Abundance in this beautiful beginning would be saying BOOM! And there it is just like the song when you logically cannot comprehend how your dreams could ever possibly come true. So, TRUST that the MAGICAL POWERS are in hand and there is 'SYNCHRONICITY' to what I need. It is my job to know how things are going to work out but it is also my job to really Know that all is well.

I BELIEVE in those who are going to make it happen and how and when it is going to happen.

I'm putting it in the hands of the Divine because once I surrender to the outcome, I will be shown the next logical step. I'm living consistent alignment with Source and I focus on 'positive thoughts', 'positive emotions' and 'career' and that is going to automatically attract these 'Synchronicities' into my life because I have FAITH in 'Synchronicities and they are there to lead me where I need to be.

Well heck yes, of course I know with this new beginning I get 'REBIRTH.'

The number 7 is a lucky number and it is in my 7th House of

'Relationships, Love and Partnerships'. So, I am keeping in mind that as I go through this new beginning I'm going to feel like a brand-new baby and a brand-new person. New life is taking that first breath of fresh air after such a time of 'transformation.' It takes a lot of energies and it takes a lot of emotions as I move through this. It is a beautiful 'REBIRTH' that is awaiting me in the month of December, my birthday month. This indicates a need to 'go within' and recognize and address any limiting thoughts and beliefs that are holding me back from experiencing Love, so I ask myself

-"Do I truly Believe that I'm worthy of Love?" I, Sagittarius, say YES! 'Joyfully and Truly'. "Do I 'truly open myself to give & receive Love?" Here I say, - "YES, YES, YES!!!"

I Am Focused to really overcome any limiting beliefs or thoughts from truly experiencing a great LOVE I have and to 'believe' that love can exist for me because love comes with me. Only when I BELIEVE does it exist, so I know this is a 'REBIRTH IN A RELATIONSHIP' ' or 'love to myself and a love with another or in a relationship'.

The AFFIRMATION is to see things through the eyes of Love and when I do it attracts more love into my life in every shape and form for the month of December. I have this whole new healing that's taking place in this 'Tapestry of Wisdom' that's building and I'm moving it to a positive outcome and abundance. So, for whatever it is that I'm thinking of I'm going to have a positive outcome, abundance and a new beginning. Let the 'Synchronicities' take its place and I will have patience.

If my energies are feeling a little gloomy I'm getting out of there and doing some physical exercise and letting the Universe help me understand and know that I am 'Loved' and will have 'Rebirth' in that 'New Beginning.' I am getting out of my way and I am done. I speak my TRUTH and I don't give up! I know what's 'Right' and I express myself at what I truly want to grow and I'm standing-up for what I say, and I don't give up!

As a Sagittarius I am curious and energetic and one of the biggest travelers of the Zodiac Signs. I am open minded with philosophical views and I am motivated to wander around the world in search of the meaning of life.

Extroverted, optimistic, enthusiastic and liking changes I can seal my thoughts into concrete actions to achieve my goals in my spirited self and 'Balance Within myself' and move on with the 'unexpected love of

Gemini'. The death of this old relationship is with the 'unexpected love of Gemini and with 'the karma' falling under my strength. This divine relationship is falling within me with 'True Love'.

Hot and heavy is coming towards me with blessings but I prevail in this present reality and I don't give-up. I have made my choice in a 'New Relationship' and they knew they slipped-up and now must choose between two people and they chose me.

I am dealing with a lot of 'healing' and emotional releasing in the head in the mind and overthinking everything and analyzing it. There was a lot of 'Gemini' deception in the past and a lot of liars, betrayals, and sneaking around me with manipulations, mind games, control games, and childish intense manipulations going on in a million different directions with games and everything in love. In the past there was a lot of this.

Now, putting it aside today I'm having my own misgivings about what went down. I'm looking towards overcoming these energies of deception, the sneaking around and the lies and I'm putting aside any mental games, and anything that would be harmful to the heart. I am putting all that aside today and it is good coming out of this toxic energy of games, arguments, conflicts and deceptions.

I am joining today in force with my friend, partner, and my love interest as a team and overcome all this deception and all the small petty conflicts from the past because I don't have time for that anymore. I don't want to waste any more energy on that this year because I have already done enough of that. I may have lost a lot of people through these conflicts but I am realizing all the people that had my back were honest and true and had my best intensions that has come to the surface.

They are the last people standing after the dodgeball games of attacks in energy and verbal ways. I'm coming out of this time with all my emotions and the heaviness of those burdens and this has been my wish. [There is healing, abundance, and wish fulfillment of what I am wanting with the person I have asked for. I will have 'Peace, Tranquility and Healing' after a very trying and testing time.

ABUNDANCE is a key word today and I am feeling the strength today with my love interest. He is feeling strong like the Lion to get through his life. He has superb leadership qualities and is very smart, very intellectual and the person I am going to be with. And here is me with an 'Abundance in Love' and in 'Wealth' as well so I'm killing all that deception with ease. I have my hand on my animal totem today the Lion which gives me 'strength and reassurance' like a support team and I'm squashing all these deceptions from the past. I am moving forward with the Lion next to me and he's quite protective and guarding over me and if something was to come along, he would attack it.

Bears & Lions are a very significant animal today. The Bear and Lion represents (Strength, Persistence, and pushing on.) A Bear or Lion could represent someone resting their hands on your shoulders saying "I AM HERE FOR YOU AS YOU NAVIGATE YOUR LIFE." I am going through a challenging time where I could not find solutions and didn't know how to move forward with my life. I may have someone come in today to help me ease those burdens and to help ease these challenges. It may be 'a good friend' or 'a love interest' and this will be the completion of a karmic cycle. I will move forward with this person. He is turning the wheel and all the stars are spinning out so I feel this support network is creating 'Healing at the Heart.'

My partner soulmate twin flame love interest is unified in the energy realm and may be protective over me through physical signs in the physical realm. This is all about the strength of the connection we have. This is a very strong spiritual bond that lasted the test of time through many hits and many fall backs with many deceptions and many mind games. Despite all of that it has such a strength that maybe only I can comprehend and the kind of connection that has lasted countless lifetimes. Today, it is a very strong soulmate or twin flame connection. It is like my soulmate and I are both wanting to put in equal management and maintenance into the relationship, with "EQUAL BALANCE.'

However, the energy feels every heavy and it is hard for me to focus. I need to depressurize and focus on 'extra breathing' today with Love and a capital 'L' front and center so there will be a lot of Love and a lot of Compassion. Whoever this is 'he loves me very much and he wants to have transformation with me.' With the LOTUS on his head in his Crown Chakra he's had a Revelation about me and about 'WHO I AM AND WHAT I MEAN TO HIM.' This person's 'Soul' may have some sort of connection to water or able to control water as an element on an energy level but he has some sort of connection to water and it is going to be one Big Emotional overload of positive emotions.

[I should respond calmly in a crisis using diplomacy and not force from an 'Archetype' perspective of character and reach out to help with accepting a different point of view with an atmosphere of caring and tolerance. It seems slightly 'melancholy' although he has much power. I seem to be missing something here in this connection with my Soulmate Twin Flame Relationship.

I am fortunate in my achievements and I have accomplished much and built a good business or career for myself and I have a stable loving family life and these things give me much satisfaction, but there is still a longing in my Heart. It is as if I have lost touch with my creative side seeking artistic and nurturing emotions that are missing in my life. I could grow bitter and resentful and I may neglect my existing obligations if I give into pouting and self-obsession rather than workable solutions. This is about Love and someone coming to the table with the rest is history.

This is someone I have not been in contact with for a while and we both took off and removed ourselves from the situation to rest and recuperate ourselves. My thoughts weigh very heavy on me today because there is a heavy mental energy on the mind. We both have lions' which represents persistence through the day.

When a Sagittarius and Gemini get together in love compatibility, move out of the way as they blaze new trails together. This is a Mutable Fire Sign of Sagittarius joining forces with the Mutable Air Sign of Gemini and both elements move very quickly. Air and Fire always create sparks together as well so all the sexual chemistry is certainly there for Sagittarius and Gemini as well. This relationship is not one that is rooted anywhere at first, and if both parties want that they will need to make some effort here. This is an energetic relationship that appears to always be in flux and finding focus on common goals and shared visions could be problematic for these flexible signs. If they can find their happy balance, Sagittarius and Gemini will create many happy sparks together.

The PROS: The Sagittarius and Gemini match are one that is marked by high energy and a lot of sexual chemistry. At the base of it we have two Mutable Signs, Mutable Fire and Mutable Air, and this brings a fresh energy into this relationship most every single day. Both zodiac signs love trying new things, and love that their partner does too! Gemini loves Sagittarius sense of adventure, their love of travel, and their spontaneous bursts of passion and affection. Sagittarius on the other hand loves how Gemini opens up their mind to two worlds no matter where they go. Gemini is the thinker and the communicator in this relationship, being ruled by Mercury. Sagittarius is ruled by Jupiter and this brings lucky energy, and an open mind to every adventure this great big world sends their way. One thing is for certain, there will never be a dull moment between Sagittarius and Gemini.

The CONS: Of course, there are always wrinkles, even in paradise, and these two Mutable Signs will have a tough time even focusing on that. Both Sagittarius and Gemini are mutable signs, which means they fill whatever vessel they are in at the time. These signs are normally easygoing and good natured, but not when they are forced out of the independent comfort zone. Both Sagittarius and Gemini need freedom to be themselves, as much as they are with each other, or this relationship will fizzle out before it starts. Gemini is a bit of a double talker which will prove disappointing for Sagittarius on occasion. Sagittarius can be lightly indecisive at time, and Gemini will not have any patience for this. Sagittarius also does not like how Gemini gets critical in a disagreement, and Gemini will not appreciate how Sagittarius runs at any sign of drama or conflict.

How to Make it Work Anyway:

As both Sagittarius and Gemini have short attention spans, this bodes well for them when it comes to problems. Neither one of Sagittarius nor Gemini are going to hold a grudge for very long. Both are forgiving enough to let things go, as quickly as the sparks start flying. That might be because the sexual chemistry in this pair is difficult to match. Andy both Sagittarius and Gemini know they will always have this to bank on when the going gets tough. And if not, then Sagittarius and Gemini will need to find a way to learn how to focus and regroup with each other when the going gets tough. If they can find that balance, Sagittarius and Gemini will be making sparks for many happy years together.

Having been stuck in LOVE today and coming out of a time of not really moving anywhere in the past my energy was so stuck. Today, it's going to be moving and it's going to be shifting and my 'Chakras' are going to start flowing my energy and I may have two people interested in me. This is about Communication so I'm going to be getting communication soon. This is about putting into action a very fast-moving plan that goes very quickly. Someone is coming into action very fast traveling to me. This man is coming in with ambition and control and power and force and could be a soulmate twin flame connection of the dark & the light energy and I'm moving forward very fast and moving on from conflicts and out of being in the cold with someone and feeling alone or single.

I may be dealing with an overly and overpowering alluring or seductive woman today and she may feel like she is far away or she' is hard to reach. But there are a lot of changes happening with me and this woman today so there is definitely 'SPIRITUAL CHANGES' happening in the energy around me today and soon it will manifest into the physical. There is going to be surprises today a communication which comes in and SHOCKS and surprises me. There is going to be a clearing away and PEACE brought to the situation like a suddenly change and then it will be 'A NEW STORY TOMORROW.' Things are going to just suddenly Boom CHANGE!

[The STAR as well is to finish off so this is about [feeling akin to a woman today who is over-powering, feminine or seductive and this woman may be 'a Wish Fulfilled' and someone that I would really like to speak with someone I get a lot of knowledge from and I feel direction and someone I feel connected to and can assist me with MY LIFE PURPOSE AND DIRECTION and very akin to 'A SPIRITUAL CONNECTION.'

– [The Star is about having a vision for the future so this person may have a vision of what they want with me and feeling hopeful in their Heart looking for a direction and guidance and so there is going to be a TRANSFORMATION IN LOVE today. This is such a 'Twin Flame' 'Soul Mate' connection and where they are at with me and seeing 'WISHES BEING FULFILLED' today means a great deal to me. I finally have Abundance and the energy of today is limitlessly Abundant. There is no end to Prosperity and there is no end to LOVE today and I will enjoy the beauty of life. My supply is unlimited, and blessings are coming to me.

My supply of whatever I am needing right now is there for me waiting to be claimed.

It is unlimited and there is no end to the bounty of my life. There is no end to the Abundance & Prosperity. If I don't feel very abundant or prosperous in my life then I need to 'redshift' my thinking and how I treat my money and how I think about everything in my life and between a millionaire or a very successful person and I will notice it is very different. 'One of them is conscious and realizing that the Abundance of Love & Money is not unlimited in their life' and 'The other person is feeling like they can never get on top of it' so there is a difference there. I may need to shift my energy as well and the supply is unlimited today. It like I CAN JUST KEEP PICKING THOSE FLOWERS FROM THE GARDEN and that I CAN KEEP TAKING AND TAKING AND THERE IS NO END TODAY. That is a great part of the Abundance.

There is a [SOUL CAGE] meaning 'Rescue & Escape from captivity & restrictions. So, I am busting it out today that has kept my energy blocked and has held my voice back.

Someone may be coming in today to rescue me and they're going to come in and pull me right-up out of all that negative energy of all that darkness and all those problems and conflicts in my life and then it's gone straight away.

Through Time and Tide Patience is necessary for today and to wait and see how I'm feeling. I am particularly dreamy today and fantasizing about Romance and Cupid's Arrow strikes, and the past is now behind me. I will Release it and Embrace New Possibilities. A new path is now available to me and I'll follow it with FAITH and see this is a New Beginning and as I noticed the 'Doves' today which is significant and coming out of this dark energy. The past is now behind me and I AM BREAKING FREE OF WHAT KEPT ME CAPTIVE AND RESTRICTIVE.

I'll say to 'my Friend' 'Soulmate -Twin Flame'

- "Let there be closeness between us, but always give each other space."
- "Love never claims it simply allows and gives."
- - Only time will tell

"I bring in 'Forgiveness' and I have stopped focusing my energy on past events for life is too precious to waste. I can create my reality by what I think through dreams & imagine."

My Spirit Guides are strongly letting me know that the past is now behind me so this is the time to bring in 'Forgiveness' and stop focusing my energy on the past events because there is a 'NEW PATH' available to me and I have "PASSION". - "A magnetic and seductive quality surrounds me at present that has an overpowering seductive and alluring feminine energy and essence that I feel drawn to IT COULD BE ME. There is a very magnetic lot of abundance energy in the air braking free of restriction's and energy blockages 'healing' my empathic heart and showing me the ability to understand and share the feelings of another.

I began receiving a 'Divine' calling of Spirituality to do 'Intuitive Healing Work' spreading 'Good Will' & Peace' to all Souls with 'Love and Understanding' and this is where it all began unfolding and this is THE STORY of MY LIFE:

I CAN SEE NOW HOW THIS TREE is TRANSFORMED and what it wants me to be aware of. We are all 'Transforming' and there are SEASONS that we transform through.

It is like this 'Timeless Earth' and knowing that I am 'Forever Transformed.' There is not a moment in time when I have stopped and to really 'Embrace it' and to 'Treasure it' and to really 'Focus on it even at the very 'smallest change' and the way I see myself or my place in the world.

With new Ideas, solutions, opportunities, and creativity and all abound pieces that I know exist in the abundance bound for me.

The Universe is limitless! I could see that it is coming and on the way. When I do all the hard-challenging work overtime continuously to find the wisdom of this positive outcome I will achieve abundance. What is my future outcome?

Well, I only know the 'Spiritual Path' that I am guided on and what the Universe is bringing to me. I had not read any books and did not know anything other than what the Universe was providing me and I began 'Thinking Backwards' in TIME exploring my thoughts in the sub-conscious and looking for TRUTH. "THINKING BACKWARDS" I was a little confused from the teachings of what I learned when I was a kid and in the differences today when I explored my thoughts of the past I found that I was spending more time in my life with struggles of FEAR and HOW OTHERS UNDERSTOOD IT. I had let FEAR to be instilled through THEIR LOVE INTERPRETATIONS WITHOUT

SENSITIVITY AND UNDERSTANDING and as a child FEAR WAS PRESERVED INSTEAD OF SENSITIVITY AND LOVE.

– If we are EXPLORING OUR 'SPIRITUAL PATH' MADE FROM AN UNDESIRABLE SITUATION or from an unfounded belief that has continued indefinitely while we are FIGHTING AGAINST THE FORCES OF FEAR - then it's hard to share one's intimate thoughts and feelings on a spiritual level and our common interests with work and income on the vibration of Love.

FEAR IS ALWAYS IDENTIFIED WITH TIME meaning I either have too much time with something I don't want or I don't have enough TIME with the things I do want or I'm afraid I'm not going to have enough time to be where I want to be. So anytime we are in this type of FEAR we are in the VIBRATION THAT CREATES SUPERSTITION and it's all about TIME. Worldview 'Beliefs' of 3rd Dimensional Religious Paradigm are in the framework of SUPERSTITION.

I see from the viewpoint of Source that everything is occurring to help me expand and that everything has been created to lead me in the direction of Destiny. That will be far more fulfilling than even the things that I can dream-up and desire. What I manifest is pre-determined by certain markers in history and what I'm meant to have and not have and is based on what inspires my sole to manifest.

The Universe has a plan for me and all of reality will benefit from my existence just by me dwelling in this body. I am taking this moment to put aside all the busy work all the Micro-Managing and just be in GRATITUDE in all and in recognition of my 'Inheriting Perfection'. This is a moment of SINCERE HEARTFELT ACCEPTANCE. I take this moment TO CELEBRATE Me as all existence celebrates THE TRUTH I AM.

As I began to love myself, I understood that at any circumstance, I am in the right place at the right time, and everything happens at the exact right moment.

New Beginnings, New Places, A New Fresh Start! It's a new door opening and a new chapter in life. I am focusing on my dreams and I am getting my new beginnings, love wishes and success. Today I know THAT IS LIFE!

"May you be safe. May you be happy. May you be healthy. May you be well."

Buddhist loving-kindness

The MIRACLES of LIFE happen to those who believe in them.

I let go of the old and open myself to the new. A new day of opportunities are coming my way and filling my creativity with peace and abundance.

You cannot have Truth without Trust.

To the Divine Source, God, the Universe the Archangels of divine light my Spirit Guides, Angels, & Guardian Angel Family Members and Friends - "I deeply 'Thank You' from my heart for your guidance, and for your mutual support and personal empowerment, in helping to bring Spirit to fruition with the abundance of 'SPIRITUAL LOVE' and 'UNDERSTANDING' and I AM Deeply 'Grateful' for your confidence, patience and kindness."

I am calm as I feel this is the time for making all recent changes available in the Spirit and being attentive to the problems of others and what is important for me. I wish to make myself available to a new person or 'soul mate twin flame' wishing to come in towards me with their feelings of FAITH HONESTY and LOVE and what they would like me to know with a deeper Understanding.

Conscience Never Dies.

Message to 'God', Source, and the Universe:

"Love in Him I live in him, am him, am him-as-me Ecstasy makes pronouns swim Snow met: gardens start swarming." Dedicated to Poet Jalal-un-Din Rumi

"When I trust in myself, I am trusting in the 'Wisdom' that created me."

The first 'award-winning poetry' I created are personal REFLECTIONS

With my deepest heartfelt Recollections of Family LOVE."

'RECOLLECTIONS'

I remember the silliest things ... golden glimpses, nostalgic scenes.

Dotted Swiss dresses, white pinafores, new black patents never worn before. The many paper dolls we called our very own,

- They were little people ... we traded, and we loaned. The middle hours of night ... teatime party of three,
- By special invitation ... sister, brother and me. Remember our ducktail bobs? Those colored, rolled-up jeans?
- Can you believe we ever wore Cracker Jack 'special prize rings?'

Hanging by our legs from that red apple tree,

- Upside down on a limb ... eating apples you and me.
  The summer lightening bugs dancing in blue mason jars,
- Made love beams throughout night ... lights of a thousand stars.
  Two wildflowers, always together, seen yearly in fall blooming pastures,
- A child's love story, Mother told, of Golden Rod and Purple Aster.

The glass perfume bottles made from a special mold,

- Hand-tooled with his love ... Dad made for us to hold. Heart full of recollections, the magic of Mother's face;
- Her hats lined with miracles ... hankies bordered with lace. A kaleidoscope of events, the clashes I do regret,
- With no defense, but respect ... the past and present have met.

Copyright 1991 Patricia Ann Monroe Harbour
"My deepest unconditional love and respect to my parents for giving me the motivation and maturity to move forward through life's process. I have worked to understand and accept who I am and who I may become in the highest manifestation with Confidence, Compassion, and Wisdom and finding Peace which unites me with Soul.

-In Separation of Soulmate Twin Flames -

I began surrendering to the change the Soul was guiding me to do with feeling free emotionally and spiritually free from the past and all the things I had been holding onto.

Big issues were coming back from the past with thoughts, emotions and spiritually. Going within to do the work, there has been an internal shift. I have put a lot of time and energy working through stability and growth. There had been a lack of growth in connections with love relationships and I've decided to move forward with new beginnings letting go of burdens that I have been holding onto for so long.

Some of what I've been holding onto I felt was not my own energy and was attached to someone else. It has been a cycle that I have been going through and entangled with another's karmic thoughts and emotions and it's tripped-me-up on my path. It doesn't mean the other person is karmic because everything is karmic in what we think about in our own energy and in the intent of the moment and now, everything is playing out. There is an awareness as to what we are willing to take-on and what we are not willing to take-on. I began to feel an awareness and a division from an attachment to this energy that's been blocking my manifestation and growth with a new beginning to BALANCE from a period of IMBALANCE. I get pulled back into that old thought process the old experiences and it has triggered those ups-and-downs and back-and-forth thoughts I've had for quite a while. I must begin releasing the causes that made massive changes in my life I'm in separation with as a soulmate and someone who has been a huge part of my past.

I've had a karmic attachment to someone in thought and something I kept going back too and couldn't let it go. It came up in my awareness and has been blocking me in my past. I had to tune-in emotionally in how my emotions were clouding my thoughts and affecting my energy with pulling me back and forth and blocking my energy from a new beginning with a manifestation needed to heal. Any 'Soul Contracts' we have with people will need to be set internally and with the things I was not trusting intuitively or emotionally.

Guidance came through God, Source and the Universe with a change in happiness. I have been standing on my own for several years in the physical separation ever sense my husband passed. After going through the eternal battle and the thoughts I had with this person from my past, I began focusing on home and stability and I saw a foundation for myself.

Everyone in life has different karma and different lives we move into with different intensions and we all have 'free will.' Through my realization, someone I've been dealing with has their own 'Timeline' and their own karmic path that they have to go through and have to experience and it's not up to me to take on their karma, their energy and their thoughts and their fears. It can block you from moving forward. This is something I didn't realize in the past and it was blocking me in some ways. Now, I am gaining a lot of psychic ability of what I've been dealing with in my awareness and thoughts.

There is a lot of movement going forward and I'm directing my energy in the way I want it to go. Change is coming in with my initiating and guiding the action with my worth for how I create resources for myself and stability, my homelife and my foundation. At times, 'Creatively', I felt lost in dreams generically and I tried hard to force things in what had been clouding my thoughts in the past.

There has been a lot of inner work and reflection on the root cause of my emotions and causes that have been coming up and triggering my reactions. I want to move forward, and I have been trying to leave the past patterns behind, consciously redirecting my energy and being aware of what I'm directing. Because of my 'PAST PATTERNS' of experience that I had fallen into my emotions were directing my awareness consciously from the past and especially with a certain person I had this difficult experience with and that I have not been in contact or in communication with. I'm guarding my feminine energy and especially 'Sexuality'.

Our relationship needs to go to the 'NEXT LEVEL.'

The other person is now seeing my worth and the energy of our connection in the past; and how it has affected the past in my life.

There is something unfolding in 'Divine Timing' and it feels like 'A Power Moment'. I am meant to put myself out there in some way. There is a change and it could be 'a creative project' I'm putting myself out there for a positive moment in changes with the Truth in some way. I'm sharing 'MY TRUTH' and something that I'm interested in that I haven't moved forward with yet. There is someone initiating a positive change for me that I can create and move forward. There is a Reunion here A SPIRITUAL REUNION like Waking-Up.

I have psychically and telepathically linked-up with someone I'm reconnected with but instead of being a burden it's with someone in control and understands this connection in a non-physical place and also directs the energy in a positive way where my path and the 3rd dimensional vice remain grounded. So, this has been a huge development from the psychic contact. I am dealing with a connection from in the physical and even though they are aware of this, they are not saying. There is definite a connection on their path, but the other person is where they are and needs to be currently. They are fulfilling their Karmic path! They are not thinking in this way and are very focused on their money and career. They are wrapping-up some sort of court situation that has ended and they feel a relief but they also feel there is no new beginning. So, they are NOT ready to take 'a leap of faith' just yet for it feels like it is a 'Soul Karmic Contract' and feeling a relief but not ready to take a 'Leap of Faith' or make a decision and are unsure which decision to make.

There has been an ending with this person. There is a change in this cycle in this connection and the role we are playing with one another. It's more of a 'spiritual' thing. We are both playing out distinct roles, but we are connecting 'spiritually, psychically' and it is part of my cyclic evolution but my partner is playing a different role and is playing out different lives.

When it comes to this person's growth period it feels more confident. This person is going to offer something emotionally but they are not going to open-up just now. They are more focused on finance and career and moving away from difficult thoughts, moving away from illusions That means a lot of things are coming up and have crystalized in the form and structure of reality that they need to dissolve and a change for the better in a cycle that has been a battle. Someone, a Gemini, felt tired. They have been trapped in their head so they have been thinking about everything.

How are they seeing me?

They are seeing me in my power and very aligned with them and are so aware, it's causing some FEAR. It's like being intimidated and having a lot of opportunities and an ability to grow. It's like they have watched me go through a cycle of feeling stuck and unworthy to move on in my life and move forward and then coming up and standing in my power. It's not something they are seeing physically or having come in contact but they are watching me and getting information on me somehow and 'the Soul awareness.' So, it's something that keeps coming up in my thoughts and with something that I'm achieving with that TELEPATHIC AND PSYCHIC KNOWING. I must trust it when it comes to certain things. I am very connected with this certain person because of the heart and with both our transformations and wellness for one another.

There is a lot of passion and desire and a lot of thinking about this with a lot of desire to connect intimately. If this is someone from my past, I had a connection with then there's a lot going on. In the non-physical realm this person has a realization and it happened very quickly. This could be a new person and not in full capacity. They wants to have contact and they're trying to get themselves set-up in 3-D life.

WHAT IS THE ISSUE HERE?

They just found there's been a lot of delusion and there is now A LOT OF CLARITY with either a lot of REGRET or JUST FEELING STUPID and that is an issue for them. They got caught in DECEPTION and things got out of hand RIGHT INTO A TRAP and feel they put themselves into a tricky situation and now they feel trapped and their guilt is in their internal self. This person is hiding it from the world and especially since they are alone and not in their power. Now, it is coming up emotionally.

They are feeling they cannot make an offer and it's torn them up emotionally inside. There has been a lot of conflict and there has been a lot of people involved. This person is having a lot of endings with this group. They've had a lot of passion and desire for quite a while to move forward and to initiate change and they feel like they have an audience and people are watching what they do or say or they have to behave in a certain way and they come off as very COLD. They were caught but at the same time, they try to come-off as they have won the Victory. The internal self is feeling very sad and unsure.

A TRUTH HAS COME OUT and a person knows and wants to see something in a separate way than what it is and it has to do with them walking away with an Ending! There has been issues with the home and business and with growth and finances and a lot of cold detached feelings of guilt with something in the past and some TRUTH that has come up about DECEPTION that was ALREADY KNOWN WITH THIS PERSON AND THIS SITUATION where there was LOVE and the karmic love of three. Someone has been refusing to look at the situation for what it is and deciding whether to leave. [This must be removed from the situation for this to elevate to the next level].

This could have been a decision that was made and is now aware of the connection and the games played in the higher self by giving into desires with their lower nature which happened in their connected relationship where there was a lot of Love. There is 'UNCONDITIONAL LOVE' between the two of us and they are learning WHAT LOVE IS and in whatever has taken place through this separation.

There definitely has been AN INJUSTICE on my end, and because of this, I feel like my ship is not going to come in OR there is going to be A CHANGE with this connection. It's a feeling that there isn't going to be TRUST AGAIN and BALANCE with this energy. The energy is very nurturing and very caring and giving time and energy but it's like NOT SEEING ALL THE CARDS, THE MANIPULATION THE WRONG DECISIONS THE COLDNESS AND AWARENESS OF ALL THIS AFTER THE FACT. It's like the playing out of a lot of things unconsciously BEING MADE AWARE of things and (the catalyst) promoting the breakdown and the feelings of the person I'm dealing with here just beginning to go through the process of AWARENESS and what they have been unconsciously creating.

Seeing THESE PATTERNS of reflection has taken me back a bit and there is a lot of pain here. This has not ended with this person but in their world, there is victory with any interference dealing with a lot of external stuff.

It's like a lot of predestined things they had to experience and what they have chosen to experience. It is part of their path and it is part of what helps them here SPIRITUALLY, EMOTIONALLY AND PSYCHICALLY to grow 'IN STABILITY' around and within themselves. It is part of the work they must put in to help them see something they haven't been seeing. It also helps them to TRANSCEND SPIRITUALLY THEY DO HAVE VICTORY and they are wanting to come in but there is A TRIGGER showing-up and whether the other person has gotten into another relationship with somebody and A CHANCE with a positive thing or a health thing or the Universe is showing them the things THEY MUST CLEAR-UP WITH THE OUTCOME OF THE 3RD PARTY.

Spiritually gifted I am just awakening to my spirituality and divinity with an overall energy on the spiritual path being all about Relationships and Connections.

With this overall energy, this spiritual path and journey has a lot to do with healing and connecting different relationships in my life. It is also where I'm connecting into members of my 'Soul Tribe' and meeting new people and instantly clicking and connecting but mostly, there is a deep healing taking place 'Spiritually for Me.'

Sagittarius is known as the 'WOUNDED HEALER' so I am given a tremendous amount of healing for a lot of different individuals helping me to restore a lot of different individuals and different relationships and connections in my life personally.

I've putting in the challenging work for myself to heal and to grow. The waiting feels like I've been spinning my wheels with the effort and of what I've been doing here. Is it ever going to take off? There seems to b e a lot of work to be done yet. There are great rewards for me and a lot of 'healing' like the reconnecting of relationships with people I have lost touch with.

I began having repeating numbers coming out and spirit is talking to me through the language of numbers. I began to see (11:11) (3:33) (3838) (1:11) (999) (99999) (299) (4:44) and (299) (22:22) are more than just a communication. There are activations going on inside of me. I am being triggered through this repetitive sequence of different numbers, so I am paying attention to how often I'm seeing the repeating numbers, and the sequences of (111) and (999) are more of a common sequence. The random number of sequences like (3798) just keeps popping up all over the place. That is a very special code that spirit is giving me because it's not common and it's not easily noticeable. When I see (11:11) everybody sees that number like that and I wouldn't ordinally notice but there is a special code that spirit is trying to give me and to TRIGGER and ACTIVATE my subconscious mind.

The very special sequence of numbers is for something like predicting dates of certain things happening and it's like 'A Prophecies' A Prediction. Some people might think these numbers are 'lottery numbers' and for some it could be true, but I'm not really focusing on that. To me the numbers are 'A Special Code' and it's more than win the lottery. It's 'a predictive' of something quite significant for me and a 'special sign' like a confirmation from spirit. It is like 'okay I trust, I get it, and I understand.

As a 'Sagittarius' it means, "Do the Hard Work!" Spirit is really testing and pushing me and when that is happening, it's because spirit is really growing me, and I'm about to take-off!"

I have conformation that I am being visited by 'PAST LOVED ONES' or by 'STAR BEINGS' and that depends upon 'my personal spiritual journey', my 'belief system' and that I'm open to spirit letting me know that there is visitation happening for me. I really resonate with the 'STAR SEEDS.' To me this is my 'Star Seed Family' visiting me in dreams and even in the day. They are giving me love even if I'm not aware of it and that is what this code is about and the work that I've got to do and must achieve, accomplish, and overcome. They are giving me that support whether it's 'Star Beings' or 'Passed on Loved Ones'. There is a lot of support coming in for me to do this work. This 'SPIRITUAL Quest' or whatever is to get me to the next step and to follow 'THE PROPHECY.'

I am meant to walk through the 'TEMPLE of KNOWLEDGE' I have rites of passage and whatever my craft is there is an 'element' of something that I must do. It is the putting 'Healing' and doing that type of emotional work. Spirit knows it's hard, but I've got to do this and get through this for the next step and follow 'THE PROPHECY.' Then I will come out as 'THE GAYA WORKER.'

'THE GAYA WORKER is a very special energy who is a 'Special Person' here to protect 'Mother Earth' and her entire kingdom and all that inhabits her animals, plants, insects, and marine life. Humans and every sentient thing that has consciousness and that exists on Mother Earth is under my protective hands.

I really resonate with animals and can walk into the forest and know the entire story and history of that forest and every plant and every flower, every insect and every piece of that forest and I can touch and get the essence of its history and its story. THIS IS MY GIFT deeply connecting with animals like 'an animal activist or an animal rescuer.' Also, I find that it's plants and trees and flowers that I really resonate and connect with a 'Special Gift.' Also, the (GAYA WORKER) Is a very special (TYPE OF EMPATH.) Sagittarius, being the 'WOUNDED HEALER' cannot only feel into another and their pain and can feel and can sense it and can bring forth the remedy that quick. Most 'Empaths' can feel and can sense what they can understand but NOT every Empath can because when

I am in the presence of somebody I know immediately the Imbalances that exist within them on every level emotionally, mentally, energetically and physically. It is like I can sense it and can pick-up on it and know the remedy. It's just that there is an element to me that is different, and that I have never felt this before and I'm really struggling. (It's like being a tender waterlily and absorbing and sensing all the vibes around me like this sweet tender energy. However, I can go like (Morph) a special form of character into this crazy beast of a 'Warrior' into the fierce protection of Mother Earth and the habitants of other human beings. This also denotes the (Psychic abilities such as Intuition, Telepathy, Psychometry, Clairvoyance, and their 'trans-temporal operation' as Precognition or Retrocognition).

Most 'Empaths' are very tender, and they can get angry, and can go from being this into that and the way I can protect the fearlessness that is in me that is unreal. I can just lay down my life to protect another person, an animal and anything in danger. I weep at the pain of others and it goes so deep because I am so sensitive and that is why I shy away from this work. An EXAMPLE is like if most people get a little pinprick, they would feel that. But for me, [I would feel like it's an entire knife being stabbed into me.] That is the difference in my sensitivity to a typical 'Empath' and because of this fact, is why I put this barrier around myself.

Spirt says, "You are my 'Special Healer." "You understand, you see, you perceive, you are so sensitive for purpose, so that you can understand and because you are a part of the 'collective consciousness of men.' You experience and you feel into others, into animals, and into the planet itself and you pull all that energy and disseminate information widely into the collective consciousness of man. It's a big job! Not just any soul could handle this. It's intense stuff and you get it."

Spirit says, "You are made for this and you came here for this. You are here to 'Teach love to all' and 'How to love everything.' Everything has consciousness on 'Mother Earth, Gala.' Everything is alive and you are elevating the consciousness of mankind with that knowledge and that information through your extreme sensitivity of perception and experiencing life because you experience and perceive all that gets filtered through and out and up to the All. You are part of the All so everything that you experience, other's experience as well. It's just that you are incredibly sensitive to all the energies around you. It's very important that you take walks in nature and connect with 'Mother Earth' and do meditations and do a lot of grounding work because you have big jobs here to do! This is like it's the heaviest load which tells me how strong of a Soul that you are. Again, this 'special code' and the visitation is coming out under your Intuition of the repeating numbers. It's like, "No, I will not go." It's like Spirit is saying "Yes, it is TIME, and it will feel like a powerful 'four-digit code' when you come into yourself. You are 'Grounded' and you are 'Balanced' and there is no stopping you. This is that inner way that you can 'Morph' into the great protector, fiercely guarding and destroying anything what attempts to harm. You are 'A Very Powerful Energy Worker.' This is your confirmation of that, but you've got to do the work and come into your power and to really ground your energy. With the 'Activation' You are a little overwhelmed by this visitation and by your EMPATHIC ABILITY."

"I just want to shut down and go back to an ordinary life because I didn't sign-up for this." Spirit says, "Are you kidding me? You did because this is WHO YOU ARE! You are so capable Sagittarius and you are 'The Dark Night of The Soul." "Follow the Prophecy!"

MANIFESTATIONS! There is something here I'm not wanting to do! "This Dark Night of The Soul" is what this work is and there is something in me that must be extracted out. It must be released, and it must be let go of.

I'm a bit stubborn because I get very overwhelmed by energies. Looking at (994) and (4499) and (99448 is like all 9's) and like I'm ready for the next step. This is like things are solidifying and manifesting and becoming real for me. So, whatever is this 'Dark Night of the Soul Work' it's time to face that head-on and do the work.

Boom! Spirits got it and I will be so happy. Spirit is going to make me rise so high, that I will feel like I'm waiting for the moment and it feels FIERCE. Spirit says, "Now the moment is upon you, my love and you've just got to let this go."

"The Dark Night of the Soul' is when you've lost the flavor of life but have not yet gained the fullness of divinity. The 'Dark Night of the Soul' is the period of - TRANSFORMATION. It's when those close (little griffons) and what is familiar has - been taken away and the 'new chapter' and 'new beginning' is not yet ours - and we must weather that dark time.

Spirit says, "I know this overwhelms and scares you. I know you don't want to go outside your comfort zone. I know you've been burned and I know you've been hurt but trust me, Sagittarius, you are 'THE WOUNDED HEALER.' Every experience that you've been through has shaped you and prepared you for this role of the "GALA WORKER." Not just anybody can fill those shoes and you need to know that." You go from 'Black & White' and then some more 'RED' Sagittarius, and it looks like life is good." (You see 'Yellow & Green' the Solar Plexus & the Heart) 'grounding' your energy and facing what you must face here so 'You must 'Think Twice.' There are some situations in your life and in the 'relationship connections' that you really activate and 'Trigger' and this is a part of this."

I began thinking to myself "Never Again." "I'm Done with That!"

Spirit's thinking, "Let's think 'Twice' about all you've got to face and as you face this there may come 'A Healing' that you had not anticipated. When you face the work on this, You'll Stand Out & You'll Rise.

Spirit wants to make me 'Rise' and Bloom. I've got to face this 'DARKNESS OF SOUL' and 'Ground my Energy in all the RED!'

I know there is something beautiful on the 'Other Side' and I know this is 'Painful' but I promise to do the work and HEAL what hurts inside of me and as I do that I naturally HEAL others, and rounding my energy is going to help.

In modern culture and adaptations of 'Arthurian legend' the character of 'Guinevere' is a 'Warrior Priestess' sworn to the Goddess of the 'Moon In Her Dark Time' and also known as 'She of the Sword Struck Heart.' Inspirational 'War Leader, Guinevere' is a (berserker) in combat. Despite her iconic doomed romance with 'Lancelot' a lot of modern reinterpretations portray her as being MANIPULATED into her affair with Lancelot, and 'KING ARTHUR' being her rightful 'TRUE LOVE.'

I need to better 'Protect My Energy' about absorbing other people's energies so that I'm only in that 'Space of Deep Absorption' when I'm doing that 'Spiritual Work.' "What is a PINPRICK for one is an entire KNIFE going through my arm."

Spirit is saying, "Ground your 'Energy Better' and learn how to protect your energy. When you're not doing 'Spiritual Work' you're NOT absorbing and it will help you out so much when you're grounding. So, don't 'give up' thinking this isn't for you, because it is! You are meant to RISE."

I don't feel it and it's not impacting me when I'm just trying to go about my normal daily life, and it is really overwhelming me. I feel like when I'm 'opening-up' and doing the work it gets to be so much that I pull back and close off in an effort of Self-Preservation.

-The person I'm dealing with must deal with something in order before the two of us can come together. -

I am the 'Fire Sign' bringing to this situation A Lot of TRUTH. I am 'Opening' and letting them know how I truly feel about this situation. 'Yes' I have a lot of PASSION for this person but is he allowing me to walk in my 'Divine Truth?' I am awake, and my 'Fire Sign' is fully awakened, and I can see the 'Divine Power' between this connection and the victory that we could have by walking in this 'Truth' with the 'Divine Reach of Success.' I am very clear about how this is a gift from 'God.' This 'Relationship is 'A GIFT.'

I have made the 'clear decision' for this relationship but he has not made that decision yet. I know that this is a gift from the Universe, and I know the power of this relationship. The 'other person' knows 'The Truth' as well but for some reason they are still fighting this connection. They could have a lot of healing they must do before this can come forward. They're feeling very guarded and they're not allowing their emotions to be felt because they are worried about the fight, they make that will happen between this decisions. They're very held back and very reserved on their emotions.

'Holy Cow!' This is 'Big Stuff' but the other person is NOT FULLY AWAKENED and this may not appear that Big. There is so much to say here and I don't even know where to begin. This situation has (come together and a part more than once or twice and we can't seem to break apart from each other fully. We come together a lot of times where there's a lot of silence and when we come together, we are all in again but then soon we separate, and this has been going back and forth).

We are coming to the beginning of a cycle where we are reaching out to each other again. There's a lot of messages going back and forth. There's a lot of decisions to be made and some are tough decisions standing in the way of making this choice because it's not an easy one and they have a lot of inner conflict about this decision. They know there is going to be success within this relationship, but they feel also they will have to constantly defend their success and they're not sure if they are ready and willing for this battle to defend their success and get out of a situation they are currently in. So, they are just sitting there. They know that they love me and want to be with me and that there is a very strong connection between the two of us but they're holding on tight because they FEAR losing it. They are worried if they allow their 'emotions to be felt' and make a decision to fight for this connection that they will lose out financially down the road. They FEAR that I'm going to think that they are not enough and don't have enough to make me happy. There're worried about finances to support this situation and support themselves. So, they're being very stingy with their time and with me right now and being very stingy with their investment in this connection and their emotions. They are trying very hard NOT to feel emotions. They are worried that if they allow their self to feel their emotions, then they will know how miserable they are going to be without me and will push them into a place that they will have to do something. So right now, it's very easy for them to numb their feelings but there're getting ready to act because no matter how hard they try to block this out the TIME is here.

The Universe is saying that "I am fully ready so it is going to push into this person's life where they will have to take action and where they are going to be there waiting because I have established and succeeded to reach my full potential at the highest vibration. This is a "TWIN FLAME SOULMATE CONNECTION" where I have fully Healed. BAM! And here we are: So, no matter where this other person is or whether they're ready or not to do the work they are going to get PUSHED into these feelings. They aren't going to be forced to move because we have this blessing of 'FREEWILL' But they're NOT going to be able to fight off these feelings anymore! They're NOT going to be able to fight-off feelings that they have to have me' and invest everything they have in me. They have already been doing this for the last three, four, five, six, seven years and trying to block-out this connection so they can stay comfortably blinded where they are. By my reaching out to them, or vice versa, is causing their tailspin and then it's 'Oh my God,' "I need this person." So now, they've thought about it, they've thought about it, and then thought about it some more and are acting FINALLY. So here we are, Take it or leave it because I'm walking away if you don't reciprocate to the energy that I'm putting into this I am going to remove myself from 'Your Options' and you are no longer going to have a choice. I'll Choose for You! See you Later! -

This is putting them into a 'thinking position.' I also know that I have a huge possibility for this opportunity and a huge abundance with this person, but I also know that there's abundance anywhere and wherever I want to create a big huge abundant life. I can do it because I'm walking in my 'TRUTH' and I'm living 'The Truth' of the Divine. I'm no longer in this confusion and in this state 'that I need this person.' It's now and you know what? If you want to be with me, we can make it great but if you don't I'm going to be great no matter where I am. So, you're either with me or you're not but you better decide, and you better make it fast because I've been waiting here for years and I'm not waiting anymore! -

This is what is causing them to make this huge move because they see me for 'WHO I AM, and I am 'taking charge' of my life. I'm tired of sitting here in silence and I'm tired of waiting on you so I'm going to take charge of my life. You're either going to build an 'Empire with Me' or I'm going to build it without you, but either way I'm Confident and I'm Amazing, and I'm Vibrating so high that I can bring anybody into my life to be sitting at my side with me on 'Our Thrones.' I'm building an 'Empire' and I AM A GIFT from the Universe. I'm building an 'EMPIRE' because the Divine is at my side. I have put in the hard-challenging work and I have 'Healed.' I have let go of so much garbage that this other person has put me through and I'm giving them 'One Last Chance.' -

SO, are you coming with me are we moving forward are we going to live this life of 'PASSION' are we going to choose to be together or are we moving in our separate ways? I know that I have the Confidence and I have the Warmth and the Ability to draw in many suitors. I am a 'Fire Sign' and I have a Confidence about me that people are drawn to me without even trying. I am Beautiful Inside and Out and I have this 'Sex Appeal' and an appeal to people because of my Mind, my Thoughts, and I am Amazing.

This energy is in the first couple weeks of June and the last part of GEMINI season is tough on me. I'm not going to lie with our planetary

'Aspects' and where we are at because it is tough. I am coming through some 'blink turmoil' and I'm realizing that outside forces were just too long. I let this person's opinion and everyone else's opinion and actions determine my happiness and I am finally coming out of that at the end of the GEMINI season and into the astrological sign 'CANCER.' I'm no longer confused. I know I can have an amazing life with or without this person and I'm not whatever this person decides I am. I'm not determined by what this person thinks of me or whether they want to be with me or whether they just want me as their 'THIRD PARTY.' I'm no longer part of that.

- I'm going to be this amazing individual and if you want to come towards me and come with me 'that's Great' but if not, I'm choosing to remove myself as 'AN OPTION' and it's going to be your loss not mine. So, as my outcome, I am manifesting an amazing situation and an opportunity to move this to a place in this relationship that has never been before and because 'I Have Never Been So Awakened.' I have never been so HEALED and I've never been through so much DRAMA and BLANKETY-BLANK!

Looking Backwards "Look how far I've come" and "Look Who I've become." I'm here, ready and willing 'to help' this other person 'HEAL' so the two of us can create a new life together. 'The Tools' I have learned through all the heartbreak and healing, and through all the Blankety-Blank Drama that I've been going through with this person in many other relationship situations and all the lessons that life has thrown at me I have attained SUCCESS in ACHIEVING A LEVEL UP.

There are a lot of dips in the road. There will be a lot of fun times and a lot of tough times Wow that hurts! I took a couple of steps back in the quiet time like a HERMIT. A lot of information is coming towards me and there are a lot of things coming out that this person did but I'm coming out on TOP and ready to start a new life, a new situation, and a new relationship, whether it be with this person or the next.

Little did I know or realize until I found 'Myself' and 'My Soul' in the HERMIT mode that anything I go through is not out of the realms of 'Healing' but because people are just drawn to my 'FIRE SIGN' that is so MAGNETIC. When somebody needs 'Healing' and when they are hurting and searching, they are consciously drawn to me because of the 'NATURAL WARMTH of my HEALING. I am gaining this 'WISDOM' because I've taken a step back from this situation and I'm finding that 'INNER LIGHT' that 'Inner Glow' and that 'Inner Beauty' and it is so drawing to other people. It's like I hold 'THE STAR' in my hand. Not only do I have a 'constant source of healing within me' but I can constantly 'MAKE MY OWN WISHES COME TRUE and that is what makes 'My Magic' so POWERFUL. I now have the tools and I now realize that whatever 'WISH' I want, I have all the tools in my hand including all the 'ELEMENTS' and the 'STAR of HEALING' within me. These 'Two Elements' together are the MAGIC of A MAGICIAN and 'My Soul' in the HERMIT. This is in my outcome and creating whatever I want is mine. Now I know and realize it's because I come from a place of Pure LOVE and Good INTENTIONS. I'm NOT using the MAGIC of A MAGICIAN to fool people and play games on people. I'm using the 'MAGIC' to build my life because I now have the tools to create it and not to fool somebody. It's at my fingertips and I'm becoming this 'transformed' individual like a 'Queen.' It is like somebody who has been through so much blankety -blank garbage and so much hurt, betrayal and disgust that people have put on me through this whole life, I'm finally getting pushed to a placed where I have to 'walk away' or move out of this turmoil and into the 'Hermit' mode. When I come out of that 'Hermit' mode and go through this 'Deep Transformation' and cut all the excrement, disgust, anger and annoyance out of life, I know what is 'True' and what the future holds because I have the power to create it. So, in this outcome, I have attained the 'Highest Level of Healing' and Ascension to this point.

- This other person is now leaving their situation and they are coming towards me to help me create "This New World" because I'm very 'Confident' and I'm creating it with or without the astrological sign of a 'GEMINI.' But no matter what this person is coming to me because they see me hold 'The STAR' for 'HEALING ' and they see 'my warmth.' My Arms are OPEN' and I'm Willing to help them 'HEAL.' I'm going to act with them in 'The Equal VIBRATION' and 'The PERFECT PAIR' so this person is acting and moving towards me. I'm going to help them get out of any situation that is causing them hurt and I'm the one that is 'pushing the oars' through the rough waters to get them out of this situation. I'm going to help them ASCEND to A HIGHER LEVEL and to help them reach this 'Vibration' they are confidently embarking on and to help me. I have 'Congratulations' on my side with getting to this point but I've had to go through some vulgar stuff to cut, divide, and separate from a relationship to HEAL.

- I'm going to act with them because they see that no matter what 'Element' this is, it's an automatically 'Equal Vibration Per Pair,' so this person may be taking action and I'm going to help get them out of any situation that is causing harm. -

- Now another way is in telling the other person to listen and "I love you but if you don't make a decision I'm Out. In my gaining this much knowledge and wisdom and healing, I'm going to create my own prosperity and I'm going to heal my own self and those who come to my 'LIGHT' and I'm cutting myself out of this situation and I'm moving away from you." -

This person will then chase me because I'm going to move away from this situation and the negativity. I am over that and my vibration is too high to deal with this nonsense and they're out. This is when they are going to realize 'I'm for Real' and they will chase me and quickly decide and will follow right behind me and hoping I give them another chance.

- The Gates of Triumph and Success are expanding in my life and I am surrendering to the Journey and releasing control. I can expect wondrous MIRACLES to emerge. 'The Guides' are saying, "It's time to let go all is well." "The Creator is at my side and I don't have to do it alone." "My life is guided and protected."

This is not the time to try and control the details of my life right now. Let it flow. There are times to hold on and there are times to surrender. I am surrendering to the greater forces of the Universe and letting go of wanting control of my future. I'm simple turning the challenges over to the 'Spiritual Source.' The Creator will escort me on my journey. Surrendering is not giving up and I'm not yielding to a force outside myself. I am opening up my 'Soul and Releasing' this hold. I am allowing my creating and creative forces of the Universe to spiral through me which brings inspiration and direction into my life. Sometimes the journey goes in a different way than expected and when it does, I don't resist. There are times you can see The Path and there are times that you can't. Not knowing where I am going can activate Inspiration, Insight and Creative forces through me. I cannot discover new oceans or the distant vistas unless I have the courage to let go of the shore and I don't have to do it all by yourself. Support is all around me. I am opening my heart and allowing it in because it is going to lead me exactly where I need to go.

MIRACLES

Just around the bend a miracle is waiting to happen. I'm releasing FEAR and UNCERTAINTY. I am expecting Miracles and they can come in unlikely forms so I am watching for them and embracing them. I trust all that is unfolding in my life right now is in my highest good and what is expected and realized. The more I become aware of the Small Miracles in my life the more they will grow in magnitude. When I celebrate and cherish they will appear. No matter how small they seem and what others see as 'Ordinary' "I look at my life in 'A New Way.' I'm letting go of the FEAR and allowing the Creator to solve all my challenges in mysterious and wondrous ways. I don't limit the way I think because all is well right now and all will always be well if I allow the Creator to bring MIRACLES into my life. I have Inner and Outer Healings on all levels occurring in my life right now and 'a situation in a relationship is going to be resolved'. I have FAITH that it is happening, and it's time for me to find the source of my challenges and transform as I find Healing Without a Heavy Heart. Even if I'm not aware of it now, I know that I'm 'A 'HEALING FORCE' for others because I hold the candle that lights another person's darkness. If I was aware of what is coming I wouldn't believe it. I like to create all the work of MIRACLES through me, so I just hold on and stay ready.

I am not giving up 'Hope.' I'm guided to my TRUTH and the divine is working through me to where I am exactly and to where I need to be. So, if I'm guided to tell 'the other person' that "I know it's Now or Never," they will come, and they will follow leaving their situation. Either way, the two of us are creating this magnificent life together and I must "BELIEVE IN MIRACLES" because "IT'S WHAT I AM." "I AM 'The Candle in Other People's Darkness' so I AM allowing that flame to burn bright and everyone that is meant for me is coming for me. I'm releasing control and expecting those MIRACLES when I surrender the outcome to Source. MIRACLES really do happen!

My person is finally asking for my take on things and saying, "Sagittarius what do you think I should do?"

"Well, I'm so glad you are finally asking me! I've been unable to help because I haven't been welcome to step in and help and only now after much resistance and distance, I am being asked to help. Well, I would like to support you and all this energy now in line with my personality and I'm free to do so after being given the green light because I have become a Master, and I'm all about Boundaries. I've become a Master in boundaries through this relationship and it has made me 'Up Level' and allow a scope of boundaries with boarders. As frustrating as this process has been for me I've sharpened into the Mastery of These Skills and I can take these resources forward into other areas of my life. I'm saying this 'With Love' so don't get me wrong for it's quite a Sagittarian trait to

'Stampede into Territory' where I might not be welcome and speak without thinking. In the past, I've trampled into boundaries and have given my opinion when it wasn't asked for. This has been 'A Huge Transformative and Dynamic Process between the two of us.'

In the highest embodiment of the TRUTH I'm being presented as the (Bear) which is the king of the 'Earth Realm' but I'm not an earth sign it is the 'Alchemical' symbol' and a very territorial protective energy. I'm not taking my eye off the process that's going on with my partner right now and he could be 'a vulnerable family member' or 'the lover' and someone who's been distant with me. So, my energy is in the protector mode and it's quit militant helping to keep 'worry' from coming through. I'm trying to stay calm and out of things but I'm finding it difficult to do as I'm rushed to the Hospital's Emergency Room twice in one week swallowing BLOOD. I don't want to be giving advice to someone when it wasn't asked for.

I have so many things to say to my person as always and I am the 'suggestive type' of Energy saying, "Hey, let's try this or have you tried that?" I have so many 'tips of advice' and 'words of encouragement' that I'm wanting to give, and it's been drooling out of my mouth like the 'BLOOD' that I am now experiencing and trying to fix.

'The Student' must be ready for 'The Teacher' to be able to speak. My person is finally opening and saying "Hey Sag, what do you think I should do here" or "Will you help me" or "What's your perspective of this?"

I've come through 'this alchemy' and this situation of dynamic interaction. I've learned when to speak and not to speak and I've become a Master without sounding patronizing. I do think I've learned so much through this process that I've been given major sets of 'life skills' and to be able to bleed-through these skills to my 'work life' and my 'family life.' We have taught each other, and this is 'SOULMATE'. It's 'A Teaching Relationship' but 'Mutually Right with Respect' and we both are teaching each other a heck of a lot of knowledge.

I do have a 'Spookiness' a 'telepathic wordless bond' which is romantic and sexual, and I know it is especially around my energy, and all that watery 'psychic telekinesis' that my Soulmate and I both share as a 'Spiritualistic Medium' without contact or other physical means. I seem to be dealing with someone who struggles but doesn't ask for help until its reached crisis level. Their own internal 'Fears' and 'Doubts' have been contractually prohibited from speaking.

This is a type of siege going down in this drama for whatever reason and if this is my romantic partner and Soulmate this GEMINI REBEL is rocking the boat and pushing the envelope and smashing through the sound barrier and shacking-up the established order. They have been biding their time and waiting till the moment is right before sharing what they must share. I think they've sensed that I'm so invested in them in this relationship and that I might be a bit possessive here.

My friend, 'the other person', has nightmares and mental disturbance around them and I've been quite concerned for them. I haven't been saying anything (which has been correct) but with this energy, there is mental disturbance, mental anguish and a lot of imaginary fears, paranoia, and sleepless nights and they are keeping a vigilant watchful eye around me. I think so much of this mental paranoia and physical exhaustion is because they've been really worried about 'how I'm going to react with their message.'

The 'Intention' for energies coming into this is a "Soulful Revolution" and the ending of old paradigms being shifted in relationships and all kinds of disruption and ending things. So now, we are dealing with the Eclipse season and (down is up) so I'm following the 'bubbles up' like being under water and I'm still follow the bubbles-up. Air goes to the surface and this is what I am doing right now to catch my breath because there's a lot of confusion going on right now. Wisdom tells me "There is no place like home."

This is a 'higher power' of coming home to a past life Soulmate. This is 'Twin Flame' energy and a reunion of coming home. This reunion is not just a union. This is a significant and meaningful interaction of past life Soulmates. It is 'Time' to come home to the reunion with my Soulmate. I could be in this energy of not really seeing it or not wanting to see it because it's going to screw with my life. It is the reunion of the 'Twin Fame' the reunion of the 'Soul Mate.' It's a very 'earthbound experience' which is why the resistance is here. It's a 'new' paradigm we are in and a 'new' place like the feeling that "we're NOT in Kansas anymore Dorothy." It's a feeling of 'Higher Power' and coming together through this experience.

I know what my TRUTH is about and 'My Wish' is being granted. I know that this is the right thing for me but there's some people I don't want to leave behind. I think this is apropos and about growing 'BEYOND' the box of what other people have put me in because it makes them feel comfortable, and when I grow outside of the box, the other person becomes very uncomfortable with a sharp pang of JEALOUSY. The jealousy thing is 'ENEY' and I think this 'envious' energy comes out when people feel my 'Good' and feel that I'm going to leave them behind and must stop it, and it's just easier for them to put their blinders on over their eyes so they don't see it.

My wish is coming towards me but they are still focused on the past and the 3rd party situation. We are in a place where we are 'Up ending' the 'Wrong Side Up.' It's not that we are going to completely eradicate the existing contracts but it's just that they have a contract with somebody else they are holding onto and their 3-d experiences went way beyond their 'expiration date'. They don't know what else to do and are trying to hold onto that because they find it comfortable. They just want me to stay in 'The Box' and to shut-up about this 'Twin-Flame' stuff and not talk about it.

I'm not that same person and if we are talking about the 3-d my whole entire body has changed. There is not a spark of feelings that is the same as it was twelve years ago in the 3-d world. In the plane of existence of old-fashioned traditional norms things must change. There is no such thing as 'Staying the Same.' Some people who are really loving and wanting to be connected and wanting to stay the same can get a little crazy when I'm moving 'Out of that Box' That is what is happening here.

I'm moving 'Out of the Box' and into a relationship with 'Twin Energy' and into 'A Higher Vibrational Love.' A past life of big 'Soul Mate' Energy is being offered to me 'unexpected' and here I am, very much closed-off. Yet, the past life Soulmate Twin Flame is around me again and coming home into this connection. 'Home is a feeling, and not a place of New Beginnings, and a 'New Direction.'

What is interesting The 'GANESA MEDICINE' Energy in Hindu Spirituality known as one that removes obstacles, but it will also put obstacles on our path and then help us to clear them in an absurd or self-contradictory way. It is like choosing what virtues we would have our wife possess, and all those faults we would desire in her which most lovers would admit that it adds a pleasantly sharp and fascinating, headstrong, stubborn, uncontrollable imperfection to 'the loved one which confusion then makes her perfect.

Yes it's a removal of obstacles but also 'A Strategic Energy' and knows how to put obstacles in our path for our ultimate 'Souls Growth Expansion and Personal Development. 'GANESA' can remove and add obstacles depending on what we need in the given moment. This is SOMEONE that I'm dealing with. This could also be SOMEONE who has the 'Fire Sign' in their sign which is the 'Upward Triangle' and Chemical Symbol for FIRE and of which is my 'element', but it's not me. If this is sexual or romantic I could look at this as 'the head-to-head meeting with 'The Other One' as an absolute full meeting toe-to-toe- on the doorstep. It's uncomfortable but exciting at the same time and it has arrived for me and the lucky break that I've been waiting for years. It's enormous but 'GANESA' is not in the process of arriving for my Soulmate. I've put it on my path and I did it! I've conjured it up out of the (abyss). It's sort of like an Indian 'Arabian Nights' 'genie in a bottle' and It's like "Be careful what you wish for!"

Bearing in mind this is the Other Person coming at me. What is interesting there is 'Ecstasy' and it has flashed-up before because of the 'Trickster' and that is me. I took a gamble of putting my chips on the table and not thinking that it would actually happen. Therefore, I'm suddenly retreating with stage fright. My energy might have been feeling a 'bit sexy' or 'horny' with a few drinks and not in my usual state. Feeling exuberant and a bit reckless in my energy I threw something out there in a reckless, flirting style with the other person and not really thinking that there would be any repercussions from it. It's that kind of energy where I flirted harmlessly and now, I'm being called in to have a chat that is not entirely professional. It's like "Oh god, what have I just said and what have I just done to bring this person stampeding towards me? I think I'm going to be shocked at the immediate response to something I thought wouldn't gain any traction so the response is not only going to be immediate from my partner but overwhelmingly massive. It's like a terrifyingly good start to my week. My energy looks sweet like the Doe (a female deer) which is flashing my 'Trickster Gnomish Self' and has potentially put me in a funny pickle here. It's my life in this partnership and this opportunity is coming into fruition and harmony. I've revealed my cards a little bit flirtatiously and I'm letting something slip. I've revealed my cards and my hand in that very 'gambler trickster way' and now what is happening is that the chips are falling Where They're Supposed to Fall.

They see me as the (muse) and the 'Penelope Dreamweaver.' The textbook definition in the formal title is 'The Inspiration Fairy' and has set armies marching here because of how much I have inspired this person to live a better life or to be with a partner like me. It might not be romantic and this whole thing could be happening in the professional workplace and is coming at me and will not take NO for an answer. They have been utterly captivated and inspired by me and my talent, my seduction, or by My Cheeky Naturalness because this is my 'Sagittarius Energy' that's in its element as an open book. There is something about 'My Cheeky Open Naturalness' that has completely inspired my partner to become fully mobilized fusing and partnering and collaborating with me as my friend and being my Lover.

A roundabout way of saying this is that I know I am perfectly qualified for what they are looking for. I'm perfect for the job without having to do any training and for just who I am as a person not only being enough but being the (X-Factor Level). I've managed to somehow present myself to this partner as having an (X Factor) being a diamond in the rough. This is huge because I've known that I'm a pretty cool lady.

There is something about me that has not been fully appreciated until now and the talent I have and the rare diamond that I am with that gorgeous blinking 'Deer Energy' and the flashing lights in me that I still haven't seen yet as the rare diamond that I am. So this is like I'm going through a 'rising ascent' sign here because of the 'Penelope Dreamweaver' on an elevated shaft and a rising opportunity ascending in an upward spiral rise.

I could be on the process of fusing with a very rich romantic partner and have been spotted as the 'cherry-pick' of his 3ʳᵈ eye, and 'Cherry-picked' by a millionaire or wealth manifested in terms of highly influential people. I have manifested a 'GANESA' partner or group of people here who are members of the 'mystical knightly order' like in the 'Star Wars' films trained to guard 'Peace and Justice' in the Universe. In my specific case, they want to open doors for me because they can see my 'raw talent' and the raw materials of 'Who I Am' which is so appealing. This personal 'GANESA' energy is one of the best-known and most worshipped deities in the 'Hindu' pantheon and I am offering it to this person to work with. They have been searching a long time for a partner like me and a colleague or a friend like me that they can work with because I've got all the raw natural traits, qualities and talent of my 'sparkly diamond self.' My GANESA partner has all the resources and the backstage pass and the financial stability.

With our true powers combined as a couple we're looking at a 'Power Couple' here and a power alliance. My wishes have come true, 'Conscious Alchemy' is like 'Genie in a Bottle' style. I know our union is imminent, but the masculine still is not here. Inner desires are going to be revealed in July with the 'New Moon Solar Eclipse.

The 'Themes' that are coming up with this particular 'New Moon Solar Eclipse' are happening. This is Spirits way of bringing me the message when it is intended for me. I like to use the astrological events as inspiration in honor of 'The Themes' coming through.

'The Theme' is being tested for the 'Collective Divine Masculine' Spirit is calling the Divine Masculine to the mat and calling for them to 'The Task'. (Where do want to go? How badly do you want it? Do you want to do what it takes to get there? Are you going to get things started or are you just going to sit there and wait for something to happen and bring something to fruition?) Are you willing to do the work for this?)"

Themes are coming up in my inner masculine or in my inner feminine no matter which energy I tend to identify with primarily. For Example: I primarily identify with the feminine energy even though there are times I need to be in my masculine energy. It's about being 'In Balance.' I need to look at this through two different lenses to get the most out of it. So right now, it's the 'Divine Masculine' and his commitment that is being tested here.

What is 'The Theme' for this Eclipse and for the 'Divine Feminine?' 'My Theme' is to give rather than take. I'm eager to see how this is going to come forth. I keep getting drawn to two different messages that are screaming at me right now.

The First Message: This is a time to continue to give whatever I'm giving whether it's 'Love,' whether it's 'Attention,' or whether it is 'Energy' to things that matter to me without expectation of receiving anything in return. This truly is 'The Energy of Giving' for the sake of giving and not giving to receive something back. The energy upon which it's given is completely different and therefore, the energetic principles are completely different.

The Second Message for Others: This is learning the lesson of receiving. Ironically enough, I'm hearing that it is time for others to give to me.

THE DIVINE MASCULINE'S PAST LIFETIME TWIN FLAMES 'SOUL' STORY is much different than mine as the feminine. The last lifetime for the masculine was very ungrateful, selfish, and lazy and I walked away I left my Twin Flame behind because of who he was to me. So, this is where there was separation this last lifetime because my Twin Flame wasn't with it and didn't live up to the full potential of what could be achieved and accomplished in this Union. So, I, as the feminine, moved on and walked away as I was offering him everything in the entire world. I don't know, but it may be that he was a very spoiled privileged person and had a lot handed to him or he didn't feel what we two had accomplished together was good enough for him. I see that I walked away from my Twin Flame last lifetime.

What was the 'Life Path Journey' for the Divine Masculine's last lifetime and the 'Life Path Journey' for his Twin Flame last lifetime.

This is so Crazy! The Divine Masculine is somebody who was meant to have a complicated and challenging path and being very argumentative, very defensive, very smug, and kind of a "show-off" like "Look at what I've got."

The Divine Feminine Twin Flame has a 'Life Path Journey' much different. Her life path is filled with a lot more stability and security, and that is why she left her Twin Flame. He just couldn't get it together and was confrontational, ungrateful, and a very hard personality to deal with. It wasn't just with me with all his relationships. It's like he signed up for a very challenging life journey regarding relationships and 'the people relating to him.' So, his life journey looks to be a bit more challenging. However, I feel the feminine felt much more pain and sadness and heartache because she really had her stuff together and was offering her masculine everything he could ever want. It just wasn't good enough for him for some reason.

LOKING AT THE SPIRITUAL JOURNEY and the SOUL JOURNEY and SPIRITUAL PATH of both the Masculine and Feminine Lifetimes and their repeating numbers for the Feminine.

Spiritually the Masculine really did desire to connect with the Soulmate to have 'True Love' but I don't feel the Masculine was able to give and offer what it is he desired at a 'Soul Level.' He couldn't, and his incredibly challenging life journey with connections and relationships gave him 'the life lessons' and 'the soul expansion' and all the 'soul growth' he needed.

Spiritually for the Feminine with repeating numbers, she was very superstitious, and very in tune with the Universe, with Instincts and Intuition, and made choices in her life based on that energy and how she felt. It was very hard for her to walk away from her Twin Flame but felt at a 'Soul Level' all the signs were leading her away from him because this energy was so distorted even though there was a love connection here. It was very 'Out of Balance' and very distorted energy.

Spiritually for the Masculine in the Past Life There is the 'Authority Figures' 'Knighthood' and 'Atlantis.'

With these energies coming through this is more than just his last life with his Twin Flame. What we experienced in this last lifetime is a part of 'A Much Bigger Cycle' and it's really coming forth strongly in your masculine reading 'Gemini.' With the 'Atlantis' being here it's like we have many, many, incarnations on the earth plane with each other. What is interesting as of this last lifetime, (it's like the Masculine was blocked to his 'Divinity) and it is like his 'Soul Tribe' has connection to everybody that really mattered to him in a 'Life Journey.' I feel he was being blocked from this because it had something to do with the 'Soul Growth' he was trying to achieve.) I feel the 'Masculine Knighthood' got into a lot of trouble with the police, and 'Authority Figures' or with 'Knighthood'. We could have been incarnated all the way back to then and that is what is coming forth, but I just see more of 'a very troubled soul' that has a tough time committing and connecting with people in and out of jail and is a black sheep in a sense.

What kept this Feminine around for so long as she was not blocked to the soul connection. She felt it from day one and especially with the repeating numbers, but her Wisdom allowed her the conclusion that her Masculine was 'Not Awakened' and there was nothing she could do about it. He may have even had her moving on and may have been imprisoned or put into jail for the rest of that life journey. There is something that caused this feminine to walk away and move on like she had no choice. It was for her highest good to do so.

To look specifically at 'The Twin Flame Journey' we have shared the last ten lifetimes with Shift Perception Inspiration Repeating Cycles & Lessons Sacred Moments and 'Incredible Heartbreak,' so this brings in your last 'Twin Flame Lifetime Journey', Gemini. It's speaking of the 'Feminine Energy' as a very inspiring, very established and a very mature person in life and in society, etc.

The Masculine 'Shift Perception' again was unable to see or learn properly. It's like there were demons that he had inside and it caused the same thing to happen over, and over, and over, even though there was the 'Sacred Bond' between the two of us, and with moments that were so precious that nobody else could come close in comparing to them. I just feel like whatever was repeating over and over was too much and the feminine walked away and brought her incredible sadness and heartbreak. So, 'The Last Lifetime Twin Flame Journey' was not easy for the Feminine. At least, (When I say the 'Feminine' it is whoever is embodied in this 'Feminine Energy' this lifetime.) The last lifetime was not easy at all because the energy was so distorted between the two and she, (the Feminine) ultimately had to be the bigger person and had to be the 'Wiser' person and how to make the call and walk away, and it devastated her. I don't really think that she every fell in love or connected romantically again with anybody else. It's just what she went through here was too much for her and I really feel like either the masculine was put in jail or was deployed like in the military or moved far away like there was this distance and is ultimately what caused her to walk away from him. 'The Last Life Twin Flame Journey' was very rough and a very painful experience. However, both parties learned a great deal at a 'Soul Level'.

Where were the Energies Left Off at This Last Lifetime? How did they Roll Into This Lifetime?

Synchronicities (33) Love, a sign of Cancer (3) 'The Trinity' sign (333). The way things were 'left off at this last lifetime and what I am feeling is there was definitely some 'Third Party' energy going on in this last lifetime and may have been what led the feminine to walk away. However, the love still existed between the two of us and there was 'Unfinished Business.' Even if this masculine tried to change his ways and begged back this feminine 'The Last Life', she wouldn't go back even if every part of her wanted too she wouldn't. Whatever happened and played out was to tragic and damaging to her. I feel that some of those energies still exist this lifetime even though there is an instant connection when we both meet, there is a lot of insecurity and weird anxious energy that the feminine can't figure out and it comes from just the way things ended. I do feel like there is either 'A Third Party' or there's 'A Third Element' that caused the separation between the two of us. This may even be where it was a family thing like where 'This Feminizers Family' is like you can never marry or be with that 'Masculine'. It's just like business was unfinished and with a 'Third Element' 'A Party Energy' or Person to this situation and it was left that we weren't finished and didn't complete everything that we wanted to get done 'The Last Lifetime.'

What is 'The Masculine's Life Path' for both of us 'This Lifetime?'

These energies are very different once again.

The Feminine is in this life journey intended to experience a lot of new energies and new people and new experiences than ever before. 'In This Lifetime' she finds 'Confusion' in who her Twin Flame is or it feels like in 'The Last Lifetime' and like she's got to walk alone because the Masculine shows same type of energy of being 'In Conflict' and being verbally abusive and manipulative and very sharp with the tongue and always having 'to be right'. Victory and success are the most important thing to this Masculine in 'This Lifetime' on 'His Life Path.' But again, it's like he didn't really learn everything he was supposed to gain from 'The Last Lifetime' and that's why these challenging experiences and relationships and connections will play out again for him 'In This Lifetime.'

For the feminine I just feel like there's a lot of new energies that I'm working with this lifetime and may not believe in Twin Flames or may feel like she's got to walk a lot of her journey alone without her Masculine.

What is the 'Spiritual Path' for both the Masculine and the Feminine 'In This Lifetime?'

For the Masculine there is an (Energy Shift) so that is positive. He is meant to overcome his challenges and struggles this lifetime and it's there SPIRITUALLY.

The 'Spiritual Mission' is on the Feminine side. Again, that is where we're working with a lot of new energies. The Feminine may be much more 'Spiritually' based this lifetime and is really focused on that and that's why she feels like she is walking alone because she feels she has a mission to complete like it's HER CALLING and whether this is in her personal life or a bigger mission for 'Humanity' at large. The 'Spirituality' on her 'spiritual growth' is unlike all these new energies that are part of her experience this lifetime.

The Masculine at some point here is going to SHIFT and he's going to see himself in a whole new and different light realizing 'Who and What He Is' and will really be 'Inspired to Change.' I think it's his 'Feminine' that is the main 'Inspiration' for him to 'Change' and become somebody different and somebody much more positive and loving.

What is 'The Masculine's Twin Flame Journey' for this lifetime?

The feminine of the Twin Flames is being very aware of her connection to the Masculine. There is some sadness and heartbreak that will take place between these Twin Flames this Life Journey, but it's like this Masculine is going to realize eventually (How he breaks his own heart based on his behavior.) This energy does indicate there will be a disconnection between these 'Twin Flames in this Life Journey.' It's a matter of 'GROWTH' and 'PATIENCE' and 'TIMING' before we come back together. Lastly, 'The Spiritually Gifted Feminine' with the 'Spiritual Mission' is showing up and looking at this 'Twin Flame Reunion' and that's pretty much like the 'Ultimate Outcome' for the two of us. There is going to be A TWIN FLAME REUNION THIS LIFETIME. The Feminine is much more focused on 'Spirituality' and may even be 'Very Gifted Spiritually', A Physic Medium Reiki, Healer, Empath. THE FEMININE is 'VERY SPECIAL SPIRITUALLY' and she is AWAKE and is aware of her Journey, and of her connection to her Masculine and just a very 'WISE SOUL'. I feel this because looking at this male and the female It's like 'The Masculine' breaks his own heart based on his choices and actions 'This Lifetime' and 'The Feminine' is being left in a place kind of waiting for her Masculine 'To Grow' and 'To Mature.' During this disconnection, I am very focused on my 'Spirituality' and 'Spiritual Growth.'

'My Spiritual Gifts' with 'Understanding Life' from this perspective I'm here as the Feminine of Twin Flames and the sign of 'Sagittarius' my 'Fire Energy' and astrologically opposite to my 'Gemini's 'Air Sign'

I see our Twin Flames coming back together in 'Reunion' because this is a temporary disconnection and not meant to last the entire duration of our lives this lifetime. Our last lifetime, I feel that we were ripped apart from each other for some 'Third Party Factor' Influence and now in 'This Lifetime', the Masculine needs to 'Grow-Up' and 'His Own Choices' are ultimately going to break his heart' which 'Wakes Him Up' and then we will come back together in this connection and 'Fulfill' our 'Twin Flame Journey this Lifetime'. So Dear Gemini Remember, 'After every storm there is a rainbow,' no matter how long it takes to show up.

THE SAGITTARIUS SOUL STORY TWIN FLAMES PAST LIFE -

I intend to look at 'The Journey' that my Twin Flame and I were experiencing 'The Last Lifetime' and the different lessons and 'Soul Lessons' that we were working on as well as how that energy plays into 'This Lifetime.'

There was awareness of the 'Twin Flame' connection in this 'Last Lifetime.' We both were very successful people this Last Lifetime' but more independent of each other rather than being super 'Emotional.' It's not saying we didn't love each other but just that we both were very successful people in life. The masculine could have been well known for whatever it is that he did professionally but with me being 'The Feminine' I held my own as well. I paid my bills and handled my own business. I didn't need anybody to help me in life. We both were very independent and powerful and strong on our own. So, if we were married, 'we weren't sharing resources.' There was some sort of 'barrier' which I didn't understand.

Again, the two of us come through as very strong personalities. When we fought, we would fight with intensity that caused 'a lot of conflict' between the two of us in our past life. It's like we just couldn't figure out how to get along and there was a lot of 'misunderstanding and arguing'. It's like together we would have been extremely 'powerful' but we both were so driven in our passions, in our career, in our life and who we were and that caused 'a lot of conflict.' It wasn't like a more dominant personality and a more submissive personality we both had incredibly 'dominant personalities'.

The 'Soul Path' for 'This Last Lifetime'.

The Masculine is coming through as having (Love Lessons)

The Feminine is coming through as (Ego hold) WOW!

The Masculine was a bit of 'A Playboy' and that had a lot to do with the fact of his 'status, power, prestige, money, and the family he is born into. He is 'A Playboy' but partly with that is with (Love Lessons) this 'Last Lifetime.' He was learning a lot about 'romantic love' and he gained a lot of 'Emotional and Spiritual Growth' through all those experiences. I don't think there was anybody he loved more than me, as the Feminine, but it's like he couldn't and the way other women would fall to his feet and put up with his second-rate negligent appalling ways.

I, being 'The Feminine', having pride, ego, and being very strong, very stubborn didn't need anyone who would cross me, even if he was my Soulmate. It was like "Who are you trying to play?" Being a very independent woman I feel 'the barrier' between us was that this Masculine 'screwed-up' and tried to play me the way he played everybody else but I saw right through it and I wasn't standing for it. I was willing to 'cut him off' and 'cut him out' of my life even though I had never loved and connected to another man more. He was 'A Playboy' and I couldn't deal with that emotionally.

What comes through in 'This Past Life' is 'Medicine man or woman' and 'Atlantis' and 'Asia.' One or both of us were doctors. There is a very talented power here and a lot of 'power money' things. Also, with 'Asia' coming through, one of us or both of us could have been of the 'Asian descent' in our last incarnation and lived somewhere in Asia or in a different Asian country and someplace like (Japan, China, Korea, Thai, Vietnam or from so many other countries that we could have originated from or lived in 'This Last Lifetime'. The 'Ethnicity' was that of 'The Asian Descent' and I do feel that goes both ways with us.

I feel we both were very driven and focused on our careers. We both could have been doctors, but I feel the fact that with 'The Masculine Being A Playboy' and 'The Feminine Being Very Independent' and with the feeling, "I'm not putting up with that" was the cause of the fighting and misunderstanding with arguing and not getting along.

The 'ATLANTIS' coming through of which I have had these feelings for many years says to me that this 'Twin Flame and I' have had many incarnations on the earth plane and that there are other planes in which we can incarnate and exist. However, for the two of us, a big focus has been on the earth plane in our journey here and it goes way-way back. We both are very 'Wise Souls', so 'In This Lifetime, we could have that 'strong personality clash' again because we're not these same 'wise powerful beings' like in 'The Last Lifetime' and suddenly then that just goes away. "NO, I'm told that we both are very 'Powerful Wise Beings' with 'Spiritual Talent' and even in different rites of passage, there's 'Magic' about the two of us even into this lifetime."

THE PAST LIFE TWIN FLAME JOURNEY

I feel that 'Our Independence' is relevant and quite important so I'm looking at 'The Twin Flame Recognition and Soul Consciousness.' I really feel like my 'Soulmate Twin Flame and I' have never connected with anybody else more than we connected with each other in a past life. However again, It is like there is 'this barrier' and it feels as though 'This Masculine' could tell 'This Feminine' "You're the love of my life" and "You're the only one I ever want to really be with to the end of my days" and he is still in other female's beds. It's as though this was the love of his life and everything else was just me as the side-dish the fun the lessons 'the love lessons that he's working on' and that 'This Feminine' really pulled back from 'This Masculine' and didn't care if she was the only one he ever really wants to be with to the end of his days with saying "you've burned me" "you've betrayed me and that's that!"

I just feel like we've both never loved anybody else more and have never felt connected to anybody else more. And again we are 'Spiritually Connected' and that's just 'The Confirmation' of the MAGIC about each one of us and the 'Wisdom' that exists in 'our Souls'. It's just that this Masculine had a lot of 'Love Lessons.' Unfortunately, having to go through that 'Last Lifetime' I'm looking at how we both ended things and if there is any unfinished business from this period.

I am feeling 'Very soon' we will have 'Growth' and we will have the future 'The Unknown'. Spirit wants me to see 'The Quantum Reality' of things going on and I told the 'spirit guides' "that is way too deep for right now." The way we both left things there was still a lot of 'growth' that needed to take place, which obviously pours over into this lifetime and with the future. This is where Spirit is not giving up any information. It's like "No the future is unknown because it's Magical and they don't want to ruin the element of the surprise or the growth or the change of mind about anything. So, this is showing where we left things. Again, it feels like 'that barrier' where we weren't together, but we weren't necessarily apart. It's just like we were two stars circling each other in a 'binary system.' It's like you can't get too close. I feel like that's where things were left off. There were still lessons of growth that had to be lived and learned this last lifetime and that comes into this lifetime.

My Gosh! 'The Masculine' is the playboy again. 'The Feminine' has very similar energy focused on career. Again, I feel 'In This Lifetime', if 'This Feminine' can't make it work and get it right with 'This Masculine' then I would rather just focus on my career and make money and focus on me. It doesn't mean I won't be with anybody else, but I just don't feel like anybody else in this lifetime will have my heart but 'This Masculine'. I feel he's coming through 'that energy' because that's 'The Love Lessons' again and I see here that he has more of that to work through.

What is 'The Spiritual Path' going on 'In This Lifetime' for both of us?

I see the 'Illuminated Mind' for the masculine and the 'Galactic Family' for the feminine. So I really feel that the masculine is going to master these love lessons this lifetime because if the masculine has the 'illuminated mind' there's a point in this Twin Flame journey with me where he is going to come into a deeper level of maturity. The Galactic Family being the 'spiritual path' for the feminine in this lifetime is somebody who is very tapped into her Spirituality going all the way back to that 'Atlantis' period. At some point in my life, I'll stop my first career and switch to a career spiritual based practice along those lines. With the 'Galactic Family' showing there I am very connected and tapped into the 'higher realms' to pass down to loved ones and my spirit guide 'star beings.' I'm not feeling like that was as relevant to me the last lifetime even though I knew I was a 'Wise' being. It comes forth much stronger in this lifetime and I really feel like I'll either do a side hustle of some Spiritual work or it's my full-time job at some point in this lifetime.

WHAT IS THE TWIN FLAME JOURNEY FOR US THIS LIFETIME?

I see the action of 'HEART ENERGY' for 'The Masculine' and the 'SPIRITUALLY GIFTED ENERGY' for 'The Feminine'.

So, there it is as 'MY CONFIRMATION.'

With this action of 'Twin Flames' if there is separation between us I feel like we find our way back to each other. It's just that there's some 'PRIDE and EGO' that needs to be overcome in me, 'The Feminine.' And there is 'The Playboy' energy that needs to be overcome in 'The Masculine'. But also, we have this 'KARMIC CONTRACT.' I feel like we almost marry other people but there's something that pulls us back at some point in our Journey because of the action of the 'Twin Flames.' This is where 'The Masculine' is 'WAKING-UP' and I Understand. I'm going to do whatever it takes to get back to my 'Twin Flame.' Again, I just see 'The Feminine', doing 'Spiritual Work' this Lifetime having 'A Spiritually Based Practice' of a kind. I am 'Spiritually Gifted', and I don't feel it was as highlighted 'The Last Lifetime' for 'The Feminine' or 'The Masculine'. Once we both fulfill our KARMA CONTRACTS 'This Lifetime' there's 'AN AWAKENING' that happens and our joining together is of a much different nature than it was before because 'The Feminine' is going to be so well-versed in HER SPIITUALITY HER INTUITION HER INSTINCTS and it's like 'This Masculine' could never cheat on me or play with 'My Heart Again.' I would notice it before he even had the thought in his mind, and what that is about would be a very different experience. It's like these 'Twin Flames' come back together later in life in their fifties, sixties, seventies, or eighties, and nobody wants to hear it like that but that is what it is. It's like we have a lot of KARMIC ENERGY that we're working on and I don't mean 'Bad Karma' like we are being 'Paid Back' for something. NO, it's like a deep lesson because we are such 'WISE SOULS' and we go all the way back to 'This Atlantean Period'. We have been incarnated on the earth plane and I feel we are joining as 'TWIN FLAMES' LATER IN THIS LIFETIME and it is more about 'Spiritual work' on both sides where we both give 'Our Heart and Soul' to Spirit and we vibe very equally in that space like the "Crystalline Children."

"Beneath Winter's Crystalline Snow Lies 'The Seed' of Spring's Kiss of Sheer Bliss Opens Its Plush Petals and Become A Rose in Full Bloom" Patricia Harbour, Author and Poet

I Am the 'Fire' sign of Sagittarius creating something and feeling a bit anxious to get it started. I'm told to be patient in whatever I'm trying to build or whatever I'm trying to influence that grows so near and dear to my heart. This is a very special time for me because there is something within me that is like the small BUD of a flower developing and growing roots from beneath the winter's icy snow and breaks through with an element of understanding and the freedom to breathe fresh air in a brand-new beginning that gives rise with a place of stability BLOOMING with an external and internal manifestation that I've been working on for quite some time. It's like a flower that is unfolding in the illumination of light opening and blossoming with its soft plush petals and becomes 'A ROSE in FULL BLOOM' in the ecstasy of an overwhelming feeling of Salvation with great happiness and Spiritual Joy.

When I move away from the situation that has brought me down to 'My Spiritual Awakening' now it's time to get out of that and use 'The Awakening' forward power of the Divine for Good. I Am going to receive 'Healing' and by helping other people it's going to bring me even more 'Healing' than what I could have imagined and to a better place than where I'm at when I'm reflecting on my past. I'm helping to share this with others, and it will bring me to my 'Destiny.' The Stars are aligning, and wishes are going to come true.

I have somebody at a distance from me that is coming in for me. I'm manifesting this person as I speak and I'm manifesting my 'TRUE LIFE

PARTNER' not the person who put into 'A Spiritual Awakening,' but the person I'm meant to build a home with and build a life with, and they are being manifested. The 'Divine Timing' is coming so it's time for me to move forward in 'my path' and allow myself to feel that victory. The person, that did NOT ACT with moving towards me Is NOT who I'm meant to be with. The person that I'm meant to be with will make me the husband that will teach me to nurture and love myself. They will come in once I raise my vibration. After I spend time on working on my finances and raising my vibration I'm going to meet this person through doing 'Spiritual Work' and through the work that I'm talking about and it's going to be the person that 'MATCHES MY VIBRATION' and the one who I'm meant to truly change lives with. I'm going to meet this person through working with the Divine and through doing my divine purpose and my Soul's purpose the two of us will build that (Yin and Yang) Balance. The Universe is trying to show me 'THE SECRETS' and trying to give me this 'Wake-Up Call.' Maybe the Contents of this Book that I am writing is my 'Wake-Up Call' but it's TIME I know that I've been hearing this call for some time now and I just haven't been able to let this go. It's time to move into 'My Path' and it's time to help others (out of heartbreak) and (out of sadness).

I know this isn't a whole lot about LOVE but I will meet my 'Perfect' person. I will meet the person who brings me BALANCE as far as my 'Love Life' goes and I will meet them while doing the work of the Divine. So, I'll step into my purpose, and step into my path sharing MY STORY however that path is for me and use 'THIS HEARTACHE' that I've experienced in the past to help people in the future. I truly have the 'Healing Power' in my own hands within me and I'm truly 'the person' that holds 'The Torch' in everyone's 'Shadowy World,' so I'm allowing myself to be this. It's going to bring me beautiful places and it's going to bring me 'Stability' and it's going to bring me the 'Happiness, Joy and Abundance' that can grow for my whole lifetime. I know this is coming in for me and they are at a distance from me right now, but I need to allow myself to move into 'My Spiritual Journey.' 'My Destiny' is calling and it's time to act.

The (Other Person) that was emotionally manipulative and lying about coming towards me in the future and keeping me 'STUCK' and waiting is 'them Lying' and trying to keep me from doing my work and it's time to step into my own path. It's time to make my own plans of the future and allow this to cultivate into my life once I release this 'Other Past.'

This is a Very Powerful Message for me and not a whole lot about LOVE but this is 'My Wake-Up Call' to start doing what is in my Heart and Soul and what 'I am' to do here on this planet. I have an 'Epiphany' of what is in my heart that changes the way I'm looking at valuable things and I'm growing 'Roots' and want to be 'Reborn.' TRUE LOVE comes in many different forms of 'Unconditional Love' and a mother's love is the 'Root of this Tree.' Unconditional Love and Spirituality is the house of MAGIC and a very positive 'Aspect'. The SUN is bringing the light into the darkness and I'll see the lights go on and see CLARITY and I will see 'my path' forward. There has been a lot of stubborn energy and all that patience is going to pay off. The Two Souls the (other person's soul) and mine are agreeing to disagree and there is a deep connection here. My ruling planet, 'Jupiter' has brought me some sort of a completion to the end of a 'Karmic Cycle' that is very slow but steady and it brings Stability, Money and Family, and a lot of Security and Support. This cycle is ending in this 'old relationship' and it brings 'JUDGMENT' and to come to sensible conclusions. Walking through that new doorway now brings 'THE TRUTH.' A message is coming through which promises something that is going to grow and is real and tangible that has potential and something to do with the past.

I keep seeing the sign of (11:11) and this is the new doorway with a message in this Transformation and the new future. I have been holding onto the past like 'a typical miser' standing in the 'hermit' mode and wishing for something to come in and bring 'Change'. I've seen 'the light' and I have become 'the elder' and 'wiser' and I'm coming out very strong. I had been holding back feelings and I've been 'soul searching' to where I'm coming out and ready to act and freeing up my life to act. The Angels are giving me this 'New Beginning' with a 'Wealth of Experience' and I'm going for my desires about someone that's 'passed on' and they are here with me 'in spirit.' I've worked hard through conflicts to expand and 'my spirit' is driving me. I have come a long way and have built on my own something that will be long standing for me. I have grown the 'Roots of The Tree.' I'm all about higher education, Philosophy and the 'love of wisdom' in whatever I've studied and have taken the first spot with the highest mark and honors with overtaking the FEAR and having the courage to do what needs to be done and moving towards it. This (other person) is coming forward offering this information and sending me a message of wanting to get together and saying "Let Talk, Let get together and see what happens." This is truly a reuniting OF ETERNAL LOVE facing the fears and having the courage to be with the person I truly love and leaving behind the old way of thinking and doing things with FORGIVING another person and FORGIVING the one who hurt me with the betrayals, the heartache, and the devastation of the past. I truly feel that both of us are honoring and loving each other and coming back together in this relationship. This is clearly A 100 percent TWIN FLAME SOULMATE RELATIONSHIP.

This change is in the wind and truth is being seen and coming out. It's a new way of living in 'The Divine Order.' Things aren't going to be the way they were in the past. This is the last time that the (other person) is going to walk away and especially with the 'full moon' on October 14th. People are 'waking up' to the TRUTH. "So, what I THINK I HAVE CREATED and can accomplish together is that we are walking and living our 'Divine Truth.' This is both of us coming forward with 'our truth' and not settling for anything less. This (other person) is coming back and asking "to work on things 'you, me, and 'the Divine' and make this relationship with a stable foundation for us to work on this together and stand in 'our truth' and no longer staying in a situation where we can't be who we 'truly are' and see the way that things need to be done. Moving forward and offering me this information is huge, and truly one of 'Eternal Love'. The door of opportunity is countless for us and we are going to show how THIS RELATIONSHIP CAN MOVE FORWARD and live in NEW AGE THOUGHTS not doing things the way that they use to be done. We will show by 'EXAMPLE' the type of 'Love & Relationship' the two of us can create. We are creating an 'Empire' and "Our Mark on the World."

I have come through this 'Spiritual Rebirth' and through the 'Transformation' and I'm spreading 'The Light' to those who need it. This is going to move forward to Victory, and it's protected by the Angels. Someone is coming in with "A Love Offer in an Apology and the Truth." Even though I have not met them yet My SOULMATE is coming in for me. I have recently experienced my life of 'SPIRITUAL

276

TRANSFORMATION' and it is coming in for me. I have FAITH in it and knowing that it's happening and will be here for me because the 'Important Things' are on the horizon.

In the past I've had a misconception of 'manifesting' my desires and I've tried to bend the desires of another and that is NOT a good thing to tap into. I've walked away from the past in a 'Respectful Way' with 'the lessons' I have learned and what my Soulmate has taught me. All this has happened in 'Divine Timing'. I'm meant to attract other new experiences into my life and I'm holding my head high as I have done this in the best capable way that I could. I'm learning by making different choices in the next situation whenever I run into similar circumstances. My 'Soulmate and I' can get to a 'Peaceful ' time later down the line in 'A Higher Universal Way' and I'm trusting in my journey and The Divine way to grow.

There has been a period of pulling back because I've needed to reverse some things about myself and wanting to communicate some truth not felt important before. FEAR was hidden deep within and I am waking-up completely and it's moving towards 'Enlightenment' of where I'm going and knowing what I want to do. I've learned a few things about myself that have been at a distance. I may have been a bit guarded even though I knew what I wanted to do but a bit closed off and pulling back. I am willing to put in the work in this situation to feel happiness. What I've discovered, IS THAT IT WAS NOT THE RIGHT TIME and that I needed to discover things about myself in this Spiritual Transformation. I've learned that I needed to 'STAND MY GROUND' over the things that were facing me with FEAR. I've been fighting in 'A Spiritual Battle.'

I am ready to walk away from an UNTRUTH the untruth about myself and the things that I wasn't really discovering. - This was about putting myself on a pedestal and the things I really admire about myself. So, here I am 'The Feminine' and waiting, while my 'Masculine' is watching from a distance and being inspired. This is about a Soulmate Partnership going towards a Soulmate and 'An Equal Partnership' and seeing each other 'with a sparkle' between us. The clarity here is This IS IN A SINGLE RELATIONSHIP. it's a 'Spiritual Relationship' with 'Enlightenment Balance and Joy that is now coming into this situation.

Through the 'Mercury Retrograde' I am slowing down and looking at things and seeing all the 'Good Things' during this time. 'My Masculine,' which is 'Me' is not rushing and wants the conflict to be over. I've been conflicted and didn't know what to do and I've been reflecting with 'Confidence' to go to battle because I know what I want. Through my 'Confidence' I have created on my own 'an abundance' for myself which is 'very solid, comfortable and a happy place' and I haven't needed anybody. I know I can take care of myself, take care of my family, and live my life in a beautiful way. But, I get this nagging that I want to do something differently and so I say, "Okay, I'm good on my own and I'm happy, but there is something missing here." This is because I need to see something a bit differently with more understanding. Spirit is calling me to be better to be fuller and to be 'Enlightened' with experiencing more than just my Self-Purpose, which is (the 3ʳᵈ dimensional) with having enough depth. I'm being called to a better stage of 'Higher' energy and to discover this about myself and to be 'Enlightened'. WOW! I'm reaching a level of 'Mastery' and feeling like I want to expand and learn something NEW.

I'm feeling good where I am but 'my soul' is bored. My own 'Masculine' and 'Feminine' in me are communicating together. 'My Masculine has been loving from 'his mind' and thinking that he is in love because his 'Heart' has been closed. The Masculine is now getting rid of the one with the 'Logical and Practical Choice' and is now following 'His Heart'. He wants to communicate with the DRAMA of his 'Heart' to my 'Feminine' and has just made the decision to get rid of 'A Logical Choice' for a more 'Practical Choice' and follow 'His Heart.'

My 'Feminine' is also being very clear. WOW! My 'Feminine' and My 'Masculine' are in the same position in their clarity. She is ready to go forward and is very clear and wants this 'reconciliation' with the opportunity to tell the 'Masculine'

what she prefers and what she wants. The 'Guidance' of Attention is significant of 'Mirroring'. The Masculine and the Feminine are both moving out of that 'Mental Energy' realm of thought and into the 'Emotional Realm' of the Heart. YEAH!

How is the Mercury Retrograde shifting the 'Masculine' and the 'Feminine' in Me.

The 'Masculine' has moved out of the 'FEAR PROJECTION' and into his clarity of the 'Divine Masculine' energy. His transition is from the FEAR and the accepted abandonment, rejection, and Unworthiness. And in line, both are separately feeling the energy of Unworthiness, Fear, and Abandonment, and both of them are starting in the energy of UNCERTAINTY and both are wanting to move this forward.

So here I am both energies of me are emerging from 'The Mercury Retrograde' through 'our own embodiment' of the 'Masculine' and the 'divine Feminine' with the energy of me being the true 'Divine Feminine'. So here's that 'Power Couple.' I know my ground here, and after an extended period of time I also want a 'Reconciliation' of uniting with restored friendly relations and 'Soul Growth' with focusing on Love and how it applies to other areas of my life. Love is an exchange of lifeforce energy between two beings and it grows extremely fast.

Day after day, I didn't have the facts of what I could understand and felt like I was sitting back in the suspense of 'A Horror Movie' and only could see what was presented in front of me and having the idea of thinking I knew what was right around the corner. After going within and linking it down to 'My Own Reflection,' Suddenly, I could understand that I have been sitting in a horrible 'State of Confusion' of walking in my own Shadow in and out with me.

Spirit says, "Open your heart and allow it to be filled. Let love in and let love flow out and new energy will enter old Relationships and new relationships will burst with the sweetness and vibrancy only encountered when winter gives presence to spring. This is a time to connect with others and share excitement and passion, and hearts full of joy with 'Respect' to Love and Partnerships' in all forms. New relationships are forming, and old ones are being rejuvenated. Love grows quickly and increases exponentially when gifts of love res exchanged. You must give and receive in order for love to flourish and grow between two beings."

The Angels say, "Call in your Soulmate! Your prayers, Your Affirmations and Visualizations will help bring you together have FAITH."

I'm truly relying on the strength of myself because the path I'm on is a 'New Path' and my life will never be the same. I'm starting to look at it in a different way and I'm learning so much about myself in this path. Looking back to years ago, I never would have imagined even three or five years ago where I'm at right now and even three or five years ago. I have come this far in my own personal journey of self-reflection and making plans of the future. It's standing between two worlds. It's like a whole new vision of what I see my future being. I'm out on my 'Hermit Journey' taking stock and asking myself "What is it that I want and how I'm planning to get it."

The Hermit comes out of the cave just to shine their Light of Knowledge so everyone below him can see. He is reminding me of my ability to inspire others with my presence, my actions, my abilities, and my good deeds. Just my being around other people is inspiring them. The lantern has that six-pointed Star in which the two triangles reflecting the top and bottom represent (Heaven and Earth). I'm gaining 'Wisdom' and the willingness to learn from my mistakes and my life experiences are going to bring me a beautiful harvest. I've been in this isolation for a purpose and I've had to meditate, and I've had to contemplate my life. I could have started this Journey Not by my choice but now I'm on it because I'm on the 'Spiritual Quest.' I've had to have this individual experience this solo voyage so I truly could be the 'Beacon' for others.

There is a 'masculine' energy that does represent the element of 'Air' but it's intellect is a rational analysis. It's pure thought and it's my actions based on my thoughts. It's thinking things through and it's being tactical and meeting deadlines, finishing projects, and being the boss but it's also somebody who emanates truth, quality, justice and a higher level of consciousness.

So, whoever is coming in for me is somebody who is of like mind, and it's somebody who is of the 'higher level' of consciousness as well, and it's somebody I'm meeting along my Journey.

It's new love, it's new life it's exchanging gifts because the two of us have gifts to exchange. The potential for this relationship is the happily ever after sweet and playful culmination of our hearts. It's a happy family dancing under the Rainbow. It's truly the fairytale happily ever after and I'm going to be very satisfied and emotionally fulfilled. However, my happily ever after is so that I know it's the potential for the relationship. It is being confident and knowing what it is that I want in moving forward and it will come in for believing in myself.

It's mature and being charismatic with a developed sense of sensuality and sexuality. People are just naturally drawn to me like a moth to a flame. It's truly the feminine mastery of fire which is passion, devotion and a spiritual person who ignite the passions of others and always remains true to me. So, I have timeless energy and loyalty to those around me. The person who is meant for me will find me by just doing what I do and being me. I'm not getting all caught up in my emotions and wacked out of Balance. I continue to work on myself to find that 'Stability' and I don't act inappropriately. Action and Idealism is me forming ideas and it's the sexy come in and save the day type of person.

When I meet this other person they aren't even going to know what hit them. If I need to complete tasks, I will get those done for this is coming in very quickly and very passionately and either 'I or they' are not going to see what hits me because this is like an amazing connection. We are on 'shared energy' both of us coming out of difficult relationships and both have been hurt but we both have healed in a beautiful way and by my getting emotions into balance and balancing out my own shadow and light and going with the flow of change and allowing things to move in and out and just going with the flow and really dancing in the time of change and being successful at it and getting my groove back I'm really getting balanced in so many different ways. I've been patient and I've healed myself.

Archangel Gabriel has the 'Sun' here in the middle of his forehead which is the promise of a new day so the 'Alchemy of Healing' is the balance the marrying of Two Souls, it's the constant cycle in life. So it's death and rebirth after the death of an old view and after being heart broken and sprung into this action forward, I am truly healing and balancing my inner self and bringing in that inner peace and inner balance and in turn, I am exuding that and able to manifest that into my life and somebody who is reflecting the same energy as me here at the death & rebirth.

I'm ready for a new life and I'm truly calling in a Soulmate. I'm looking for STABILITY something STRUCTURED STABLE, that is STURDY RESPONSIBLE RELIABLE and something REAL. I'm walking away from something that did not give me that realness. It gave me a lot of emotions and I put a lot of investment and a lot of time into this (other person), but I'm walking away. They couldn't give me MARRIAGE or a STABLE HOME. I want the WHOLE PACKAGE because I know that I deserve it and STABILITY in my own life, and I'm going to take control of my life. I am the 'Hermit' and acting after coming out of a time of silence and I'm ready for a BALANCED relationship. I am letting go of the old ways of doing things and I've now paid my 'Karmic debt' and I now know 'my lessons' and RELEASING anything that didn't serve me. I'm taking action towards somebody that is going to treat me right and be FAIR to me and be TRUTHFUL to me and keep this scale BALANCED between the two of us.

After I take time to reflect and heal the 'HEARTBREAK' that is in my overall energy I'm taking time to rest and recuperate is going to bring in this 'happy-ever after.' I'm taking things slow and not rushing in with full guns a-blazing because it could scare this person away. Also, they may have come out of a divorce in their recent past and don't want to rush things either and it has to be built slowly and I will get there.

Spirit says, "Just sit in my power" "I have what it takes to draw in the person that is meant for me, so just be confident that is coming for me and know that I deserve this and that I am manifesting it." "My ships are coming in with my blessings on it." "This person is at a distance from me now so be confident know what I want and set my intentions now in this new moon of October 30th and of which goes on for two weeks thereafter."

What I don't see coming is my releasing the emotional rollercoaster that I have been experiencing and I'm getting on that path and I'm walking away from anyone whose EMOTIONS were out of line or acted in an IRRATIONAL BEHAVIOR and I'm no longer putting up with somebody who is doing that to me. I'm setting out in search of the REAL DEAL and I will find it. I'm ready to follow my passion to my true heart's desire and no longer wanting sex. I'm wanting something REAL and something STABLE and it will come in after I get out of this delay and a time of pause. I've had to take sometime away from the world and I had to retreat in order to get my mind right and my emotions healed and know what it is that I want. So, I'm moving in the right direction and I definitely have somebody here who is ready to love. I am coming in with the same vibration and intentions and we are both wanting the exact same thing and it has been cut and clarified.

Yes, the (other person) broke my heart but they weren't seeing what I had to offer so I'm healing my heart and balancing out my emotions and taking the time for that SELF-LOVE and to HEAL The Heart so I can love again and bring me a huge opportunity. The Universe is giving me a 'BIG TIME LOVE' and a beautiful blessing. I'm seeing the WAKE-UP CALL and I'm walking away from what I didn't see and what I had to offer.

The Angles are most definitely bringing the two of us together and to give me that opportunity to give me this BIG LOVE that I deserve and the STABILITY and the HAPPY HOME that I have been in search. I am open to it and know that I will find this STABILITY on my path that I have somebody who is going to love me UNCONDITIONALLY and may be meeting them in November. I am taking that CHANCE and know that THE STABILITY is coming in for me when I take the chance and I am calling in 'A BEAUTIFUL SOULMATE' where I can start a new life and where I EXCHANGE GIFTS equally and where I GIVE as much as I take and TAKE as much as I give for a beautiful connection together. This is A NEW LIFE A NEW OPPORTUNITY for STABILITY, for COMMITMENT for A REAL RELATIONSHIP with A SOUL MATE that is coming in for me. CUPID has shot me in the 'booty' with his bow and arrow to be very focused on SOUL CONNECTION with a '100 %' authentic connection and is what I'm giving out. It's all about the return of the past and time for TRANSFORMATION with a purge of HEALING and for RELEASE and RECONNECTIONS.

My Soul Journey ends, and I am having mixed emotions. There is something I didn't understand in a committed relationship with a person and a commitment that I've had history with so it's not like a brand-new relationship. I see NEW LOVE. It's like there is a discussion taking place about what the next step is for me and THE EVOLUTION of our relationship advancement and growth.

One person says, they are ready for the new relationship! The other person says, they have mixed emotions!

Mixed Emotion could mean so many different things like "Do we have the money for that? Is this the right thing for us? Am I ready to be committed ready to be a parent ready to get married ready for the next step in this relationship for the EVOLUTION and GROWTH of an existing connection?"

The EVOLUTION of an EXISTING CONNECTION is on the forefront

One person says, It has to be REAL and RAW and AUTHENTIC. - What are we and where is this headed? I'm ready for this NEW PATH and NEW JOURNEY with you. Let's do this! This is an existing connection going forward and going to the NEXT LEVEL or to NEW LOVE

& ROMANCE. This person is ready and 'Super Excited.' Mercury's Retrograde through Scorpio is bringing LOVE to a single and it's like 'the end of dating now we're connected or the end of 'bachelor and bachelorette' life and is like moving in together. I'm ready to leave the past behind and start out with new paths and the Journey with you. Lets do this! This is an 'Existing Connections' going to 'The Next Level' or 'New Love & Romance' coming in. This person is ready and I'm ready I'm yours and I'm ready to be committed and step it up and do whatever I need to do.

In the Existing Connection We choose each other and we're taking the next step whatever that means for us and the past doesn't matter. Nobody else matters it's just all about us. This is really about the PRESENT, THEN, and NOW and releasing the past and not bringing it back in the lessons we have learned.

The 'Mixed Feeling' person says, It's not that I'm bored but there's something inside of me that isn't quite resolved. I've been sitting on the fence and going back and forth in FEAR-based energy. It's the 'Magician' and that is not a confliction of the emotional connection but it's more like "Is this going to work " "Do we have enough money" "Can we make this happen." The Fear-based is more about "Resources, Longevity and Stamina. Do we have what it takes? And "Do I really care about 'the other person?' "NO" It's more like "What are we getting into with this EVOLUTION and the Next Venture?" There is weariness and concern in this person. Are you for 'Real' You're too good to be true and I'm scared the other shoe will drop? This person feels this connection is very MAGICAL. This person has finally made that decision and that 'we do belong together' and there is no better person for each of us. This FEAR-based energy is about going to the NEXT LEVEL and truly trusting the MAGIC here. It's like they're going to snap out of it and their perception is going to SHIFT and they will come into the same thought, the same emotion and realization as like the other person and ready to go and let's do this (if they're going to get on board). It's a decision of choosing each other "like we belong together" and "Nobody from the past really matters" "It's all about you and me today."

For OTHERS There is a New Romance for the SINGLES and you can follow either side. There is this 'Desire' to be committed or to be connected however there is some FEAR-based energy around it. It's not picking-up on a relationship so much like a reconciliation or of a past returning but it's an EXISTING CONNECTION that is going to THE NEXT LEVEL. There is A NEW ROMANCE for some with the FEAR-based energy and it's about Resources, Longevity, and Stamina. The question is: "Do we have what it takes?"

The 'Karmic Flame' in the Journey is Loyalty, Patience, and Timing Twin Flame Recognition and SHIFT PROJECTION.

In the Existing Connection and 'Karmic Flame' coming out I don't feel this is speaking about a current connection in our life whatsoever. It's more like us and the other people we were involved with and it's coming into the realization that the Relationships of the Past were 'Karmic & Fleeting' and not as important and 'Significant' as this connection right now.' Also, there is 'New Romance' coming in. I thought 'one particular person' in my past was my 'Twin Flame' and was The One I Belonged' with' but this NEW PERSON coming in could be the one after quite a while of being single or disconnected from the person I THOUGHT was my one. OH MY GOSH I am where I belong and my PERCEPTION Shifts. So, I get my sense and WHO I THOUGHT I was supposed to be with 'Aren't the One' and like my mind is totally changing because of who is now coming into my life. It's all about TIMING and I wouldn't have wanted this person to show up any sooner because I wasn't over the past but after going through TRANSFORMATION with the Death and Rebirth I am ready and once I meet this person 'My PERCEPTION SHIFTS' and I realize this is where I've always belonged and I'm so happy that the old relationship didn't work out before because it wasn't ever LOYAL to me and it wasn't HEALTHY for me.

I don' feel like I could have some XX's coming back because that's part of the 'Mercury Retrograde.' If anything, it's like "Put me in a SPACE of not wanting that X soulmate anymore or realizing that's not where I'm meant to be. There's a satisfaction like this 'NEW ROMANCE' that is coming in or this 'NEWER ROMANCE' that has entered my life like this is 'Who I Belong With' 'This is where I am supposed to be' so it's like a huge purge and Transformation of Past Connections and Healing. I elevate and in 'that space' My Perception Shifts and what I used to want or where I use to think I belonged is not there anymore. You've in a different space and that actually allows me to align to a much better connection for me.

This is about- A New RELATIONSHIP A New BEGINNING A New START and this is where I belong. So, whoever it was in the past

I thought I was supposed to be with or who I've had a really hard time letting go and moving on all that is changing in November with all this Change in Astrology and I'm going to be able to RELEASE and let that go

Because there is this New ROMANCE coming in that feels like A PERFECT FIT and it's EQUAL it's MUTUAL so for us, it's bye-bye past 'Hello' brand New Beginnings 'Hello' Future. Yes, I'm overcoming bunches of DRAMA from the past and choosing each other and going to the next level. A lot of emotions are involved very, very, very, Authentic and Raw, and that definitely is what is the next step which is making me a little nervous and afraid. I can't make babies right now so we are taking 'Our Relationship' to the next level. - There is an Evolution and it's all about the INNER WORLD It's the SOUL CONNECTION, the EMOTION, and that is where we are relating with each other as well as completing a Cycle and that allows THE SHIFT in Perception. WOW! I'm Breathing Deep!

Heart and Soul Messages are the words that are in the 'Heart and Soul' of the person coming in that hasn't spoken to me.

SOUL MESSAGE: We have known each other before in a life apart from this one. This is 'Soul Mate' coming through - in Twin Flame Recognition.

Right here is this 'Karmic Flame' in my life from my past that I may have thought I was supposed to be with or that I wanted to return back to and it's like this 'Inescapable Connection' and now it's either there is this Newer Romance that is coming into my life that is really going to help me realize 'that other person' is not where I belong.

And my friends and family do not think 'that other person' is where I belong.

In the EXISTING CONNECTION

Whether I'm committed or not we do have History.

I feel this is a Progression and an Evolution of a Relationship that is in the process of developing and moving gradually towards a more advanced state that is going to the 'Next Level.' It's not about the connection it's just a worry or concern about resources, or wondering "What are we going to do?" "How are we going to make this?" "And the 'one person' that I thought I belonged with and that I've been disconnected from so long I'm going to 'change my mind' about it and "No", this isn't where I've always belonged and I don't care about the past anymore. It's just, that I'm changing my mind and I'm in the present. I have really thought about this and have been hung up on this 'specific person' for so long and now that 'Here it is,' I'm saying, "No." That's not where I belong and I don't want that anymore and it doesn't hurt. I'm ready to release this and I'm ready to let this go because it's time for a 'New Love' the love I belong too.

We have had a relationship in past life before and in this connection we have history going to the 'Next Level' that could be getting committed, speaking, "I Love You" being intimate for the first time moving in together having a baby getting engaged just whatever the next Evolution of our Relationship would be and that is what is taking place and whatever I was hoping for in the past or our incompatibilities of that is washing away.

We are coming into this beautiful union and recognition of each other and going to the 'Next Level' and the Magic is there.

So, the 'Mixed Emotions' and whatever is this Fear-based energy is going to dissipate and all as well.

So, I'll just be open to it and know that I will find stability on my path and that I have somebody who is going to love me Unconditionally and is coming in for me this month. So, I'm taking that chance and I'm calling in a beautiful 'Soul Mate' where I can start a new life where I exchange those beautiful gifts equally where I give as much as I take take as much as I give and have a beautiful connection together and really be a 'Power Couple' and influence people in a huge way! The two of us are really just made for each other. This is most definitely a relationship that will Value, and Love, and Honor, and be Faithful and not only that we have huge potential for success with the coming together of this relationship, and like I said Cupid's arrow is hitting very quickly. The two of us are falling for each other very fast. This is a New Life A New Relationship for Big-Time Love with opportunity and stability for a happy home and commitment for 'A Real Relationship' with a 'Soul Mate' that is coming in for me. This relationship is going to give me a life full of passion and love and truly my happily ever after and a positive outcome to our continued 'Love Story' meant to be told where two hearts have a continual LOVE beyond the unknown and the ultimate sacred connection of God's Universal LOVE.

THE END

The Epilogue

An Evolution – 'The Happy Ending' of a heart and soul connection through 'dark night of the soul' and getting through the badly burned experiences and the intense energy of a broken heart from the past. Clearing and purging out karma, she goes through a transformation of healing a broken heartache and works through the lower vibrations – the challenges, the tragedies, the trauma, the drama, and the intensity to resolve karma growing through soul lessons into a spiritual connection as good friends and lovers as well as a stable and fulfilling marriage built on truth and honesty in a match and a forever ever happy ending.

THINKING BACKWARDS – like the winter energy that is lifting the final purge into a time of spring where everything starts blossoming once again like – A Rose in Full Bloom – she rises like 'The Phoenix from the Ashes' reaching up to a new level in dimension and spirituality to an experience she could not have ever imagine. Her gifts will become stronger, visions will become clearer and voices will become louder with intensity. She is ascending and the dimension is opening, and she sees the truth for what it is and what it is meant to be. Her whole life is leading up to this opportunity – in a lifetime of happiness and blessings over relationships and connections.

Trusting and believing in herself, her intuition and vibes – she awakens to the spiritual gift she went through with the 'dark night of the soul' and walking through the fire activated by the heavy relationships and experiences. Emerging as 'A Lightworker' for her to turn on and shine in the world of opposites and with her time through living experiences, comes healing shifts in perspective and the importance of TRUTH. It is light at the end of the tunnel.

Our lives radiate ripples of tolerance and respect and paves the way for us to grow through life's soul lessons lifting a final purge. Her spirit's tremendous courage inspired her decision to light the way, sharing the wise experience learned -- embraces with humor, common sense, compassion, empathy, forgiving herself and others with unconditional love – awakening to a better version of herself.

This is definitely 'A Love Story' for a reunion and a heaven-sent relationship and soul mate energy following her passion and heart with a new person coming through that old energy and into the new world in perfect union and harmony. It is a new way of doing things with a twin soul. Our purpose was to come together during this time to do our soul's work.

We are healing separately and come together to help get through this 'New Wave' – this next push and it is all coming for a reason. We are only here for so long and what you say and what you do creates your own reality around you. You can change your life by changing your thoughts. Those in a separation are coming out of karmic relationships and karmic partnerships and ending with the 'New Wave' of Energy. A strong physical love connection is growing a new beginning. It's 'true love' and a new job – and definitely a windfall starting a business with 'a lover.' This is the right thing and the start of something big because her ship has come in with her talent and skills – teaching other people her skills. Before she was 'the learner' but now 'the teacher.' There is magic in this relationship and it's going in an absolute new direction.

The Soul Mates: She takes back her power and has the blessed gift to see amazing possibilities embracing her uniqueness and allowing it to serve her. She is the Sage – (wise through reflection and experience) – and she is the Shaman – (the medicine woman, healer, and witch doctor having access and influence in a world of good and evil spirits practicing -- the Celtic art of divination and healing.) She is the spiritual leader in a lot of ways knowing the mysteries of the world and 'ancient knowledge' but not everything is revealed right away.

The other person is wise, insightful and a wonderful sense of humor, and offers a lot of life experiences. He has withstood pressure and has transformed – reaching emotional maturity and not playing games. He is ready to communicate his feelings for her – elevating this love relationship to a higher level of commitment.

This is a relationship of 'life partners' and who they are meant to be with – going through this journey together with real love in their true sacred union and the authentic emotional freedom to be who they are with each other – allowing them to sour and live well and free constraints, the nine-to-five job, the expectations and rules of it all – and counting their blessings, enjoying life, taking pleasure in the simple things and always expecting the best.

What an incredible start of 2020 – and a brand-new decade and why this is such a pivotal time in our awakening as a consciousness. It is all about unconditional love, emotional fulfillment and how to make it real and bring things into balance with healing past situations and offering that cup of love connected at the soul. It's the start of a new beginning.

– The End –

Printed in the United States
By Bookmasters